MAO ZEDONG'S WORLD VIEW

From Youth to Yanan

Jianfei Xin

University Press of America,® Inc.
Lanham • New York • Oxford

Copyright © 1998
University Press of America,® Inc.
4720 Boston Way
Lanham, Maryland 20706

12 Hid's Copse Rd.
Cummor Hill, Oxford OX2 9JJ

Library of Congress Cataloging-in-Publication Data

ISBN 0-7618-1034-X (cloth: alk. ppr.)

CONTENTS

PREFACE

The reasons for me to choose Mao as my first book-length research in English academic world are: (1) I belong to the generation of Chinese intellectuals, which is called the sixth generation or "Red Guard generation" in the history of Chinese intellectuals in the twentieth century. This generation had been living under Mao's shadow during their childhood, teens and most of their youth. Apparently, everything related Mao was, is and will be a permanent theme impacting their life. No matter what kind of experience you had, how would you like to identify Mao's historical position, You can not escape from Mao's influence, just as you can not get rid of a part of your life. (2) Probably, I am among a group of the persons who have sensed the above-mentioned situation most. I started my academic interest in and reaped some harvest from Mao studies in later 1970s and early 1980s, when I was a college student in Fudan University. I did not continue my study on such a very politically sensitive subject in the rest of 1980s for some obvious reasons in China. In October 1993, Dr. Allen Whiting, my major advisor, suggested me to go back Mao studies for my doctoral thesis on East Asian Studies, particularly on the study of China's foreign policy-related issues. On one hand, Dr. Whiting's advice was a knowing about my early interest. On the other hand, his suggestion was based on his professional foresight; his recognition of Mao's historical importance for China's international relations and his acute vision of the academic needs on the subject.

The main thrust of this research is to explore Mao Zedong's world view from his youth to Yanan (1941), a relatively neglected period in academic circle. A thorough examination of Mao's writings, speeches and behaviors is believed the most complete and systematic discussion of the subject. The findings, through the analysis moving from vertical to horizontal, from micro to macro, from concrete to abstract, have bridged the gap in our knowledge.

Two interrelated hypotheses are suggested at the outset: (1) Mao had built up a long-time international sense and perspective since he was very young. (2) Mao had shaped his own world view during the defined period at both concrete and abstract levels. They have gained factual and logical validation.

A chronological, periodized, and overall outlook portrays Mao as a lively world observer, an enthusiastic commentator, and a bold predictor. Mao's judgments, inferences, and perceptions, whether accurate or erroneous, were the reflection of the connection between the real (objective) world and Mao's mental (subjective) world, either concordant or discrepant. Mao's subjective world was compose of various elements, mainly, nationalist mentality, revolutionary interest and values, historical and cultural heritage, and personal experiences and characteristics.

Mao's perceptions of the world as a whole and his images of the major powers, especially Mao's relations with Soviet Union, provide a concrete framework of his world view at empirical basis. A macro analysis of world view-related three groups of concepts (foreign affairs related concepts, famous revolutionary concepts and philosophical concepts) offers abstract principles of Mao's world view at conceptual level. His belief of "understanding the world and changing the world" shows distinctive philosophical ground. Mao's preference of change, struggle, unevenness, and flexibility had particular significance for featuring his world view.

Four intellectual sources contributed to Mao's world view, such as: older Chinese traditions, the newly emerged tradition in modern China, western thought and learning, and Marxism-Leninism. Each of them functioned to influence Mao's world view in one way or another. Mao proved to be an eclectic with the label of sinicized Marxism.

The project was started in later 1993, a year of Mao's centenary of his birth. It is a great joy for the author to be informed in 1996 that the thesis will be published. As we know that 1996 is another anniversary of Mao-- the anniversary of his twentieth death. The coincidence makes more significance for the book, I believe.

ACKNOWLEDGMENTS

In the course of preparing and completing this research, the author is deeply indebted to professor Allen S. Whiting, professor Charles Hedtke, and professor Chia-lin Pao Tao for their reading and criticizing the manuscript. It is impossible for the author to accomplish the task without their help and encouragement.

A special gratitude should go to professor Whiting and his wife, Alice C. Whiting. My family and I have accumulated personal debts for their love, support and guidance over last six years, while we were living in Tucson--a lovely but exotic place for us. In addition, I would like to thank all the people who have assisted my studies at University of Arizona, particularly Dr. Jing-shen Tao, who made my entering and staying in the Department of East Asian Studies possible, both academically and financially.

The research is based on many original and secondary, English and Chinese sources. Particularly, we quoted Mao's words from the book: *Mao's Road to Power, Revolutionary Writings, 1912-1949* (Volume 1, The Pre-Marxist Period, 1912-1920), which was edited by Stuart R. Schram and published by M.E. Sharpe, Inc.

INTRODUCTION

The significance of the subject--Mao Zedong's world view, on the one hand, is embodied in modern Chinese history, politics, ideology and culture in which Mao played *the* most significant role.[1] On the other hand, the weakness of scholarly research on the topic necessitates a serious, systematic, and comprehensive study.[2] The research undertaken for this thesis intends to fill the gap in our knowledge.

Through an examination of Mao's writings and behavior from his youth to Yanan era (up to 1941), this thesis aims to sketch a chronological, periodized, and overall outlook of Mao's world view. It will discern Mao's judgments, inferences, and perceptions, whether accurate or erroneous, and explore Mao's world view on the empirical and conceptual levels that were the reflection of Mao's cognition-based knowing and thinking.[3] To reach these designated targets, two general but unconventional assumptions are set out before conducting this research. The first is the belief that Mao had built up a long-time international sense and perspective in his perceptions of both domestic and foreign affairs from the time of his youth. The second is to recognize that Mao had shaped his own world view during this period in both a concrete and abstract sense. Later on, Mao's world view of this period had a great impact on the Chinese Communist Party (CCP) and the People's Republic of China (PRC) foreign affairs. Apparently, these two points are at odds with widespread but superficial viewpoints regarding Mao's relations outside China, especially in his early life.[4]

In this thesis what we mean by world view is neither the formal system of doctrine subscribed to by Mao and the CCP, nor the practisable foreign policy pursued by them. In fact, neither case existed at its full sense in the period of our discussion. The term world view employed here carries loose, broad, and complex meanings. It can be defined as Mao's mental imagery of the world order and assumptions about the factors which shaped it. With its mixed aspiration of Chinese nationalism and Chinese communist revolution Mao's world view is politics-oriented. Many factors, such as Marxist-Leninist ideology, the societal-cultural environment, domestic power struggles within and without the CCP, personal experiences and characteristics, and international situations all contributed to form a world view. From a dynamic perspective, shaping a world view is a continuum from receiving the stimuli of international information to the inference tasks of thinking, sensing, symbolizing, intuiting, and finally, to the output of cognitive process. The process of shaping a world view is the result of certain types of connection between the real (objective) world and the mental (subjective) world, either concordant or discrepant.[5]

By definition, shaping of Mao's world view of the period was the process of his world knowledge-acquisition-activities. In other words, the process was his purposeful reaction to varying world information which included information on many crucial events and influential figures on the international scene, information on the established world systems and its changing world situations, and particularly, the information's meaning and significance for the Chinese nation, the Chinese revolution and eventually, himself. Mao's reactions, judgments, inferences, perceptions, and conceptions evolved accordingly. This process may not wholly accord with Yaccov Vertzberger's modal during the chosen time period--from Mao's youth to his Yanan time by 1941, but Mao's early life contains adequate data to satisfy our inquiry into his world view as an "operationally-relevant" dimension.

Factual and practical factors legitimized cutting off the time period at the end of 1941, a monumental point in world history. A political and military line had been drawn in the wake of the German and Japanese attacks on the Soviet Union and the United States respectively. The alignment of the two camps, though temporary, cleared the dust from the stage of world politics. This new situation made world watching easier and simpler. Also 1941 was the time of decline in the relations between Yanan and Moscow. The record shows that after Zhou Enlai and Ren Bishi returned from Moscow in

March 1940, the CCP had no formal or high ranking representatives in the Comintern. Thereafter, Mao alone had telecommunication access with Moscow. The communication only functioned to keep Yanan and Moscow informed on each other. Even this communication had been reduced substantially after the second half of 1941.[6]

In 1941, while the external situation was undergoing a remarkable change, the internal situation of the CCP became stable for Mao. Although Mao weathered various challenges, particularly the crises within and without the CCP from late 1940 to 1941,[7] he had managed to free himself from the shadow of the crises. The most salient achievement was the gradual recognition of his sinicized Marxism-Leninism in the early 1940's, which gained a permanent place as "Mao Zedong Thought" later. The trend toward Mao's complete domination of the CCP began after the Zhun Yi conference in 1935. It developed significantly three years later in the Sixth Plenum. Eventually, by the end of 1941, the trend had become pronounced. Mao had convinced his comrades at the top level and he was now ready to launch the Rectification Movement. The acceptance of Mao as an authoritative thinker and the establishment of the Rectification Movement at the beginning of 1942 was a confirmation of Mao's power.

Thus, both objective and subjective environments in 1941 are momentous factors for discussing Mao's world view in his early life. The following two or three years were relatively an internally oriented time for the CCP and Mao. Not until late 1943 and particularly 1944, did external relations draw the attention of Mao and the CCP.

Two questions arise at the outset. First, does Mao's world view reflect an effort to define a new Marxist-Leninist perspective or does Mao substitute his own perspective for a traditional Chinese one? Second, how can we differentiate the various context-functions of Mao's statements, e.g., following Comintern-Soviet demands, playing tactical lines for specific audiences, or showing his own beliefs, values, and cognition?

Although a chapter will introduce and interpret Mao's theoretical world view, this thesis is not designed to present Mao's world view from a philosophical or cultural perspective. It offers a practical and empirical view of Mao's perceptions and conceptions of the world within the framework of international relations relevant to China. Nevertheless, a relatively abstract assessment of Mao's world view compared with Chinese tradition and Marxism-Leninism is useful for identifying the role of Mao's world view in modern China.

In common parlance, the traditional Chinese world view refers to the Chinese self-image, the Chinese perception of the world order and other states, and China's early foreign relations and behavior down to the 1890's. One well-marked feature of the traditional Chinese world view was its preservation of the conception of Sino-centrism that included the middle-kingdom self-image, a concentric or hierarchic structure of world order with the Son of Heaven at the center or apex. Extended notions of kingship and kinship were linked to its peripheral areas and neighboring countries. The cultural base of Sino-centrism and politically oriented foreign relations, crystallized in a unique tribute system, reached a height of classical refinement in the Ming and Qing dynasties.[8] The traditional Chinese world view was alien to Western conceptions of world view as developed in international relations and diplomacy in Europe since the Middle Ages. The common Western conceptions of the world order, built at the Westphalia Treaty (1648), were the principles of national independence, national sovereignty, and national equality, upon which modern international laws are built.

The Chinese traditional world view is generally recognized by most western authoritative scholars with little substantial divergence.[9] This thesis does not challenge these points. Nonetheless, several less noticeable aspects need attention for a better understanding of the Chinese traditional world view. First is the traditions other than Confucianism. China closely resembled the emerging multi-state system of fifteenth-and sixteenth-century Europe during the Spring and Autumn and Warring States periods (C.800-200 BC). It also had the "hundred schools" with Confucianism being only one of the major schools. Some of the cosmological and methodological ideas, such as the two-division notion of Yin-Yang, must join the complex and vague concept of Chinese tradition.

Second, some traditional strategic and tactical teachings and principles relevant to the Chinese world view were at the operational level. In essence, the importance of the ancient period of a multi-state system was "the emergence of many of the concomitants of a multi-state system including a rudimentary science of international politics and efforts to achieve collective security."[10] Among the "hundred schools," the legalists, the military "experts,"" international affairs experts" or "state Craft" (*Zhong Heng Jia*, "experts in horizontal-vertical relations") produced remarkable examples of handling internal and external politics for their descendants.

Third is the discontinuity and retentivity of older traditions in modern Chinese history, especially after the second half of the nineteenth century. Although it continues to live on behind all the shifting ideologies and commitments of twentieth-century China, Benjamin I. Schwartz suggests that the older Chinese world view has suffered fundamental collapse as the internal and external bases of Chinese world order decisively crumbled. Discontinuity might be most basic in the area of international political behavior where survival may depend on adjustment to new realities.[11] Therefore the third aspect was not part of the older tradition, but represented a transitional time, an intellectual context or a *new tradition* produced in earlier modern China for later generations.

The intellectual context of this transitional time was exactly what Mao, born in 1893, had inherited. The decade of the 1890's marked a sharp and revolutionary break with the older tradition. It was the beginning of Chinese nationalism. The revolutionaries, reformers and constitutional monarchists were willing to accept the multi-state system. In the meantime, building a strong Chinese nation as a replacement for the Middle Kingdom had gained nation-wide momentum. Furthermore, from the 1910's onward, many Chinese intellectuals wanted China to receive equal treatment as a nation-state in the international system.[12] National sovereignty and international equality became the major instruments for the Chinese to seek national revival through international competition, national reverence in the multi-nation-state system, and national re-unification after political and territorial disintegration.

However, although in general the traditional Chinese world view had faded away, it was still connected to the nationalist mentality. There were two reasons for the connection. First, the older Chinese world view had its root in the very marrow of the average Chinese life and in the deep-laid habits of Chinese thought. This is what Joseph R. Levenson meant when he wrote that traditionalism justified modern nationalism on an emotional plane.[13] Secondly, non-mainstream ideas, such as Legalism, the *Bing Jia* (military experts), and the *Zhong Heng Jia* (international affair experts), which were relevant to the older Chinese world view on an operational level, gained importance in the areas of international relations, because of the Chinese belief in the harmony of heaven and the human being (*Tian* and *Ren*), the identity of internal and external principles, and the stress on practical and empirical utility.

Through the study of Mao's world view from his youth to 1941, it is possible to see the connection between Mao's world view and the traditional Chinese one. Like many of his predecessors and contemporaries, Mao encountered the dilemma of the interrelation and confrontation between nationalism and traditionalism. This dilemma was typical of a post-traditional epoch and could be called a *new tradition* in modern China. Mao's approach was to hold a proper tension between the two. He persisted in nationalism for the denial of both Sino-centrism in the past and foreign intervention in the present. He adopted an eclectic approach when it came to cultural tradition, especially on the operational policy-making or tactic level. Mao's world can be viewed partly as a product as well as a dynamic of the *new tradition* of modern China. To say "partly," one can see that Marxist-Leninist ideology served as another source of Mao's world view.

The introduction of the Marxist-Leninist perspective to China in the twentieth century was an important and complicated element for shaping Mao's world view. On the one hand, Marxism-Leninism was officially *the* exclusive ideology and guiding line for Mao's revolution; on the other hand, the term Marxism-Leninism, including its world view, has an ambiguity of identification. Could the two, Marx and Lenin, be identical? Was the Marxist-Leninist perspective acquired by Mao containing the very essence of the original?

In the literature relevant to these questions, Stuart R. Schram's view is convincing. He tends to treat Mao's "Marxism" as one component of thought among many others and tries to make light of the fact that Mao's "Marxism" was a combination of Marx, Lenin and Stalin.[14] Therefore, we should neither overlook nor overstate the impact of the Marxist perspective on Mao's world view.

Originally Marxism was a theory rooted in Western society and culture but it rebelled against the current Western system. The writings of Marx embraced almost every conceivable domain. Although there was no established world order in the modern sense until the Hague Peace Conference of 1899, and the Eastern nations did not receive much of Marx's attention until very late in his life, Marx had proved himself a prominent internationalist and his doctrine a cosmopolitanism with his masterpiece, *The Communist Manifesto* (1847-1848). Central propositions with respect to Marx's global-historical perspective are his theories on materialist concept of history, the nature of the capitalist state, the world-wide working-class revolution, and the international communist movement.

Abstractly speaking, the major appeal of Marxism to Chinese revolutionaries, who held mood of nationalism and anti-traditionalism in parallel during the early twentieth century, was its criticism of the western system and its non-Chinese origin. Yet the influence of Marxism could not have been effective without the impression the Leninists made on the less privileged parts of the world. Therefore, Leninism, interspersed with Stalinism, had a practical as well as ideological impact on Mao's world view.

Leninism differs greatly from Marxism in its doctrine and its world view. The reasons for the divergence were its objective context and subjective focus. For instance, Lenin's theory of imperialism was a development of Marx's point on capitalism from a different dimension. For Lenin, an international environmental dimension had replaced Marx's economic and social dimension within the capitalist system. Lenin's interest in weak and non-western countries was in opposition to Marx's western-centric stand in terms of international revolution. More important, Leninism retreated from the Marxist cosmopolitanism that held the nation-state was a capitalist superstructure, possessing little value in revolutionary praxis, that must be abolished. Lenin recognized that national and state differences would last long after the socialist revolution. His doctrine was to strengthen the nation-state after the revolution so that the differences would vanish automatically in the future. Through Stalin's enhancement of Leninism, nationalist themes have predominated in the communist world. The function of the central state became a key for a socialist nation-state.

While Marxist-Leninist views had a positive impact on Mao, none was the sole or exclusive source of his world view. There were other intellectual sources, such as western political theories and Chinese traditional thinking, co-existing in the framing of Mao's vision, along with his personal efforts to mesh Chinese tradition, Marxist-Leninist teachings, and western political thinking. Practical and empirical aspects as well shaped Mao's perceptions of the world.

Such aspects have logically been linked to the question of distinguishing Mao's statements on a contextual-functional dimension.

Affected by the modern cognitive revolution, the study of international relations has centered on the cognitive perspective. The cognitive perspective is a subject-emphasis approach. In addition to objective and specific conditions, it takes a subject's beliefs, values, emotional sentiments, personal characteristics and cultural attainment into full account. Following the cognitive perspective in an empirical inquiry into means and ends, a subject of research makes choices about the situation that he or she faces. This challenge confronts a student trying to infer this subject's world view.[15]

The question of differentiating between the context-functions of Mao's private and public statements on internationally related matters from his youth to 1941 is a task of drawing inferences about Mao's perceptions and conceptions of the world by empirical research and cognitive inference. The task requires attention to Mao's world view on subjective elements: Mao's perceptions and identification of particular situations that involved his ends and means, beliefs and values, likes and dislikes, etc., in addition to data-collecting and data-driven objective induction.

A brief explanation of the materials used in this research is necessary. All official and unofficial published writings of Mao, his speeches, and chronological records within and without China are indispensable primary sources. A careful comparison had to be made between different versions and editions of Mao's works. These primary sources include: (a) *Mao Zedong Xuanji* (*Selected Works of Mao Zedong*) compiled by the Committee for the Publication of the Selected Works of Mao Zedong, Central Committee of the Communist Party of China (Beijing: People's Publishing House, 1966), and its English translation--*Selected Works of Mao Tse-tung* Volumes 1 and 2 (Beijing: Foreign Language Press, 1975); (b) *Mao Zedong Shuxin Xuanji* (*Selected Letters of Mao*) compiled by the Department for Research on Party Literature, Central Committee of the Communist Party of China (Beijing: People's Publishing House, 1983); (c) *Mao Zedong Nianpu* (*A Chronicle of Mao Zedong's Life*) Volumes 1 and 2, edited by the Department for Research on Party Literature, Central Committee of the Communist Party of China (Beijing: People's Publishing House and Central Party's Literature Press, 1993); (d) *Mao Zedong Waijiao Wenxuan*, (*Selected Works of Mao Zedong's*

Diplomatic Writings) compiled by Foreign Ministry of PRC and the Department for Research on Party Literature, Central Committee of the Communist Party of China (Beijing: Central Party's Literature Press and World Knowledge Press, 1994); (e) *Reverberation, A New Translation of Complete Poems of Mao Tse-tung*, with Notes and Translated by Nancy T. Lin, (Hong Kong: Joint Publishing Co., 1980); (f) *Mao Zedong, 1917-1927, Documents*, edited by M. Henri Day (Stockholm, 1975); (g) *The Political Thought of Mao Tse-tung* edited by Stuart R. Schram (Praeger Publishers, 1971); (h) *Mao's Road to Power, Revolutionary Writings, 1912-1949*, Volume 1 (The Pre-Marxist Period, 1912-1920), edited by Stuart R, Schram (New York: M.E. Sharpe, Publishers, 1992); (i) *Mao Zedong Ji (Collected Writings of Mao Zedong)* Volumes 1 to 10, edited by Takeuchi Minotu (Tokyo: Hokubosha, 1970); (j) *Mao Zedong Ji Bujuan (Supplements to Collected Writings of Mao Zedong)* Volumes 1 to 5, edited by Takeuchi Minoru (Tokyo: Sososha, 1986); and other major collections of Mao's documents in the period after 1941. Efforts were made to cover Mao's writings and speeches as completely as possible based on the sources available at the time. This effort extends to many classical and new secondary sources, such as Mao's biographies, records of Mao's interviews, memoirs about Mao's activities, and so forth.

Context and content analysis showed that Mao's thinking about the world and international affairs fell into several categories with regard to his subjective goals and ways to "characterize the choice situation" he was confronting in light of the theory of cognitive balance.[16] These categories were: (1) Mao's private letters to and conversations with his teachers, friends and fellow students, especially in his youth (Private I); (2) Mao's personal writings, such as classroom notes, reading notes, poems, and publications in his own name before his political life in the political parties (Private II); (3) Mao's writings and speeches in a very limited scope, such as his directives in Politburo conferences, his telegrams to the highest ranks like Zhou Enlai (Private III); (4) Mao's publications in the public media, articles for the newspapers and magazines of the CCP and the KMT from 1923 to 1927, and his writings on behalf of the CCP authorities during the Jiangxi and Yanan periods (Public I); (5) Mao's reports and speeches on the Party or governmental conferences, the CCP schools, the mass rallies (Public II); (6) Mao's conversations with foreigners who visited Yanan and interviewed him (Public III); (7) Mao's theoretical writings that refer to his conclusions, syntheses, and arguments on the subjects that linked his world view at the conceptual or theoretical level (Public IV).

After Mao embraced communism, the absence of Marxist-Leninist ideology and practical partisan consideration in the pre-communist period is apparent. Differences in his private delivery and public statements are also apparent, as in the private situation he would be more free to deliver his "real" views and less concerned with the effect of propaganda. However stopping with these two simple lines of context and content analysis of Mao's writings leaves much to be accomplished in exploring Mao's world view from various dimensions, especially from his subjective perspective. To be specific, the analysis should include aspects of his beliefs, values, emotional sentiments, personal capabilities, and cultural attainment. While discussing these subjective aspects, one must be concerned about the concrete and changing objective conditions or situations for the integration and interaction between the subject and the object.

Two clusters of content--philosophical belief and ideological faith--made up Mao's beliefs. The former consisted of Mao's beliefs of ontology, epistemology, methodology, and the application of the philosophy to his political, historical and human-life thinking. Although his philosophical beliefs were part of his ideological faith about Marxism-Leninism after the 1920's, there were much evidences that Mao's philosophical learning and thinking in his student time had much to do with his philosophical achievement in the Yanan period.[17] Mao's philosophical beliefs were composed of his comprehensive interpretation of Marxism-Leninism, Chinese tradition and western influence. They directed his world view in many ways, especially on the world-wide situation and its general trend, and appear frequently in his writings and speeches, particularly, in the text of Private I, II, and Public I, II, and IV.

The second cluster of Mao's beliefs was his ideological faith in Marxism-Leninism including the communist ideal, the global-historical perspective, some methodological approaches such as class analysis, some Russian practical experiences. Mao had performed these ideologies for about two decades. In the meantime, he had reduced and reinterpreted the ideology. This dual attitude toward Moscow was apparent after 1927, especially in his Yanan period. Mao's words reflected his stance to the Comintern-Soviet line, particularly when he was talking about Soviet Russian related matters irrelevant to CCP issues. Those cases can be found in the texts of Public I and II.

Mao's values were a multi-factor concept that guided his evaluation on world politics, international events, and their impact on the Chinese nation and the CCP. Although this was a combination of his belief, intellectual background and emotional sentiment, the dominant factor was China's national and revolutionary interest. This was particularly true after Mao became a career revolutionary and communist leader. In the texts of Private I, II, III and Public I, II, III, Mao's values were manifested in various degrees.

Mao's emotional sentiments derived from two main sources: a nationalist mentality that was produced in modern Chinese history and external elements, and Mao's personal experience as a result of his relationship with the Comintern-Soviet line. The nationalist emotional sentiments are apparent in almost all texts, especially Private I, II and Public I, II. His emotional sentiment toward Moscow is found in the text of Private III and Public III and IV. The negative mood was rationalized with the mixture of interest-orientation and sinicized Marxism.

Other subjective aspects of Mao's cognitive perspective in respect to his personal characteristics and cultural attainment were reflected in writings and speeches to various degrees but cannot be concisely identified in any specific text. In sum, the classification of the subjective elements and identification of these elements by text comprise an important step for the further study of Mao's world view.

This thesis is divided into three parts. Part One is descriptive and chronological. Three chapters show the periodization of Mao's early life up to 1941. This is based on the interaction between Mao's subjective positions on China's political platform and objective world situations that were relevant to China. The chapters believed to be the most complete and systematic display of Mao's writings and speeches on the subject of world view thus far in academic circles. The main thrust, however, portrays Mao as a long-time world watcher and a conscious commentator on international affairs, and it describes Mao's sense and use of the relationship between internal and external affairs.

Part Two is issue-based and analytical. In short, it discusses the issues between China and the world. They are broken down into two sub-issues within three chapters, viz., Mao's general prism of the world (Chapter 4) and Mao's perceptions of the world major powers (Chapter 5 and 6). The first sub-issue contains: (1) Mao's approach to the world as a whole, (2) Mao's perceptions of the existing world order from the Versailles-Washington system through the later 1920's and 1930's to the Atlantic Charter in the middle of 1941, (3) Mao's stereotypical patterning of the world system contained in the three pairs of concepts: colonialism and imperialism, capitalism and socialism, and fascism and democracy. These concepts were used alternatively, some times in parallel. With regard to the second sub-issue, the analysis of country-reference in terms of Mao's explicit or implicit value reference enhances comprehension of his perceptions and images of the world and its relationship with China. Within international society, six countries relevant to China's politics were selected for discussion. The Soviet Union was the most important for Mao and the CCP and therefore occupies a full chapter (Chapter 5).

Part three is focused on the conceptual level. Mao's conceptions of the world stemmed from his world watching, his perceptions of the world, and his practice and theory of the Chinese revolution as he guided it. Two chapters deal with Mao's revolutionary practice and its theoretical base, related to his world view. In Chapter 7, the first question is directly connected with CCP activities in foreign affairs. Mao's defining and exercising of "*wai jiao*,"" nation-state," and "sovereignty" before 1941 in his nationalist and communist revolution are treated as a prelude to the CCP formal diplomatic activities. Then the major concepts of Mao's brand of revolution are re-explained in Chapter 8 from a new perspective linked to Mao's world view. Mao's famous revolutionary concepts are considered important components of his conception of the world. Chapter 9 synthesizes Mao's theoretical thinking of the world. Understanding the world and changing the world are two strands of Mao's philosophy. The two philosophical strands were epistemological and methodological means and ends for Mao to approach the world. By connecting Mao's thinking in his youth and his Yanan days, the thesis pinpoints Mao's consistent thinking about three notions: dialectical unity of the objective world and human beings, contradictions of the world, and development of the world. Through these notions, Mao's *shi jie guan*--his world outlook gained philosophical base. Meanwhile, Mao appeared as an eclectic of various thoughts with a sinicized Marxist label. Mao's theoretical thinking of the world was not systematic, but it provided a completeness of his world view during a defined period.

PART ONE

THE WORLD THROUGH MAO'S EYES

From 1893 to 1941, Mao emerged as a key figure and a potential world-class politician on China's political stage. It would not have occurred if Mao had isolated himself from the world outside China. A chronological review of Mao's early life, along with the broad historical context, offers evidence of Mao as a tireless world watcher. Such a review is a natural starting point for our thesis.

Chapter 1

World Watcher (1): Mao as a Radical Youth (1893-1920)

The two decades ending the 19th and beginning the 20th century coincided with the development of a new relationship between China and the world that was manifested by a series of remarkable events within and without China. In China there occurred its defeat in the Sino-Japanese War (1894-1895), the founding of the Tong Meng Hui (the Revolutionary Alliance) (1895), the Wu Xu Bian Fa (the Hundred Days Reform in 1898), the Boxer Rebellion (1900), the first tide of Chinese overseas student movement, and the collapse of the Qing dynasty (1911). Outside of China there was the emergence of New Imperialism (the so-called "Informal Imperialism" and "Finance Imperialism"), the declaration of the American "Open Door" policy, the scramble among the powers for spheres of influence in China, the explosion of the Russo-Japanese War and so on. Mao Zedong was born into this tumultuous world in 1893.

What Chinese called "the New Age" featured a complex transitional political culture in reference to her international relations. While she was undergoing a profound but painful change, she maintained old basic traditions. China's humiliation in foreign relations reached the apex with her war losses to Japan. However, China redirected her way toward modernization solely by studying the West and emulating both the West and Japan. The learning emphasis switched from modern technology to modern ideas. Started from the Tong Meng Hui, China's Nationalists initiated their modern shape and invited sympathy from outside China, particularly from Japan. Since then, Sino-Japanese relations have contained a dual phenomenon: hostility and friendship. Although the Reform of 1898 was aborted and China's four-thousand-year empire had exhausted its credit, a new generation of intellectuals, represented by Liang Qichao, traversed crossroads between rich tradition and advanced Western ideas. What was more important was that these intellectuals educated the next generation--the May Fourth generation, including Mao Zedong. The Boxer movement shows how the interwoven crises of domestic politics and foreign affairs could engage the most apathetic and most multitudinous social class--the peasantry. This group was mobilized and manipulated by certain groups to stimulate either anti-imperialism or xenophobia, nationalism or nihilism.

At the turn of the century, especially through the overseas student movement, China's 20th century elite was born. They, to a large extent, mixed their images of foreign powers with personal experiences and leanings. Eventually, the overthrow of China's last Emperor opened a new era of nation-state and political chaos as well. After that, China's three-decade disintegration offered a variety of crises and opportunities for ambitious and competent people, such as Mao, to play a role on both the intra-national and the international stages.

The environments surrounding Mao Zedong's birth and childhood were inauspicious for conventional success in China's politics. His birth place--Shaoshan Chong, in Xiangtan Xian, Hunan Province, was a comparatively poor and barren village. His family, particularly his father, was the product of a rich-peasant mentality. His childhood was spent as a farm laborer and student.[18]

As a student in a local primary school, Mao was educated in the Chinese classics. What he enjoyed most through his early readings was the romances of old China, especially the stories of rebellions. In a political sense, through his readings one may assume that Mao would find ideas of social classification and justice of rebellion (*Shuihu Zhuan, The Water Margin*), the narrow meanings of nationality and patriotism (*Yuefei Zhuan, the Yuefei Chronicle*), the elemental skills of military strategy, power struggles, and relationships between states and politicians (*Sanguo Yanyi, the Three Kingdoms*). Nevertheless, Mao had little knowledge of the world outside China before he left home at the age of sixteen. A book that particularly impressed him was the *Shengshi Weiyan* (*Words of Warning*) authored by Zheng Guanying, a late 19th century reformer in China. *Shengshi Weiyan* called for the introduction of Western instruments--railways, telephones, telegraphs, and steamships--into China. Moreover, it advocated political, economical, and educational reforms to compete with the world powers.[19] It was probably the earliest sense of the world that Mao obtained. Apparently, the youth was stamped with its mixture of westernization, nationalism and traditional tales.

At sixteen Mao left his home village deliberately to seek a wider world. After that, he had received much new information about the world. In a new school, Dongshan Xuetang, Mao studied new subjects--Western learning, such as foreign history and geography and read of Napoleon, Catherine of Russia, Peter the Great, Wellington, Gladstone, Rousseau, Montesquieu, and Lincoln from a book *Great Heroes of the World*.[20]

In Changsha, the capital of Hunan province, Mao read his first newspaper, *Minli Bao* (*People's Strength*), a Japan-based Chinese nationalistic journal. From then on, consistently and meticulously reading different newspapers became Mao's personal hobby.[21] In his early Changsha days, Mao had half a year of self-education in the Hunan Provincial Library through the writings of world-class thinkers, such as Adam Smith, Darwin, John Stuart Mill, Rousseau, Spencer and Montesquieu. He later recalled, having mixed poetry, romances, and the tales of ancient Greece with serious study of the history and geography of Russia, America, England, France, and other countries. The world was very attractive to Mao. When, for the first time he saw a great map of the world, he realized that Shaoshan, Xiangtan, Changsha, Hunan, and even China occupied only a small portion of the whole. From then on, Mao realized his activity in China had a cause and effect on the world, and he kept an eye on the rest of world.

Many people and events in the world, particularly great powers, political heroes, and influential thinkers, decidedly impressed Mao in his youth. Meanwhile, Mao began to formulate his style of commentary and criticism through lessons he learned of the world either from "*Gu*" (ancient China) or from "*Yang*" (foreign things). For instance, Mao's earliest known writing, "Essay on How Shang Yang Established Confidence by the Moving of the Pole," was a lamentation on the four thousand years of Chinese government and its effect on the people. Mao expressed his earliest vision of state and law with reference to "various civilized peoples of the East and the West."[22]

The next stage in Mao's development of his knowledge of the world was his five year stay (1913-1918) at the First Provincial Normal School of Hunan from which he graduated. In this school, Mao continued to extend the knowledge about China and the world he had gained through his earlier self-study. He studied the relations and the differences between China and the rest of the world. His perceptions of foreigners, foreign nations, and foreign countries became concrete. He developed his perspectives on the world.

In Mao's writings at this time, his knowledgeable outlook on various subjects of the world emerged. Among those writings are three remarkable ones: "Classroom Notes" (October-December, 1913), "Letter to Xiao Zisheng" (July 25, 1916), and "Marginal Notes to: Friedreich Paulsen, *A System of Ethics*" (1917-1918).

The "Classroom Notes," although merely extracts, recorded Mao's knowledge about the world that interested him, such as the earth's longitude, the Observatory of London, time differences, the position of Japan in longitude, world-class figures such as Caesar, Napoleon, Columbus, Newton, Franklin, Watt, etc. Mao was also impressed with the first generation of Chinese diplomatic officials such as Li Hongzhang and Guo Songtao.[23]

The historic philosophy Mao appreciated then was seen in his quote from a famous Chinese history book, *Shi Ji (The Book of Historical Document)*: "Absorb the weak, and punish the willfully blind; take their states from the disorderly, and deal summarily with those going to ruin."[24] Mao believed "injury begets grace" because, in history, the stronger nations have wiped out other countries. A stronger nation took over weaker ones, colonized them, treated them as it's own and brought prosperity to these people, as far as the people were concerned, it was "grace."[25]

Nonetheless, it would be a mistake to believe Mao's Notes were a eulogy of classical China. In Mao's youth, the mainstream tendency was to criticize old China. Mao apparently belonged to the mainstream. For instance, talking about the importance of vigor and the cure for bodily weakness, Mao recorded these words: "This is the case of our nation now,"" Our nation has suffered greatly because of this for many years past," therefore, "she cannot compete with foreign countries." The unfavorable comparison was made with Japan and

Western countries.[26]

Thereafter, Mao adopted a comparative approach to express his world view. He believed that "understanding thing A might help us to understanding thing B. Comprehension of one truth might lead to another." This proposition is "understanding the interrelationship of things."[27] To approach the proposition, one needs to acquire experience of the world through various ways: traveling all over the globe; befriending the eminent scholars of the world; learning all the things of the world both East and West, the ancient and the modern, and so forth. Mao did his best in his student era.[28]

The "Letter to Xiao Zisheng" (July 25, 1916) recounted current domestic and international affairs. Although it is Mao's earliest available commentary on international politics, it would not be the only one. The historical context also provided rich and fresh sources for a radical youth such as Mao Zedong for "fingers pointing at scenes unfolding."[29]

After the revolution of 1911, China's politics meshed with international politics. On the one hand, this situation was a mutual interaction where world powers shaped their policies on East Asia with a focus on China. Sometimes these policies were coordinated but mostly they confronted each other. On the other hand, different factions of Chinese politicians wanted to ally themselves with certain foreign countries. The most renowned example was the connection between Yuan Shikai's ambitions of political power and Japan's greedy demand on China. Moreover, the period when Mao was in the First Normal school was an eventful era internationally. The information on world events spread, sooner or later, into China, due to the liberated first generation of Chinese journalists. It provided Chinese youth with newspapers on a daily basis; as Mao said in his Letter, "There are at least seven or eight newspapers in the Hunanese capital."[30]

In his letter, Mao recounted Yuan Shikai's attempts at restoration for the current political chaos in China either at the central government or through local warlords. It was believed by many Chinese radical youths that Yuan's political fate was inseparable from Japanese policies in China. This long-cherished ambition to ascend the throne could not be achieved without Japanese support. This was the reason for Yuan's acceptance of Japan's "Twenty-one Demands" on May 7, 1915. This event was a watershed for China's general image and attitude toward Japan.[31]

In his Letter, Mao reported "some astonishing news in the world" by commenting on a secret treaty between Japan and Russia, concluded on July 3, 1916. This treaty signaled a closer co-operation of the two powers since the Russo-Japanese War of 1905. Their target was a "third power hostile to Russia and Japan."[32] However, China became a pawn for their negotiation. China was no longer considered a nation on an equal footing with Japan or Russia. After reading the content of the pact, Mao told his friend in his letter that "the Japanese are really our most formidable enemies!" He listed China's tangible losses and intangible humiliation under Japan's action and behavior in China. To avoid further humiliation, Mao called for the Chinese to awaken from their sleep and pay attention to eastern affairs. He warned, "We must sharpen our resolve to resist Japan."[33] In the wake of this, Mao expected a Sino-Japanese war saying, "Without a war, we will cease to exist within ten years."[34]

Mao turned his eyes from the East to the West where the on-going World War I caught his attention. Actually, Mao had followed the war closely from its beginning. A fellow student, Xiao Shan, recalled that Mao once narrated clearly to him the cause, the procedure, and the major incidents of the War.[35] Mao noted that although they had suffered great losses, Germany and Austria had yet to be defeated. Both sides tried to persuade other countries to join their forces, but "It looks as if the West will not have a terrible war." Mao made another prediction, "According to economists, from the perspective of the economy, the war cannot go on another year."[36]

Regarding the situation in North America, Mao recorded the uprising in Mexico and its results in terms of relations between Mexico and the United States. In talking about the United States, Mao appeared to be familiar with it. He told his friend that

> Wilson's term is up, and they are in the midst of elections .... I think since the Americans are unwilling to enter the war in Europe, and the public opinion on expanding military preparations is not yet mature, the policy will not change, ...Therefore, Wilson might as well continue in office for another term.[37]

Nevertheless, Mao's comments on current affairs in the West, particularly the United States, emerged from a Chinese interest orientation. Mao calculated that the United States had no willingness to put forces in Europe at this time; instead, "Their time will come in ten years, and the place will be the Pacific."[38] To enhance this point, he mentioned rumors of a possible war between the United States and Japan. Mao's view of strategic considerations and the international order in the Asian-Pacific area was optimistic. He assumed that in ten years,

China will wage a war of revenge [on Japan] and they [Americans] will respond to the righteousness of their comrades. We will attack on land, they will attack on sea. When the three islands [of Japan] are subjugated, the two republics of East and West will draw close in friendship and cheerfully act as reciprocal economic and trade partners. This will be the great endeavor of a thousand years. What we give up now, we will no doubt see again at that time.[39]

The accuracy of Mao's vision remained questionable, but it reflected Mao's world view at that time and had its impact later.

The "Marginal Notes to: Friedreich Paulsen, *A System of Ethics*" was a "crucially important document" for tracing the evolution of Mao's thinking,[40] revealing his concept of the world as well. Differing from the summary, "Classroom Notes," Marginal Notes was a commentary based on Mao's own thinking. Compared with the "Letter to Xiao Zisheng (July 25, 1916)," Marginal Notes was a contemplative work at a deeper, more philosophical level. Mao expressed his concept of the world indirectly and abstractly, and this philosophical base provided a lasting foundation for Mao's world view. It lasted, to some extent, his entire lifetime.

The vision of "thing-in-itself" (understanding the thing from ontological perspective) led to Mao's historical and political philosophy. This philosophy had a remarkable emphasis on differences and distinctness, a naturalistic attitude toward contradiction and confrontation, advocacy on change--reform, evolution and even revolutions, optimistic insight of death and destruction. Mao remarked "excellent" on the German philosopher, Friedreich Paulsen's points: "All historical development is a function of differentiation. ...All philosophies originate in the conflict between the beliefs of individuals and the common beliefs of their nationality."[41] Logically, the differentiation and conflict mean changes and costs that were what Mao favored and for what he was well prepared.

Departing from here, Mao challenged the importance of moral senses, existing traditionally in both the East and the West. For instance: the idea of selflessness toward others, the sense of duty toward society, the concern for one's reputation in history, the ideal of *Da Tong* (the Great Harmony) for the world. Instead, Mao advocated teleological ethics. Using the terms of Platonic and Aristotelian theory Mao made notes in his writing based on individualism and realism that were the two principles Mao thought one needed to follow. Only the concordance of these two principles could be called a "true freedom,"[42] a freedom of will that Mao always appreciated.

Mao's "Marginal Notes to: Friedreich Paulsen, *A System of Ethics*" was a theoretical conclusion of his student life, an absorption of Western and Eastern thought no matter what nation or academic school, a high commitment to changing the world and the Chinese nation, a non-system philosophical interpretation of everything with the faith of two core ideas: individualism and realism. Whatever changes his specific ideas might have thereafter, Mao made no rejection to the change because he was committed to the importance of change. Mao's structure of his conscious and subconscious had taken shape thus far.

The next stage of Mao's life was marked by activities through which his world view and other related ideas obtained wider context and practical significance. Within China, there was an unprecedented situation faced by the so-called "May Fourth Generation" that included radical youth like Mao. There were political chaos around the issue of a united or disunited China, a national crisis created by the Paris Conference after the War World I, and cultural perplexity because of the backlash to discredit Chinese traditions and an over-flow of western fashions. Outside China, the international scene was filled with great events: the new rivalry in the Asian-Pacific arena between Japan and the United States, an unbalanced ending to World War I, and the Russian Revolution with its worldwide consequences. This historical context and Mao's active participation in Chinese events broadened his horizon substantially.

In his later days at the First Normal school and thereafter, Mao began to build his influence and reputation in the society he was living and the course of the modern Chinese revolution. His first published article in *New Youth*, "A Study of Physical Education," and his leadership of the Xin Min Xue Hui (New People's Study Society) were proofs of his ability and ambition.

Upon graduation, Mao appeared as a leading activist among

groups of radical youth in Changsha. While in Beijing and Shanghai, he attempted to spread his personal contacts with national-class figures, such as Chen Duxiu, Hu Shi, and Li Dazhao during the May Fourth era. As an organizer, Mao, with his friends and comrades, strengthened the New People's Study Society, the Hunan Student's Association, and the Socialist Youth Corps (later Communist Youth League) in Hunan. As a social activist, Mao led the movement to expel the Hunan military governor, Zhang Jinyao, and promote Hunan autonomy. He took part in the heated discussions about Ms. Zhao, a helpless woman, who committed suicide because she was under pressure from her family and old doctrine to enter into a marriage not of her choice. As a practitioner of new ideas, Mao tried to establish a New Village under the Yue Lu Mountain and promoted a work-study mutual aid movement. Mao also promoted the overseas student movement. As an educator, Mao became the principal of an elementary school. More importantly, he enthused over popular education by founding a Worker's Night School, a Hunan Self-Study University.

In his pursuit of the Russian model, Mao became a close follower of the *New Youth* and its major sponsors. He joined activities of the Philosophical Society, Journalist Society, and Marxism Studies Society in Beijing University while he was working in the university library. He was a founder of the Russian Studies Society and Cultural Book Society in Changsha. As an editor and writer, Mao published and performed as editor-in-chief of *Xiangjiang Pingrun* (*Xiang River Review*) and *New Hunan*, two short-lived journals with great importance in May Fourth era. He wrote numerous articles for each issue, which were carried by many newspapers and journals in Shanghai and Changsha.

Through these activities, Mao presented his world view in larger scope and developed a concept of the world with several distinguishing features, such as: reformism with profound faith of constant change, pragmatism with boundless thinking, Pin Min Zhu Yi (an *ism* for ordinary people) showing his social grassroots, and major concern about human beings.

Mao won credit for his love of Chinese history as well as for his attitude toward world history. A typical, it not unique, way for Mao to show his intellectual background and to enhance an argument was to cite history. In the "Manifesto on the Founding of the *Xiang River*

Review" (July 14, 1919) Mao reviewed world history "since the Renaissance." He expressed his ideas of reform in many domains, his opposition to oppression of every description, and his belief in a current global political flow:

> In the political arena, autocracy has been replaced by representative government, and a restricted suffrage has been replaced by universal suffrage....In the realm of society, the dark society of the dictatorship of a minority class has been transformed into an enlightened society in which all the common people can freely develop....In the area of thought, we have moved forward to pragmatism, and internationally, there is now a League of Nations....The time has come! The great world tides are rolling in even more insistently!...The vast and furious tide of the new thought is already rushing along both banks of the Xiang River!...Those who ride with the current will live; those who go against it will die.[43]

The message of this historical overview could be summarized by a single word: change.

Mao's preference for reformism was reflected by his mild political stand compared to what he had learned from Marxism in later 1919. His moderation was soon replaced by the radical idea of "class struggle" in 1921. Nevertheless, reformism coincides with the idea of constant change. In view of this, the difference between reform and revolution, for Mao, was not as great as peoples' imagination from philosophical perspective.

In addition, Mao analyzed "the tide of change" in the current world. He recalled:

> In recent years, the European tide has flowed to the East, and new schools of thought have emerged daily. Scholars all over the country have been enthusiastically responding to the new trends and engaging in reforms....As world intellectual trends are changing constantly, the New Culture movement in our country has emerged. The reform of literature and the liberation of thinking are rapidly sweeping the country.[44]

China had benefited by accepting this intellectually eastward trend. Politically, Mao noticed an eastward trend too:

> The world situation clearly tells us that the tide of change is already

sweeping through wild Siberia, and Korea, which has lost its national existence, also wants self-determination. This is a general trend, and no one can resist it.[45]

Not only a political change, but a social change involving every aspect irresistibly occurred and put the people's focus on the East, particularly, China.

Mao took the stand that China was a representative of the Oriental civilization in contrast to the Occidental civilization. The political change as well as social change had also moved from the West to the East. Mao attributed this trend to "the great European War and the Russian Revolution" sparking the waves of the eastward change.[46] Excited by the trend, Mao announced:

> Our Chinese people possess great inherent capacities!... I venture to make a singular assertion: one day, the reform of the Chinese people will be more profound than that of any other people, and the society of the Chinese people will be more radiant than that of any other people. The great union of the Chinese people will be achieved earlier than that of any other place of people... Our golden age, our age of glory and splendor, lie before us![47]

Pragmatism was the most influential western philosophy during the May Fourth period. This was partly due to the advocacy of Hu Shi, an American-educated, prominent Chinese scholar and reformer. Also, the spreading of pragmatism was partially because of the salient utilitarian tradition of Chinese culture, though it lacked a modern scientific basis in contrast to pragmatism in its original western context.

Mao was once a follower of Hu Shi and had various leanings toward Chinese classic traditions. Therefore, his attitude toward pragmatism was positive. He welcomed John Dewey, an authority on pragmatism, and his visit in China. On July 31, 1920, Mao said, "Dr. Dewey of America has come to the East. His new theory of education is well worth studying."[48] This comment contrasted with his criticism of Bertrand Russell's political theory expressed as Russell lectured in China during the same period.[49] Mao expressed nothing negative about Dewey then, or even later after Mao had converted to Marxism in 1920-1921.[50]

Another notable instance of Mao's favoring of pragmatism was his response to Hu Shi's famous proposition--"more study of problems, less talk about *isms*," in spite of his admiration and sympathy with Li Dazhao and Li's view, which was the opposite of Hu Shi. Responding to Hu Shi, Mao created "Statutes of the Problem Study Society" (September 1, 1919), in which he listed dozens of specific research problems, most of which had practical significance.[51] Besides a practical orientation, another feature of Mao's pragmatism was the flexibility of his intellectual commitment. In the May Fourth era, "Downwith Confucian and son" was the most resounding slogan in the circle of these radical intellectuals. Mao did not break away entirely from Confucianism. He affirmed the practical school of thought in the later Ming and Qing, which was evoked by the term *jing shi* (statecraft), emphasizing practical application and this-worldly activism in light of current reality. Regardless his economy was in a very sorry plight, he visited Confucius' home town, Qu Fu, on his way from Beijing to Shanghai. What Mao did was to criticize Confucianism in his own way. He condemned the intellectual hegemony of Confucianism and wrote after few months back from Qu Fu:

> The principle of freedom of thought and freedom of speech...is mankind's most precious treasure, the source of utmost satisfaction....The Confucian orthodoxy is the repressive despotism of the intellectual world,...we oppose Confucius for many other reasons as well, but for just this one reason alone, for his hegemony over China that has denied freedom to our intellectual world, that has kept us the slaves of idols for two thousand years, we must oppose him.[52]

Ironically, Mao created another intellectual hegemony in Chinese society with his own thought later; however, he was consistently against any type of repressive despotism other than his own. "Thought knows no boundaries," said Mao in July, 1919. A year later, he told his former teacher the same idea, "[Herbert] Spencer hated to be confined by national boundaries, and I feel that the boundaries between fields of study are also very harmful."[53]

Pinmin Zhuyi, which spoke particularly for the average people, that was one of the most frequently and faithfully mentioned "isms" in May Fourth China. It was another combination of the current situations in Chinese society and the influence of world politics, especially the Russian Revolution and the Russian brand of Marxism.

Mao's lower class origin and his non-elite educational experience contributed to his sense of sympathy for the common people. This sympathy produced a realization of the social and political strength of the masses during the May Fourth period. The international tide stimulated by the Russian Revolution reinforced Mao's idea of the masses. For him, what occurred in Russia was the most salient, but not the unique way to approach the new tide of change and politics in the world from a social class perspective. At this time Mao was still unfamiliar with the Marxist-Leninist concept of class. Mao wrote on September 3, and September 27, 1920, respectively, "Now we know that most of the big countries of the world have fallen apart. Russia's flag turned red, and it has truly become an internationalist world for the common people." Mao called it "a storm of change" throughout the entire world."[54] Three weeks later, Mao connected the Russian Revolution to *Pin Min Zhu Yi*; "In Russia, all politics is controlled by the Russian workers and peasants." Mao saw this change as a result of World War I.[55]

Mao's *Pin Min Zhu Yi* reflected his evaluation of changing world politics. First of all, a unified political power in the modern world ought to have a popular base, or "grass-roots organizations."[56] Secondly, all politicians "must employ the technique of union."[57] Here, union meant "the great union of the popular mass"; the technique was a political tip on how to mobilize the popular masses. Thirdly, the benefits for the popular masses are a matter of basic rights, among various human rights in 1919. Mao wrote, "What is the greatest problem in the world? The greatest problem is that of getting food to eat. What is the greatest force? The greatest force is that of the union of the popular masses."[58] Besides the problem of getting food for feeding the popular masses, Mao was concerned with other problems related to the rights of the popular masses, like popularization of education. The reason Mao stressed these basic humanitarian problems was Mao's sympathy with the miserable life experienced by the common people, but the recognition of the political utility of the popular masses was most likely Mao's major concern.[59]

With faith in constant change (reformism), a combination of practical priority and ideological flexibility (pragmatism), and a realization of the political function of the common people (*Pin Min Zhu Yi*), Mao formulated major principles for his world view during the May Fourth era. With these principles, Mao made his commentaries on the China-related international affairs in the same period.

Mao's graduation in 1918 from the First Normal school coincided with the end of the War. Mao, as a practitioner, was busy looking for a wider world. He paid his first visit to the two most important cities in China: Beijing (from August 1918 to March 1919) and Shanghai (from March to April 1919). The travel provided him access to a higher political stage and made Mao a very active and important person in Changsha during the May Fourth Movement. He was conscious that what happened in China was not isolated from what happened in the rest of the world. In *Xiang River Review*, his first owned journal for speaking freely and publicly, Mao wrote most of the articles in its total of five issues. The "Review of Major Events in the West" column and most of the "Miscellaneous Commentary on World Affairs" appearing in each issue came from his pen. A Shanghai based monthly magazine--*Hunan*--referred to the *Xiang River Review* saying that "if you want to learn the current trend of the world...you cannot but read it."[60]

The outcome and aftermath of World War I caused Mao to hold an ambivalent attitude about the war. The great rejoicing Chinese felt at the war's end turned to disappointment due to the sense that they had been betrayed by the Paris Peace Conference. The extreme indignation which followed gave birth to the May Fourth incident. Mao's position toward the Paris Peace Conference was quite negative. He described the conflict between the [Triple] Alliance of Germany, Austria-Hungary, and Italy and the [Triple] Entente of France, England, and Russia as "using oppression to overthrow oppression."[61]

Mao's attack focused on the victors because they became new oppressors. Mao pointed out that new international powers (in Chinese terms: *Qiang Quan* or the powers with oppressive force) emerged as a result of the War:

> Before 1919, Germany was the most powerful nation in the world. After 1919, the greatest powers in the world will be France, England, and the United States. Germany's power was political and international....After 1919, the power of France, England, and the United States will be social and economic power.[62]

According to Mao in 1919, these new powers, including Japan, intervened in the affairs of Poland, Czechoslovakia, Arabia, and Siberia under the banner of "national self-determination," but ignored the Jews and Korea's desires for their interests. In view of this, Mao censured: "I think it is really shameless!"[63]

The reason that Mao stressed social, economic, and national aspects of the new powers was his expectation of on-coming social revolution and class struggle based on his positive assessment upon the aftermath of the War. Although he had not yet embraced Marxism-Leninism, there was some partial introduction of Marxism-Leninism that delivered ideas of social revolution and class struggle, especially since the Russian Revolution. Furthermore, Mao was expecting another great war that would based on class, "If there is war after 1919 it will be a class war. The result of class war will be the victory of the ideology of the states of eastern Europe, the victory of the socialists."[64]

With such an expectation in mind, Mao recorded a long section on labor strike movements of the day in major western countries. He saw "the present wave of strikes in various countries" as a two-sided coin: "the strikes pushed the political magnates and financial tycoons of the new great powers into an awkward situation" where they "dare not take the labor too lightly," although "they were having a great time concentrating all their efforts on the Paris Peace Conference." This was a positive side of the strikes. The negative was that the strikes were too short-sighted with a focus on some economic benefit. "The mainstream faction all laugh at the workers of Britain and France as simple-minded. It is impossible to get chewed-up meat from a tiger's mouth."[65]

For Mao and the Chinese radical youth, the Russian Revolution was no less important than World War I. In mid-1919, Mao had not yet reached the point of being able to distinguish different types of socialists, such as Rosa Luxembourg, Eduard Bernstein, and the Russians. Moreover, he held a fairly conservative point about the socialist revolution. Despite his incomplete acceptance of the Russian Revolution, Mao's writings were full of Russia during this period. His viewpoint on Russia and the Russian Revolution possessed an enthusiasm that is discussed later in this thesis.

A salient example for illustration of Mao's practical world view was Mao's attitude toward the overseas student movement, the second wave of its kind during the 20th century. A long-held myth derived from two opposite extreme viewpoints asserts that Mao's absence from such an important movement as a Chinese intellectual youth was either because of his foresight,[66] or his short-sightedness.[67] Both extremes are far from the truth.

Mao was an activist and became leader of the Diligent Work and Frugal Study Movement in Changsha not long after his graduation from the First Normal school. In 1918 and 1919, going abroad, particularly to France, was an exciting topic for Mao and his fellows at the New People's Study Society. In September 1918, Mao paid his first visit to Beijing for preparing to go abroad. In April 1919, he left Beijing for Shanghai to meet with friends departing for France. Later, Mao lost the chance to go with them for various reasons, most likely, the shortage of money. It had little to do with Mao's personal intention of staying in China at that time. In his letter of September 5, 1919, Mao told his former teacher Li Jinxi, "There seems to be good hope of putting together a group of students from Hunan to study in France. Sending students to study in France would bring new life to education in Hunan."[68]

Nevertheless Mao did have his own opinion on the issue of going abroad, especially a few months later when he was deeply involved with the problems of Chinese politics and society.[69] Meanwhile, Mao learned more about the Russian Revolution from various sources, including letters he received from his intimate friends such as Cai Hesheng.[70]

Two letters Mao wrote in early 1920 expressed his points comprehensively on the issue of going abroad. One was to Tao Yi, Mao's first sweetheart; the other was to Zhou Shizhao, a fellow student at the First Normal school. In the former letter, he wrote:

We comrades, in the preparatory stage, should have a goal of `outward expansion.' I have a number of thoughts about this question. Many people talk about reform, but it seems to me to be only a vague goal....If we want to achieve a certain objective (reform), we have to pay attention to proper methods. One of them is how to place people properly....Some comrades in Paris are trying very hard to convince others to join them there. If they attract more people from the general public to Paris, that is fine. But if they attract more comrades there, it will inevitably lead to some errors. We comrades should be scattered all over the world to conduct investigations. Some of us should go to every corner of the globe; we should not all be in one place. The best way is to have one or several comrades open up a certain area. We should open up all 'fronts.' We should send people to act as our vanguard in all directions.[71]

In the letter to Zhou Shizhao, Mao expressed his viewpoint on studying abroad further:

> In my opinion, there is really no reason why one has to pursue knowledge at a 'prescribed place.' Too many people are infatuated with the two words 'going abroad.' There are no fewer than tens of thousands, or even hundreds of thousands, of Chinese who have been abroad. Only very few of them are really good. As for the majority, they are still 'muddled,' still 'unable to make head or tail of it.' ...Therefore, I am thinking of staying in China at least for the time being, in order to study the essentials of the various disciplines. ...I am not, however, absolutely opposed to studying abroad. On the contrary, I advocate a policy of studying abroad in a big way. I think the only correct solution is for each of us to 'go abroad' once, just to satisfy our craving for it. I consider Russia to be the number one civilized country in the world. I think that two or three years hence we should organize a delegation to visit Russia.[72]

Clearly, Mao did not give up his idea of studying abroad and still admitted his "craving for it," while he differed from most of the others. He termed his idea as "a policy of studying abroad in a big way" that contained three points: (1) A necessary "outward expansion." France was not a favorable place for Mao, because his destination was very political and pragmatic. Therefore, Mao suggested opening up all "fronts" in many directions. (2) A practical orientation. Mao treated the action of going abroad as a preparation for reform with a "certain objective." He referred to a Russian-type "reform," which was not only political but also social. In the meantime, he tried to establish a well-organized political force for the reform, with a center in Changsha where he was currently staying. (3) A criticism of the ongoing fever about going abroad. Mao realized the importance of the "essentials of the various disciplines," such as: grasping new theories, commanding foreign language, and especially, acquiring good knowledge about China. The reason Chinese culture was so important for people going abroad was that it would be "a useful frame of reference when we then go to study in the West."[73] Besides the foregoing issues, the confrontation between the Eastern culture and the Western culture was another unavoidable issue for every open-minded intellectual. During the May Fourth Era, there were two extreme schools: one called for "wholesale westernization"; the other insisted on "preservation of the national quintessence." Mao had close contact with the leading figures of the former school, but, instead of going to an extreme, such as the school of "wholesale westernization," he employed an attitude that took in everything that was good for him. This attitude was part of his practical characteristics, but it was nonetheless the result of his theoretical thinking. Mao made a philosophical assumption; "For the ultimate principles are the truths of the universe; the peoples who live in the world are each an integral part of the universe, so the universal truth resides in the heart of every man."[74] Logically, error should be universal too. Mao extended his sight to the realm of world culture,

In light of the interrelationship and identity between diversified cultures, Mao always quoted either Eastern or Western theories and anecdotes as proof for his arguments. He did not distinguish different schools. He opposed taking any authority for granted. Comparing his *isms* to current politics, using his own words, his cultural adoption was quite "broad-minded." Mao's flexibility in his scope of culture was a dissenting element at that time, given the fever for Westernization. Moreover, Mao put his concentration on China, realizing that Chinese culture would be, for the Chinese intellectual youth, a frame of reference to study and utilize world culture.

Nevertheless, it would be a misinterpretation of Mao's focus if one looked at Mao merely as a patriot whose ultimate goal was in China. Conversely, with the world as his political destination, he started from China, the place he had best access to begin his political long match. Holding such a destination, Mao opposed "patriotism" while he promoted "worldism" for carrying out "Socialism." Mao hoped that the New People's Study Society had an "international flavor," so as to produce radical changes all over the world. Mao's pen had gone to Russia, Korea, South Asia, as well as Mongolia, Xinjiang (Uygur), Tibet, and Qinghai.[75]

Mao wrote these words in December 1920. This was, according to Mao's recollection, the time he converted to Marxism. In the sense of seeking a road to political power, Mao's self-identification was trustable, because Marxism at that time was just another word for a Russian-type revolution. Therefore, it is clear that Mao was ready to enter a new period in his colorful life.

Chapter 2

World Watcher (2):
Mao As A Revolutionary (1921-1935)

In July 1921, at age 28, Mao took a boat to Shanghai. The trip was an important departure to join twelve others for the founding of the Chinese Communist Party, and also it was an extraordinary start for Mao on his revolutionary career.

Revolution was a fundamental concept in Mao's whole life, which colored and framed Mao's world view in many perspectives. As noted before, he had been a faithful believer in constant and permanent changes of the world from his student days onward. Since 1920-1921, Mao had discovered the most efficient way to practice his philosophical belief of change. The way was revolution instead of reform that he used to promote. Nevertheless, labeling Mao as "a revolutionary" from 1921 to 1936 in this chapter is a research-oriented consideration: First, Mao played a prominent revolutionary role during this period on both of two remarkable stages: (1) From 1921 to the mid-1927, Mao was a nationalist with Marxist-Leninist Faith, (2) From the mid-1927 to 1935, Mao was a communist in peripheral position. The stages were divided by the break off the First United Front between the CCP and the KMT in 1927. In both stages, Mao was deserve to have this label in the full sense of revolutionary. Second, the label implied certain limitations of Mao's role. Mao was not in a position to deal with top level affairs, including foreign related matters. Mao began developing his beginning thoughts on the Chinese revolution, but had limited opportunity to develop his own world view. Compared with the period of his radical youth, Mao's concept of the world in this period was less colorful, but more utilitarian. Compared with his next period as a communist leader, Mao's world view was less personal flavor but more Marxist-Leninist orthodoxy. Frankly, it is a comparatively less exciting period to explore Mao's world view. Nevertheless, one should not jump over these sixteen years if he wants thoroughly to review Mao's concept of the world in his early life. Besides, the features of utilitarian and Marxist-Leninist were important parts of Mao's world view, let alone the fact that Mao made some interesting points during this period linking a radical youth's world view to that he held as a communist leader.

(I) A Nationalist with Marxist-Leninist Faith (1921-1927)

Mao's activities in the pre-1927 period contained three components. First, he experimented with social reform, especially educational and cultural reform, a concern Mao had held since his student life. The noticeable instance was the founding of the Hunan Self-Study University (August 1921). In April 1923, Mao established the monthly *New Age* (*Xin ShiDai*) in the name of the Self-Study University. Second, he tried to build the Chinese Communist Party (and the Party's peripheral organization--the Socialist Youth Corps) in Hunan and carry out the directions of the CCP Center including his involvement in the Hunan labor movement from 1921 to 1923 until he was expelled by Zhao Henti, the warlord Hunan Governor.

Mao's flight from Hunan allowed him to participate in the affairs of the First United Front, established with the help of the Soviet Russians via the Comintern. Thus, a third focus of these years was Mao's active participation in the joint cause of the CCP and the KMT to carry off the National Revolution to achieve a re-integrated and independent China. From mid-1923 to mid-1927, Mao retained high posts in both the CCP and the KMT and his opinions were influential, but not crucial. Mao had more say regarding the issues of Party propaganda and the peasants' movement in the KMT than in the CCP, although his ideological and political loyalty belonged to the CCP alone.

Mao's writings appeared in the documents on political

organizations (the CCP or KMT's conference documents and the documents of activities of labor and peasants' organizations), in some public periodicals (such as *The New Age, The Political Weekly, The Guide, The Chinese Youth, The Chinese Peasantry*), and some letters and poems. For a world view, these writings represented three important interrelated theses: revolution, imperialism and the popular mass. These theses were not new for Mao but they had more practical significance and ideological complexity compared with those in the previous period.

On January 21, 1921, Mao wrote a letter to his comrade-in-arms Chai Heshen, who greatly influenced Mao in basic Marxist theory. Mao discarded Anarchism for Historical Materialism, the social and historical theory of Marxism. He believed that revolution was the vehicle of social and historical transformation. In Marxism, revolution required for political organization and political power; otherwise, one "cannot launch the revolution, cannot protect the revolution, cannot complete revolution." Politics was the content of revolution. The applicability of politics was universal, either for a nation-state or for the whole world. Therefore, revolution gained its universality, too.[76]

Five years later (1926), Mao still held the idea of universality of revolution. His famous article, "Analysis of Classes in Chinese Society," was first published on February 1, 1926. It was officially selected in the early 1950's as the first article in the CCP version of *Selected Writings of Mao Zedong* with some substantial revision, including all the words quoted here. Mao wrote:

> The attitudes of the various classes in China towards the [national][77] revolution correspond almost exactly to the attitudes of the various classes in the capitalist countries in Europe and the West towards the social revolution. This at first sight seems strange, but there is nothing strange about it. That is because the revolutions of today are one, their aims and their means are similar; similar in that they have the overthrow of international capitalist imperialism as their aim and similar in that they adopt uniting the oppressed nations and classes to wage war as their means. This is the point wherein today's revolution and all past revolutions most differ.[78]

Through interchanging the terms of three (political, social, national) revolutions, Mao indicated another meaning of universality of revolution that embraces every important aspect of human life in the world.

Mao expressed his understanding of the current (mid-1920's) Chinese revolution as a reflection of China's politics. His focus shifted from societal problems to domestic and international politics because these dominated China's situation. In the mid-1920's, China's political situation meshed with major external powers and internal political or military forces of different factions or warlords. Therefore, the goal of the Chinese revolution was, as articulated by Mao in the first issue of the *Political Weekly*,[79] to liberate the Chinese nation, to bring about the rule of the people and, to see that the people attained economic prosperity.[80] Apparently Mao's concept of national revolution then was just another expression of the goal of Sun Yat-sen's Three People's Principles.

Mao's thinking about revolutionary strategy and tactics was quite distinguishable for its Chinese type of Marxism-Leninism. In his "Introduction to the Series on the Peasant Question" on September 1, 1926, Mao wrote:

> ...the primary object of the revolution in an economically backward semi-colony is the rural patriarchal-feudal class (the landlord class). ...the imperialists externally and the ruling class internally rely entirely on the whole-hearted support given them by the feudal landlord class in order to realize their oppression and exploitation of those within this territory who are the objects of oppression and exploitation, i.e., mainly the peasants....Thus the rural feudal class of an economically backward semi-colony constitutes the sole firm base of the domestic ruling class and the foreign imperialists; if we do not shake this base, we certainly can never hope to shake the superstructure built upon it.[81]

Here, Mao applied Marxist terms to Chinese reality that was distinct from other nations. He set a fundamental objective for national, political, and social revolution, which was to eliminate foreign imperialists and the domestic ruling class by destroying their social base--the rural feudal class.

According to Mao, to do this one needed to use revolutionary means:

> A revolution is not a dinner party, or writing an essay, or painting a

picture, or doing embroidery; it cannot be so refined, so leisurely and gentle, so 'temperate, kind, courteous, restrained, and magnanimous'. A revolution is an insurrection, an act of violence whereby one class overthrows the power of another....To put it bluntly, it is necessary to create terror for a short period. ...Proper limits have to be exceeded in righting a wrong, or else the wrong cannot be righted.[82]

In Mao's mind, revolution was generally ruthless, although ruthlessness would not cover all of Mao's ideas about the revolutionary approach.

Mao was sophisticated enough to clarify various political and social forces. Another famous quotation from Mao's writing was used as the first sentence in all *Selected Works of Mao Zedong*:

Who are our enemies? Who are our friends? This is a question of the first importance for the revolution. The basic reason why all previous revolutionary struggles in China achieved so little was their failure to unite with real friends in order to attack real enemies.[83]

Mao believed his conclusion was to have learned a lesson from previous Chinese revolutionary strategy.[84] In the mid-1920's, Mao approached the "friend or enemy" question-related revolutionary strategy through two important issues: imperialism and popular mass, namely, the issues of revolutionary object and revolutionary subject.

Imperialism is a word no politically crucial figure of modern history, especially modern Chinese history, can avoid. It was even more necessary in China of the 1920's. Imperialism then referred to foreign powers with their respective "dirty-ends" intervening in China's internal affairs. Therefore the term became a synonym for the "ganging up" between internal and external political forces. Either Soviet Russia or the Western Powers could be guilty of imperialism-- "Red Imperialism" "Capitalist Imperialism,""International Imperialism" etc. Thus "imperialism" in Chinese politics of the 1920's was a practical and functional term associated with particular issues, especially domestic ones.

In Mao's writings, the concept of imperialism was some times used as a watershed for distinguishing revolutionary and counter-revolutionary, friends and enemies. Sometimes, imperialism became an antonym for Communism. To make the new vocabularies include words, such as "imperialism," comprehensible to the peasants, Mao used the countryside dialect; He translated the slogan of "Down with Imperialists" into "Down with the Foreign Moneybags" (*Dadao Yangcaidong*).[85] However Mao and other revolutionaries might have absorbed Lenin's theory about the relationship between imperialism and the Oriental revolution.

At the age of thirty, Mao wrote "External Force, the Warlords, and the Revolution." Three and half years later, in December 1926, he drafted "Declaration of the First Congress of Peasant Representatives of Hunan Province." With these two documents it was possible to understand Mao's concept of imperialism in that period.

In the latter article, Mao linked a political-economic perspective to China's modern history:

> From the time when the forces of imperialism first committed oppression against the East, destroying our `policy of national seclusion' and laying open our agricultural economy,...foreign oil, foreign cloth, foreign nails, foreign soda, foreign pottery, foreign iron....The lists of foreign goods are endless, have already flooded our cities and are beginning to invade our villages....Moreover the imperialists ally themselves with the warlords; ...have extended many loans to the warlords and the warlords have increased their exploitation of the peasants in order to repay them. The warlords use the unemployed peasants to organize private armies and the imperialists supply the weapons to create military power as a tool to oppress the peasantry.[86]

In the "External Force..." article Mao stretched his vision by putting China's problem into the context of the international order. He anticipated that in the next eight to ten years, the warlords would still rule the roost and China's situation would be even worse. He gave two reasons for this: the new world order settled by the Washington Conference, and China's extreme backwardness in the current political-economic situation. He wrote:

> You see how reactionary the political situation of international capitalist imperialism was! They are coordinating their moves for invading China. Before, their steps were uncoordinated, today they became coordinated through negotiation of the Washington Conference. Although the coordination will break up eventually, at present and in the near future, they definitely need to adopt coordinationism (Xietiao Zhuyi) in order to compensate themselves

for the loss from the previous great war and to shore up their energy
for the next great war. A conspicuous evidence was the `Open Door'
policy of the United States that could go so far as to get through
Britain, France and Japan who all have had respective spheres of
influence in China. China's disintegration would be not so good for the
invasion of international capitalist imperialism. However if China is
united by the democratic group, it will be comparatively worse for
international capitalist imperialism than the case that China remains
in chaos because of the struggle between the democratic group and the
warlords. The only case that will be the most beneficial for them is
that China is controlled entirely by the counter-revolutionary
politics.[87]

Mao consistently expressed his optimism while facing negative
pressure. He concluded his article with his "revolutionary dialectics":

The only thing we know is that it is a time of chaos, absolutely not a
time of peace and unification; politics will be more reactionary and
tumultuous. But this is the source of peace and unification, the mother
of revolution, the holy medicine of democracy and independence. It
should be known to everyone.[88]

How do you make everyone "know" revolution? Whom is the
major force in the society for carrying out revolution? The question of
the revolutionary subject is no less crucial than the question of the
revolutionary object. For Mao, it was the peasantry that would be the
major force as revolutionary subject. He became well known for the
stress he placed on mobilizing the peasantry.

People tends to explain Mao's rural complex with his family
background or sinitic Marxism. But a problem arises when tracing
Mao's class analysis in the 1920's, as was suggested by an article
written by Mao, "The Beijing *Coup d'Etat* and the Merchants,"
published in the *Political Weekly* in mid-1923. Here, Mao put the
merchants in the leading revolutionary position for "the whole
country."[89] This point was not Marxist-Leninist and sharply conflicted
with his emphasis on students, workers, and later, peasants.
Nevertheless, Mao's point of temporarily highly regarding merchants
were coincided with his great attention to the popular mass in his
article "The Great Union of the Popular Masses" in the May Fourth
era.

For Mao, a three-division approach was basic to observing people in the world. He felt there were three categories of people, rather than many classes, in China and in the world as well. In April 1923, he said, "If we analyze various domestic political forces, there are nothing more than three groups: revolutionary democrats, and non-revolutionary democrats, reactionaries."[90] In February 1926 he wrote: "In all countries between heaven and earth there exist three categories of people: upper, middle, and lower."[91] In any kind of revolution, revolutionaries, friends, and enemies are another triple division. Mao's strategy was to employ as many various political and social forces as possible to fulfill the revolutionary goal. The popular mass, which included everyone, except for revolutionary selves and enemies was the decisive force between the two extremes.

Utilizing the popular mass demands extraordinary skill to elevate a group of people for a time to a more important position among the popular mass. Therefore, promoting merchants to a special role when necessary, or lifting up peasants in most period of his pre-1949 revolution was the same example of Mao's strategic skill for attaining his goal. However this skill was based on Mao's understanding of Chinese reality and his belief in the functional importance of popular mass. The skill was not pure Marxism, but a lesson Mao learned from the Russian Revolution.

Later, Mao improved his idea with the point of "class struggle" that is simply part of Marxism. However while it was an idea Mao accepted in his early Marxist career, he understood this concept with his own interpretation. For Mao, the function of class struggle was to mobilize the popular mass, either in part or as a whole, depending upon the revolutionary needs. The function of the mobilized popular mass was an instrument for achieving his revolutionary goal. The popular mass was equally important revolutionary philosophy to the concept of class.

For instance, as cited before, Mao, in his famous article "Analysis of Classes in Chinese Society," at first divided people into three categories: upper, middle, and lower, and then classified "five categories" of social classes. This point appeared in the first and second edition of the article published in *Ge Ming* (*Revolution*), December 1, 1925, and in *Zhongguo Nongming* (*Chinese Peasantry*), February 1, 1926, respectively. A month after the publishing in *Zhongguo Nongming*, the point of the three categories was left out when it was re-printed in *Zhongguo Qingnian* (*Chinese Youth*), March 1926. Possibly it might have been Mao's meticulous consideration for matching his ideological commitment, because *Zhongguo Qingnian* was an organ of the CCP; it required more of a Marxist flavor.[92]

Besides responding to three major issues, viz. revolution, imperialism and popular mass, Mao had held some foreign-affairs related ideas, which had, to various degrees, significance for his later external perspectives. For instance, he criticized a well-known political faction in China's New Foreign Policy Clique, which was led by an early Chinese diplomat Gu Weijun, "who represented the interests of British and U.S. imperialism, especially those of the latter,..."[93] Mao advocated a nationalist proposition--anti-Christianity. He regarded the activities of foreign missionaries as an invasion by foreign religions. He appealed to his fellow countrymen to prevent further loss of territory, to eliminate all unequal treaties, and to protect national industries.

Mao grew to dislike the persons who were sent to China by the Third International (the Comintern). He had not much personal contact with Moscow's envoys such as Gregori Voitinsky, Jahn Henricus Sneevliet (Marin), Adolf Joffe, M. N. Roy, and Mikhail Markovich Borodin. Although he enthusiastically followed the directions of the Comintern, especially before 1926, Mao called a representative of the Comintern *yang guizi* (foreign devil), a derogatory term for Chinese to express their detestation with foreigners for a long time, when he was speaking to his colleague Zhang Guotao.[94]

Ten years later, when Edgar Snow asked him whom he considered most responsible for the failure of the Communist Party in 1927, after placing the greatest blame on Chen Duxiu, the head of the CCP, Mao listed the mistakes made by Moscow's envoys:

> Borodin stood just a little to the right of Chen Duxiu...and was ready to do everything to please the bourgeoisie, even to the disarming of the workers, which he finally ordered... M. N. Roy ...stood a little to the left of both Chen and Borodin, but he only stood.... and he talked too much, without offering any method of realization. ...Roy had been a fool, Borodin a blunderer, and Chen an unconscious traitor."[95]

The man behind these envoys was Stalin who had taken over the leadership of the Comintern from Grigory Zinoviev in 1926, and sent

Borodin and Roy to China. Apparently Mao knew the political background of these persons but he started his dissatisfaction with them.

(II) A Communist in a Peripheral Position (1927-1935)

The political events of mid-1927--in Shanghai (April 12), Changsha (May 21) and Wuhang (July 15)--marked a catastrophic failure for the Communist Party and the triumph of the Nanjing dictatorship that was led by Chiang Kai-shek. The political storm was a remarkable opportunity for Mao to test his abilities, to project his own political cause, and to develop his style of theory, including his world view.

Mao's "long, open struggle for power," in his words to Edgar Snow,[96] had three targets: all imperialists, especially the Japanese, the Nationalist government (particularly Chiang Kai-shek's regime), and many Communist leaders who were Mao's opponents on his road to power. The most criticized group was the so-called "Russian returned students" backed by Moscow or the Comintern.

From mid-1927 to late 1935 Mao finally emerged at the center of the political scene. He had been opposed within the CCP for many years, finally establishing his dominant position at the Zhunyi Conference on the Long March in January 1935. From one of the KMT's most wanted "red bandits," he became the leading representative of a major political force not in office. What Mao did was more conspicuous than what he wrote during this era that might be called either "Red Army era" or "Jiangxi Soviet era." However in fact Mao produced a number of writings that detail his first steps toward developing an independent theory of his own.

As Kenneth E. Shewmaker shows, there was worldwide ignorance of Mao and the CCP, "From 1928 to 1936 they [i.e. foreigners, particularly Americans] could not see much beyond the Nationalist-inspired bandit-remnant thesis....It seems clear, moreover, that Chinese communism was not a topic of international concern."[97] Conversely, Mao continued with his enthusiasm for current affairs. The few available letters show his eagerness to obtain newspapers and magazines while he was living in remote and backward Jinggang Mountain. He used desperate words, "We want to have newspapers and books as if thirsting or hungering for something."[98] After he had access to daily newspapers, he wrote, "The happiness is indescribable like brushing aside the clouds and seeing the blue sky."[99] Therefore, Mao always displayed his knowledge, understanding and perspective of international situations, no matter how ill-informed the objective environment he was in.

On October 5, 1928, Mao drafted a resolution for the Second Party Congress of the Hunan-Jiangxi Border Area. He briefly, but clearly reported the international situation, including Japan's dispatching of troops to Manchuria, the Naval Agreement between the British and France, and the American confrontation with Japan, Britain and France on issues of China and Europe.[100]

On October 26, 1930, Mao analyzed another chapter of international events and of world revolution in a document for the Red Army and party. He mentioned the international disputes among the world powers such as Italy and France preparing for war and Britain's denouncement of the United States for increasing its tariff. He noted worldwide tensions between the working classes and the capitalist class.[101]

In March 1932, Mao gave a lecture on behalf of the Provisional Central Government in the border area controlled by the CCP. He analyzed the political situation after Japan's occupation of Manchuria, "The tension of confrontation between the United States and Japan reached the extreme....However, imperialists will never forget to launch their offensive on Soviet Russia..."[102]

On August 30, 1933, Mao telegraphed an international conference held in Shanghai. He believed "the panic of world capitalism has become deeper; the temporary stability of capitalism since post-world War I was over." This was reflected by the worldwide economic crisis and the fascist craze in capitalist countries, especially, Germany, Italy, and Japan. An imperialist war would be the only outlet for them to overcome the economic crisis.[103]

On January 24, 1934, Mao, as the chairman of the Chinese Soviet Republic, gave a report to the second All-Chinese Congress of Soviets at Ruijin, Jiangxi Province. He stressed the confrontation between the socialist world and the capitalist world. As a representative of the socialist world, Soviet Russia achieved victories in its "First" and "Second" five-year plans. Conversely, the capitalist world was in a stage of economic panic; as a result, even the United States, the most obstinate among imperialists, had to establish diplomatic relations with Soviet Russia. Meanwhile, there was frenzied preparation for the war to re-divide the world among the capitalist countries.[104]

A few months later, on June 19, 1935, Mao drew up a declaration for the Chinese Soviet Republic to attack the KMT policy on the Northern China issue. He delineated the policies of the powers for China and showed that these policies would help either to monopolize China or to carve up China, neither of which would be good for China. Therefore, the anti-imperialism program should include a twofold mission: oppose Japan's movements in China and reject the League of Nation and the United States.[105]

Given the difficult political and physical conditions of Jiangxi, it is impressive that Mao maintained his attention on world affairs and developed his thinking about the revolution and imperialism that he had discussed in the early 1920's. Although the information he received was fragmentary, his viewpoint was full of communist ideological color.

The basic assumption underlying Mao's world view was that of integrating China and the world. Mao gave a brief explanation about this in his article "On Tactics Against Japanese Imperialism," written shortly after the Long March on December 27, 1935. He said, "Ever since the monster of imperialism came into being, the affairs of the world have become so closely interwoven that it is impossible to separate them."[106] Clearly, this is a Leninist view about the outcome of the emergence of imperialism.

However, Mao contributed his methodology, with the linkage between Marxism-Leninism and Chinese revolution, to the CCP's experiences in the modern world. His general approach was to use external elements to illuminate the internal revolution. With this approach, Mao gave new meaning to the combination of Marxist-Leninist revolution and Chinese nationalist revolution. In other words, Mao constructed his revolutionary road on an original but solid ground.

Two themes, the understanding of China's semi-colonial society and dealing with the problems of revolution and war, played a crucial role in shaping Mao's thought in this period. They were also the main components of his world view in the connection between his domestic thinking and international outlook and the complicated relations between Mao and Soviet Russia. These two themes are discussed in

Chapter 7. The significance of the themes in Mao's divergence with Moscow, through the so-called "Russian returned students," is covered in Chapter 5.

One of the most notable issues in China's external relations was her reaction to Japan's increasing intrusion into China's political and geographical territory. Japan had been recognized as a major potential threat to China since 1915, the time of "Twenty-one Demands." Japan became a real threat beginning in the late 1920's, and the Japanese issue became one of the major theses in Mao's writings in this era. Mao did not deal with this thesis only in the narrow patriotic sense. Rather, he used the Japanese challenge tactically and called for a united front in response to Japan's aggression. Thus, external threat was utilized for the CCP's internal political quest--moderating the civil war and giving the CCP a shelter under the nationalist flag. Mao also perceived the Japanese issue philosophically as the major contradiction that could resolve the key tensions in the complicated political environment.

In October 1928, a few months after Sino-Japanese clashes at Jinan, Shandong province, Mao answered the question, "Why is it that red political power can exist in China?" His major contribution was his semi-colonial theory. Japan's dispatching of troops to China proper was one of international facts Mao cited to prove his point. He asserted that impending external conflicts would lead to a new world war, but that it would be good for the survival and growth of Chinese Communism.[107]

In February 1932, following Japan's invasion of Manchuria and Shanghai, the "Soviet Government" in Jiangxi formally declared war on Japan. Clearly, the statement was no more than a posture, given the very difficult situation Mao and his Red Army were facing. However, they won credit for this stance that was repeated again and again in Mao's writings. Now Mao shrewdly seized the nationalistic banner to attack his main enemy, the KMT led by Chiang Kai-shek.

In addition he connected the Japanese issue to his semi-colonial theory, as he had in the late 1920's. Mao now specified the contradictions between Japan and other powers in early 1930's. He clarified different policies that the powers were carrying out in China. He pointed out that the Japan's policy of building monopoly China, by clashing with the "open door" policy, would produce tensions between

the United States and Japan. The situation would alter China's
international standing positively. In Mao's words:

> The Chinese revolution is part of world revolution. Because of the
> deepening of her national crisis, the overall crumbling of the nation's
> economy, the victory of the [Chinese] Soviet movement, the
> revolutionary situation in China is developing father and the Chinese
> revolution has been pushing to an extra outstanding status.[108]

A few months later, Mao and his comrades launched a political
and military relocation, known as the Long March, during which Mao
gained leadership of the Chinese communists. On December 27, 1935,
Mao gave a report at the conference of Party activists held at
Wayaobao in northern Shaanxi. At this meeting, one of the most
important ever called by the CCP, Mao started to talk about the
possibility and the importance of re-establishing a united front with
the national bourgeoisie. He also explained the connection between the
nation-wide struggle against Japan and the world-wide struggle
against fascism, and the relation between self-reliance and
international support. All these expositions and argumentation had a
philosophical base--"We must turn to good account all such fights,
rifts and contradictions in the enemy camp and turn them against our
present main enemy."[109]

Chapter 3

World Watcher (3):
Mao as a Communist Leader (1936-1941)

In October 1935, at a time when the Long March had almost reached its destination of northwest China, Mao wrote a poem "Kun Lun." He was still at a distance from the top of a central sub-range of the mountain, viewing Kun Lun, the largest mountain range in China and the sources of the Yellow and Yangtze rivers. The poem speaks of Mao's deepest thoughts and dreams regarding the world. More politically, as Mao said in a note about the poem in 1958, it addresses a theme of anti-imperialism. But, what else?

> I should put in a word now,/ Kun Lun:/ You don't need that height,/ Not so much snow./ If only I could lean on the sky/ And,/ sword drawn,/ split you in three-/ One part as gift to Europe,/ One part to Americas,/ One for the Eastern lands to keep-/ That Great Peace might reign on earth,/ A common heat and cool for the globe entire![110]

Does this sound like a hero who was elated with success and pride, or does it sound like a superman with a superiority complex and an egalitarian ideal looking down at the world of humankind? A few months later in February 1936, Mao chanted in another famous poem--"Snow" in similar mood: "All are past and gone,/ For manhood florid and full,/ Look--the galaxy today!"[111]

Truly, Mao was no longer the radical youth or a regular revolutionary; he was a crucial figure of modern China, the top communist leader. With this new position, his world outlook climbed to a new height. From 1936 to 1941, many important political dramas were enacted within and without the CCP, China, and the Far East. Mao followed these events closely and displayed himself as the head of a political force with a remarkable, and sometimes decisive voice.

In the Chinese Communist movement, Mao had solidified his dominant status through: (1) skillfully purging his political opponents, first Zhang Kuotao, then Wang Min, (2) expanding several self-sufficient red regions and the strength of military power, and (3) constructing a new ideology branded with his own name. This ideology was a hybrid of Marxism-Leninism, nationalism, and Chinese culture.

In relation between the CCP and the KMT, Mao tried to contend with Chiang Kai-shek in the second United Front and to carry out political struggle between the CCP and the KMT. The consequence of the two-party alliance and competition was favorable for the CCP because of Mao's political proficiency, the sentiment of nationalism, and the ever shifting context of the international scene.

With regard to the CCP controlled part of China and the outside world, Mao had a clear sense of how to juxtapose domestic affairs with international society. He was reasonable in ideological principles and a realist in practice inside and outside China when the CCP needed to react to international events. From 1936 to the end of 1941, Mao and the CCP tried to sell their politics and ideology to the public, to build a primary structure of principles, strategies and policies for their foreign affairs, and to be involved in the world's most significant politics.

Meanwhile, Mao rose in the Chinese Communist movement as a new authority with absolute power. His sinicized Marxism-Leninism, "Mao Zedong Thought," seemed ready to emerge at the call of Mao's supporters.[112] By now his world view had taken shape. Compared to the previous two periods, it had a richer factual and theoretical ground. Also his concept of the world had a practical significance on CCP activities, including foreign affairs. Moreover Mao's world view was embedded in CCP ideology and strategy. From 1936 to 1941 it consisted of three basic components: his practice of foreign affairs-related matters; his reactions and responses toward international politics; and his theoretical conclusion about his world outlook.

Because of the abundant materials available in this period, a chronological approach is employed in this chapter, and conceptual observances are discussed in the last part of this thesis.

1936 At the Seventh Congress of the Comintern in July-August, 1935, an anti-Fascist united front was the major issue raised by Comintern leader Georgi Dimitrov and its important members such as Wang Ming, who headed a delegation of the Chinese Communist Party in Moscow. A new direction of the Comintern served as a milestone for Stalin's efforts since 1934 to move towards rapprochement with the capitalist democracies and to build a favorable environment for Soviet Russia.

The new direction of the Comintern was recognized by Mao with some important reservations. The year 1936 became a period of shaping the Second United Front in China and a time for talking about an international united front. On May 15, 1936, a meeting of the Standing Committee of the Politburo was held to discuss international relations and foreign policy of the party. Mao's speech indicated common ground for a united front in and out of China that involved the interests of different nations in China and suggested a united front of anti-Japanese invasion to China. Mao annouced that the CCP would talk to those nations based on their interests in China.[113]

A few months later, when he had a formal conversation with Edgar Snow, Mao extended his point by stressing China's real independence. First, Mao pulled together all those with the interests on the Pacific Ocean who suffered from Japanese invasions. They "can be organized into anti-war, anti-aggression, anti-Fascist world alliances." Second, Mao delineated friendly or hostile powers by their attitudes towards China's anti-Japanese course. The line would be used to determine which powers could enjoy mutual advantages with China after the war. Third, Mao described a bright future for both Chinese and foreigners based on one important condition--China's real independence. Fourth, Mao invited external assistance while keeping a strong dignified mood of nationalism. He ended the topic by saying: "China must also seek assistance from other powers. This does not mean, however, that China is incapable of fighting Japan without foreign help!"[114] These were not merely empty words. They implied that the CCP had an uncomfortable relationship with Moscow at that time.

In another talk with Snow about the relationship between the CCP and the Soviet Union, Mao's attitude was even clearer. He defined the Comintern's function as a consultee and asserted that the CCP could only speak for the Chinese nation, not for the Russians.[115]

1937 The Xian Incident (December 12, 1936) and its aftermath were a consequence of the effort of the anti-Japanese alliance. The united front was established after the Lugouqiao Incident (also known as the Marco Polo Bridge Incident) on July 7, 1937.

The most remarkable speech regarding the CCP response to international politics was Mao's interview with Agnes Smedley on March 1, 1937. He reasserted the continuity of the CCP policy of a united front since his talk with Snow. He declared that the basis of the united front on the international level was that "the countries like Britain, the United States, France, and the Soviet Union pay their sympathy for China's anti-Japanese movement, or at least do not oppose it." Mao believed war with Japan was inevitable because of Japan's warlord government and because of the newly signed Anti-Comintern Pact of November 25, 1936 between Germany and Japan. He refuted the Japanese notion of a "Far Eastern Peace," which, Mao asserted, was a dream of "subjugating a nation without fighting." To obtain a real peace, Mao suggested an alliance such as a "Pacific Collective Security Pact" embodying all the major nations concerned, rather than maintaining treaties containing merely moral sanctions. Mao pointed to five nations: China, Britain, the United States, France, and the Soviet Union for establishing a Pacific United Line. This would help China as well as the others.[116]

After July 7, 1937, with the breakout of the full-scale Sino-Japanese War, Mao gave a new title to his foreign policy: anti-Japanese foreign policy. It was consistent with what he had announced a few months previous, "Immediately conclude a military and political alliance with the Soviet Union and closely unite with the Soviet Union, the country which is most reliable, most powerful and most capable of helping China to resist Japan."[117] Mao's appeal had its factual ground a month later when the Soviet government concluded a non-aggression pact with the Nanking central government and granted it military and technical assistance.

1938 The year was a relatively stable time for the united front internally, but the external united line in the Pacific Rim which Mao hoped for was far from materialized. The main political domain was Europe; however, Germany and Italy were in an offensive mood, while Britain and France acquiesced and accepted the *fait accompli*. Under these circumstances, Mao extended his reading and writing from military affairs to philosophy. Netheless he continued to be interviewed by foreigners and to express his observations on international politics.

In an important conversation with Evans Carlson on May 5, 1938, Mao made several predictions about international politics. After the Austro-German crisis in March and the conclusion of the Anglo-Italian Pact in April, Mao developed a deeper skepticism about Great Britain whom Chinese felt was unreliable. He flatly dismissed Carlson's anticipation that if Germany invaded Czechoslovakia, Britain might declare war on Germany. Mao asserted that Britain would not fight Germany for Czechoslovakia. Mao's judgment was proven correct a few months later by the German-Czech crisis and the dismemberment of Czechoslovakia. The second predication Mao made in his talk to Carlson was that war between the United States and Japan would break out in the future. Another predication was the fate of Japanese imperialism in China. He likened China to a gallon jug which Japan was trying to fill with a half pint of liquid.[118]

Mao's optimistic foresight had an international basis. In his article "Problems of Strategy in Guerrilla War," he says,

> If on the international plane we can create an anti-Japanese front in the Pacific region, with China as one strategic unit, and the Soviet Union and other countries which may join it as other strategic units, we shall then have one more form of encirclement against the enemy than he has against us and bring about exterior-line operations in the Pacific region by which to encircle and destroy fascist Japan. To be sure, this is of little practical significance at present, but such a prospect is not impossible.[119]

Such an anti-Japanese front in the Pacific region was suggested by Mao in 1937. Although it became very unlikely in 1938, Mao still expected it would be realized with a protracted war. The idea of a protracted war was the most important theory about the Sino-Japanese War in particular and about the political theory in general.

After Munich's little entente, which fatally discredited the governments of Britain's Chamberlain and France's Daladier, Mao addressed a political report on behalf of the Politburo in three days of mid-October, 1938. The report was "On New Stage." From the perspective of Mao's world view, this essay offered his insight into world politics rather than a concrete analysis of current affairs. Mao was aware that:

> The world center of gravity is in Europe, the East is an important part around it....Every country, big or small, in the West is placing the resolution of the European problem on the number one priority; the Eastern problems have to be temporarily put in second place.[120]

The priority of world politics had a decisive impact on Sino-Japanese war. Mao taunted those who thought that China would soon turn to counterattack the Japanese. They mistakenly took the Soviet-Japanese tension and warfare on the frontier of eastern Siberia and Manchuria during July 11 and August 10 (the Zhanggaofeng Battle) as the outbreak of War.

Mao called on all Chinese to be concerned about the relationship between China and the world, especially to show solicitude for the current changes of European affairs. He wrote:

> The result of two groups of imperialists fighting each other (referring to the World War I) was to yield a new international circumstance. The development of the post-war politics and economy has generated a new result that brought the world in front of a new great war....After the Japanese invasion of the four provinces in Northeast China and the stepping up of Hitler, a new war of re-carving up the world has begun....Under such a situation, on one side, Japan, Germany and Italy have lined up an invasive camp, and started their war of aggression. On the other side, those democratic countries want to keep their vested interests, they are preparing war in the name of peace, but so far, they are unwilling to use their actual strength to impose sanctions against the invaders. Especially, the British policy of appeasement has, in fact, helped the aggressors...[121]

The result was that many intermediate countries became the first victims. Mao condemned Chamberlain's policy severely:

> The Munich Pact is the outcome of British policy of appeasement. If Britain does not change its policy, it will result in a larger scale war of adventure by the Fascist countries. The war between those big powers may not break out for the time being, the process of invading those intermediate countries is still on going. But it will be bound to have an unprecedented ruthless war in which all those big powers will be

involved. This is the certain prospect.[122]

Relating world politics with China's situation, Mao identified three key facts: (1) The war thus far involved about six hundred million people. In other words, one can say that a majority of the whole world has been mobilized. (2) The contradictions between Japan and the four powers, namely Britain, the United States, France and the Soviet Union, were deepening. Although Britain may compromise with Japan to some degree, complete appeasement was impossible, given the monopolistic policy of Japan. (3) Because of the Japanese offensive, China, the United States, and the Soviet Union, had an opportunity to unite.

Thus far, Mao's comments on international politics were factual and logical. However he never forgot he was a communist leader, particularly when he was talking publicly within the party. After the above remarks, he warned his comrades:

> But, we should not forget, number one, to be conscious of the difference between capitalist countries and socialist countries; number two, to distinguish the government and the people in capitalist countries; number three, it is even more important to be aware of the distinction between the current situation and that of the future. On the former, we should not place hopes too high....'rely mainly on our own efforts while winning over foreign assistance' should be the basis of our guiding principle.[123]

1939 In 1939, Mao believed there was a growing tendency for capitulationism in China and an increasing possibility of appeasement in East Asia. These tendencies were linked with an anti-communism movement. Despite the fact that the Munich period was gradually replaced by relatively strong attitudes adopted by Great Britain and France toward Germany in the West, especially after the annihilation of the Czechoslovak State and the Danzi-Polish Crisis, Mao believed that "the problems in the East and the problems in the West today are somehow different on concrete situations."[124] He saw what was happening in the West from an eastern viewpoint. Therefore, Mao thought the growing tension between the great powers and Germany in the West would bring about a compromise between those powers and Japan. Again Great Britain played a major role at this point. Mao warned:

There is still an isolationist point in democratic countries like Britain and the United States. They do not know that if China is defeated, then they would not be able to shake up the pillow and have a good sleep....The fire of war among these powers comes into view day by day, no country will be able to stay aloof from the affair. We agree with President Roosevelt's Declaration of Protecting Democracy, while firmly opposing Chamberlain's concession policy towards western Fascist countries. Up to today, Chamberlain has still retained a psychology of timidity and overcautious toward Japan.[125]

In June 1939, Mao wrote an outline for his report to a high-ranking cadres' conference in Yanan: "Outline of Opposition to Capitulationism." He connected a potential KMT surrender to Japan with recent KMT anti-communists' activities, and considered these trends the biggest danger in the current situation. According to him, an element to shape the situation was international pressure. The pressure would come from capitulationists of Britain, the United States, and France.

The term "capitulationist" was ambiguous. Sometimes Mao used it to criticize a specific person such as Chamberlain. In many cases, Mao complained of the policies of the three major western powers with this term. Nevertheless he might exclude someone such as Roosevelt. It was quite usual for Mao to pick up a term such as "democratic country" or "pacifistic nations" and refer to them in terms such as "imperialist"or "capitulationist," under different circumstances.

In mid-1939, Mao worried about a "Far Eastern Munich." He warned that "the `Far Eastern Munich' promoted by Britain, the U.S., and France, is about to reach a critical time." In regard to the situation in the West, Mao thought that "Britain, France and Soviet Union may reach their agreement," but one could not be too optimistic. "Even though the agreement has been concluded, it will still be possible to break up. The danger of a new Munich has not yet been eliminated." Mao believed that the major powers wanted war between Germany and the Soviet Union. Then they could take advantage of losses on both sides. It was a strategy of those so-called capitulationists.[126]

A series of important events had occurred. From August 20 to September 1, the Danzig-Polish Crisis; August 23, the Nazi-Soviet Pact; September 1, Germany attacking Poland, September 3, England and France Declaration of war on Germany. Mao and the CCP responded. Mao's contributions were "Interview with A *New China Daily* Correspondent On the New International Situation" (September 1, 1939), an editorial for the *New China Daily*, "The New International Situation and Our Nation's Anti-Japanese War" (September 7, 1939), a lecture at a cadre conference in Yanan, "An Outline of the Speech On the Second Imperialist War"(September 14, 1939), a conversation with Edgar Snow (September 25 and 26, 1939), and an article in *The Liberty* (Jie Fang): "The Identity of Interests Between The Soviet Union and All Mankind" (September 28, 1939).

The main CCP analysis systematically elaborated several points. First, the new European War was another imperialist war like World War I. Thus Mao called it "the Second Imperialist War." But according to his view, the second imperialist war actually started in 1931, the year of Japan's aggression in Manchuria. Participation of the major western powers after September 1, 1939 brought the second imperialist war to a new stage. Certain features differentiated it from the the first stage: (1) it was not a one-sided war but an all-embracing war so far as Europe was concerned, (2) it became meaningless to distinguish between fascist and democratic countries because of Britain and France's participation of European War, and (3) Great Britain masterminded the war and became a chief criminal.

Second, the Treaty of Non-Aggression between the Soviet Union and Germany was justifiable and had great political significance in international politics. On September 1, 1939, in an interview with a correspondent from Yanan's *New China Daily*, Mao gave his interpretation of the causality between the Soviet-German pact and Anglo-French-Soviet talks. Mao insisted that in recent years, Britain and France had consistently pursued the policy of "non-intervention" towards aggression by fascist Germany, Italy, and Japan. It was a policy of "sitting on top of the mountain to watch the tigers fight;" a downright imperialist policy of profiting at other's expense, including sacrificing the Soviet Union. This policy finally collapsed in the recent the Anglo-French-Soviet talks. The Soviet-German treaty came as a result.

Mao believed the treaty was the outcome of the growing socialist strength of the Soviet Union and the policy of peace persistently followed by the Soviet government. He expected the situation to develop into direct conflict between the Anglo-French and the German-Italian blocs. The significance of the treaty was great: (1) it halted the interference of Chamberlain and Daladier who sought to instigate a Soviet-German war, (2) the treaty had broken the encirclement of the Soviet Union by the German-Italian-Japanese anti-Communist bloc. It strengthened peace between the Soviet Union and Germany and encouraged further socialist growth in the Soviet Union, (3) it had a substantial impact on politics in the East.

Third, from a Chinese nationalist perspective, Mao thought that the recent events in the West had dual consequences. On the one hand, the Soviet-German treaty was a blow to Japan while helping China. Two factions within Japan were fighting over foreign policy. As Japan's difficulties increased, China refused to compromise. The stage of strategic retreat had ended for China and a strategic stalemate began. The new stage was what many Chinese, who accepted Mao's three-stage theory of the Sino-Japanese War, looked forward to in 1939. Mao argued that "with the breakout of the European war, the subjugation of Poland, continued fighting between Germany and Britain and France, if China will fight to the end and never give up halfway, China will set the second stage of anti-Japanese war."[127] Two months later the international situation Mao expected became a reality.

On the other hand, the stalemate stage was not a rosy time. In Mao's eyes, the European War raised the growing possibility of a British-Japanese compromise in East Asia. Since a Far Eastern Munich was the objective of British policy, the dangers of surrender of the greater part of China and of internal division would increase enormously.

As a Chinese communist leader who had just received official recognition from Moscow about a year ago, critical to determining the inner party struggle, Mao defended Soviet foreign policy and diplomatic action.[128] There was a great deal of suspicion about Moscow's actions in August and September 1939 within the Chinese Communist Party. Four points were under attack:

(1) The treaty with Germany, a leading fascist country, was a big shock for most. It is unlikely that Mao was informed by Moscow in advance, nor had Mao expected the treaty. When it became public, the Politburo was having a two day meeting, but gave no response. A week later, another Politburo meeting was held to assess the event. After which Mao justified Moscow's decision.

(2) Soviet trade with Germany and Japan raised questions. Mao's

article "Identity of Interests between the Soviet Union and All Mankind" and his interview with Edgar Snow followed the principle that "trade must not be confused with participation in war or with rendering assistance." The principle sounds acceptable, but Mao was unable to convince Snow that Soviet war-material sales to Japan and Germany were not harmful and could be considered normal trade. Mao also failed to differentiate such trade by Moscow from similar trade by Washington for which he had sharp criticism. Understandably this conversation was not published by the CCP; though Mao told Snow that he "does not care to have his point publicized."

(3) The Soviet invasion of eastern Poland, as Mao admitted, bewildered many people in China. In defense of Moscow, he used the word "enter" to downplay this aggression, and said that "As for the Soviet Union, its actions have been perfectly just." Three reasons were given for acceptance of Moscow's actions: to recover Russia's long lost territories, to emancipate the oppressed Ukrainian and Byelorussian peoples, and to check the eastward drive of the German fascist troops.[129]

(4) Another concern was a possible Soviet-Japanese non-Aggression treaty. In 1938 and 1939, Moscow faced two military conflicts with Japanese in Manchuria and Mongolia respectively. They brought two truce agreements: Zhanggaofeng on August 11, 1938 and Nomonhan in September 1939. The latter truce was concluded at a very delicate time in international politics, especially for Stalin. To answer the understandable Chinese concern, Mao idealized a possible Soviet-Japanese non-aggression treaty. He was unwilling to admit the realization of such a pact while it was only a rumor, in answering Snow's question concerning a Russo-Japanese rapprochement in late 1939. He knew that the Soviet Union had been proposing such a treaty for many years and a section of the Japanese ruling class might want it. In view of this, Mao had to use the term "Leninist possibility" to idealize the matter.[130] He affirmed that Moscow's decision would be based on the interests of the Soviet Union and the majority of humankind, especially the Chinese people. "Even if such a treaty were to be concluded, the Soviet Union would certainly not agree to anything that would restrict its freedom of action in helping China."[131]

In September 1939, Mao spoke very highly of Russia to such an extent as to be incompatible with his usual attitude toward Moscow and with his own personal characteristics. Mao's idealization and justification of Moscow was so shallow and weak that Snow concluded his report of the interview with a derisive tone: "Well, everything will go very well, [because Mao told him that Hitler was in Stalin's pocket] unless people discover later that there is a hole in Stalin's pocket."[132]

Although Mao was inconsistent in his attitude toward the Soviet Union, he was consistent and pragmatic about China's foreign policy. He announced, "As regards the aspect of diplomacy, `befriend all those helping us, be hostile to all those assisting our enemy,' this is our incontestable principle."[133] Mao reaffirmed this principle one week later. While it was a true reflection of Mao's priority outside the CCP, it was too narrowly defined to be the basis line of a political party.[134]

Almost immediately following Mao's defense of the Soviet Union on European politics in August and September 1939, Stalin and Hilter divided Poland between them on September 29. Two weeks later, the Soviet army invaded Finland and began the war that continued until March 12, 1940. No further materials are available on any argument by Mao in favor of Moscow's actions in the West.

1940 In 1940, the political scene was unclear and remained so until mid-1941 when the world divided into two relatively solid camps. On May 10, 1940, Neville Chamberlain resigned as prime minister and Winston Churchill took office. On November 5, 1940, Franklin D. Roosevelt was re-elected president of the United States for a third term. These events foreshadowed a tougher western policy in response to world fascism that concluded a three-power pact, known as the anti-Comintern Axis, on September 27, 1940.

The impact of world politics made China's politics confusing at first glimpse. Roosevelt escalated the "diplomatic war plan" against Japan by granting more loans to China and restricting the sale of strategic materials to Japan in 1940. Stalin reduced his aid to the Chinese Nationalist government to meet the increasing German threat in Europe. This aid had been substantial and had the additional affect of checking Chiang's desire for a showdown with the CCP. Japan had increased its pressure on the French Indochina and the Dutch East Indies colonies so it could be free from dependence on the United States for raw materials. In the meantime, Tokyo extended recognition to the puppet regime of Wang Jingwei in November of 1940, and encouraged a civil war in China to free Japan's troops for Southeast Asia.

At this point, as an American historian noted, as Chiang Kai-shek "became more certain of American support in 1941, he showed an increasing willingness to tolerate an `armed truce' with the Japanese and resume his long-standing conflict with the Communist."[135] Facing this situation, Mao and the CCP made important changes in their stand on China's relationship in world politics to fit the international and domestic situations that occurred in later 1940.

First, in place of his two-front division of world politics,[136] Mao began talking about three fronts. In mid-1940 Mao took advantage of the third anniversary of China's anti-Japanese war to update current affairs with a three-part division of international politics:

> Currently, the feature of the international situation is the struggle of three lines. One is the line of Germany-Italy-Japan imperialism, one is the line of Britain-France-United States imperialism, one is the peace line of Soviet Union....We can use the conflict between two imperialists' lines, especially, the growing contradiction between Japan and the United States in the Pacific area."[137]

This changed view of world politics was more elastic and realistic, although it was still full of an ideological tone.

Second, Mao changed his assessment of the possibility of a Far Eastern Munich, long a major concern. It had driven the CCP attitude toward the western powers, particularly Britain, in the latter part of 1939. Now in mid-1940, Mao told his followers;

> Britain, the United States, and France are no longer the important elements to lure China's surrender. Although British and Americans want to sacrifice China, in return for conserving Nan Yang (Southeast Asia), Japan does not want to obey.[138]

Instead of the Eastern Munich which Mao formerly attacked, new factors would be a fresh source of China's capitulationism--Japan's pressure on Chinese nationalists and the Germany-Italy policy of peace inducement on Sino-Japanese issue.

Third, at the end of 1940, Mao abandoned his opposition to Britain and the U.S., but still rejected joining the Anglo-American group. In November 1, his directive on the current situation implied that regardless which side Chiang allied himself with in the imperialist clique, neither one would be good for the CCP. But two days later, Mao instructed his subordinates, "Do not stress opposition to joining the Anglo-American clique, stress opposition to capitulationism immediately." On November 6, Mao telegraphed Zhou Enlai:

> For us, Chiang's joining the Anglo-American clique will gain everything and lose nothing, while if he joins the Berlin-Rome-Tokyo clique that will lose everything and gain nothing. We should no longer oppose him joining the Anglo-American group; however, we should not advocate it either (because that is an imperialist-war clique). Today, our Communist Party, Chinese people, and the Soviet Union, these three forces should unite, but they also need to have diplomatic connections with Britain and the United States, so as to stop capitulationism and to beat the activities of pro-Japan and pro-German groups.[139]

1941 Having made these important changes, Mao led the CCP into 1941, a year for settling the dust of international politics. Eventually a war unprecedented in human history began. Nevertheless the process of clearing the line of world politics between two groups of powers was complicated. As a result, Mao kept a close watch and commented on events, particularly on those related to China. His directives were, in most cases, distributed after discussions in the weekly Politburo meeting or every two weeks Secretariat meeting. On occasion a special conference might be summoned for a matter of great urgency.

The first event to which Mao and the CCP reacted harshly was a domestic affair known as the New Fourth Army incident, or the South Anhui incident. This occurred at the beginning of 1941 and was climaxed a long-standing controversy between the CCP and the KMT. The KMT attack on the CCP force resulted from growing Nationalist resentment over Communist expansion during the Sino-Japanese war, which contrasted so strikingly with the KMT losses. A deeper but more apparent reason was the long insoluble hostility between the two major political rivals. Generally, the incident had less to do with foreign factors. However Chiang's assurance of increased American aid and his decreased dependence on Soviet help may have encouraged his action.

Mao attributed the incident to foreign forces and subordinated domestic politics to international politics. On January 18, 1941, without a clear referent, Mao asserted that imperialists must have incited the KMT. On the 20th, the instigator became specific. He spoke publicly about the long-time plot of Japan and the pro-Japanese group in China since the Tripartite Pact of September 1940. In the next couple of weeks, on many occasions, Mao attributed the incident to Chiang's desire to have a free hand to handle the communist problem. His inconsistent explanations might have reflected poor information. But, more importantly, it manifested a process by which Mao and the CCP could formulate a flexible policy to fit theirs varied needs. Mao used the international element as a tactic to explain domestic events or as an excuse to transfer domestic problems wherever suitable for CCP needs.

The incident showed that at this critical moment neither Moscow nor Washington nor London was prepared to support a large-scale civil war between the CCP and KMT. The powers' refusal to endorse the KMT attack ensured that the CCP could retain what it had held since 1936. Thus the CCP could continue to raise the banner of nationalism, strengthening its power.

The negotiations between Moscow and Tokyo caused Mao and the CCP concern about their relationship with the KMT and the influence of the negotiations on the war. Mao's reaction prior to the conclusion of the Neutrality Treaty was twofold. On the one hand, he thought talk between the Soviet Union and Japan had softened Chiang's attitude toward the CCP, because the KMT, Britain, and the U.S. all appeared unwilling to see such a treaty signed. They needed, according to Mao, the CCP influence in the communist world. On the other hand, Mao believed that if the treaty was signed, it would have negative impact on relation between the CCP and the KMT, and between China and Soviet Russia. From the CCP interest, Mao preferred that the pact would be limited to economic scope.[140]

On April 13, 1941, the Soviet-Japan Neutrality Pact was signed by Foreign Minister Matsuoka Yosuke and Foreign Minister Vyacheslav Molotov. It was not an economic treaty. For Japan, it was designed to strengthen its position vis-à-vis the United States. For Soviet Russia, it avoided fighting on the eastern front and had a positive consequence for the war with Germany a few months later.

There was a mixed reaction to the pact in China. The KMT government protested that a declaration accompanied the pact implied

Soviet recognition of Manzhouguo as being under Japan's protection. Molotov's explanation of this matter and his assurance of continued Soviet supplies for China eased Chiang Kai-shek's mind. The CCP said nothing about the violation of China's sovereignty in Manchuria issue by the Pact. Once again, the combination of ideological and practical considerations prevailed over abstract principle.

Mao's immediate reaction was an unqualified endorsement. He correctly pointed out the favorable results for the Soviet Union. But he contradicted his analysis of previous weeks when he thought a political pact would be bad for CCP-KMT relation. Now he indicated that the pact would serve to stop capitulationism in China and to reduce the danger of the anti-Communist tide.

One practical aspect for the Chinese was whether Soviet aid would remain unchanged? The CCP answered publicly:

> The Soviet-Japanese Pact has not restricted the aid that the USSR renders as independent and just resistance....The hope of the Chinese people for aid from abroad rests, above all, on the USSR...by this treaty the USSR has not disappointed and will never disappoint China.[141]

The CCP faith had no time to be tested because of the outbreak of the war between Germany and the USSR, but the unqualified pro-Soviet attitude was, to a large extent, merely lip service. Mao was never truly satisfied with Soviet aid from the beginning of the Sino-Japanese war. For instance, On January 30, 1941, a time of increasing tension between the CCP and the KMT, Mao sent a telegram to Zhou Enlai, complaining that "if the Soviet Union still sends arms to Chongqing, that is too bad. Please ask the military attaché to find a way to stop it."[142]

With regard to the pact, Mao also had some unspecified reservations. When he spoke at the Politburo meeting on April 17, four days after the pact, he warned that Russia and Japan won freedom, but China's problems had not been solved. Even in the CCP official statement, the language used by Mao conveyed a hint of reproach to Moscow:

> We should not, as some opportunists do, hope that the Soviet Union will go to war with Japan and we shall reap the harvest, and get disappointed and blame the Soviet Union when she states that she will

not attack `Manchukuo'... We must recover all our lost territories, fight to the bank of the Yalu River, and drive the Japanese out of China.[143]

Recalling some of Mao's self-contradictory statements on the same issue, readers must have tried to keep in mind, "Separate the propaganda and the policy," as he advised on March 4, 1941.[144]

The year 1941 was also a time for intensified negotiation between the U.S. and Japan. Both sides were preparing for war, while trying to avoid it. Understandably, Mao and the CCP were unable to cover the entire process. For instance, Mao's writings criticized the U.S.-Japanese talks in general, and specifically mentioned a meeting in mid-May between the U.S. Ambassador to Japan, Joseph C. Grew, and Foreign Minister Mastuoka. In fact, the meeting was only a minor one and reflected the tough attitude of Mastuoka toward the U.S. Mastuoka's hard line position was the opposite of what Mao called the U.S.-Japan compromise on China issue.

Some suggestions arose regarding negotiations between China and Japan, but Mao refused all proposals for peace talks. He revived the abandoned term, "Far Eastern Munich," to oppose this. A typical statement was his article on President Roosevelt's "fireside chat" of May 27, 1941:

> This `chat' had a dual character: forcing German compromise and preparing to participate in the war....The purpose of Britain and the U.S. was still to solidify their command of the sea, and to restore their air domination, then to force Hitler to light the fire eastward....The `chat' of Roosevelt embodied a trick of a Far Eastern Munich too. According to the Associated Press, in his talk, Roosevelt only said that the U.S. had not yet examined relations between the U.S. and Japan,...the reason for saying this is to make room for Japan. In essence, it embedded a great plot; that is to sacrifice China in order to have a compromise between the U.S. and Japan. People must deepen their attention.[145]

Mao even dismissed the recommendation of Cordell Hull, then U.S. Secretary of State, who suggested peace between China and Japan and promised cancellation of American extraterritoriality in China. Mao gave Hull's promise a name--"the long-term rubber cheque," and said, "Uncle Sam, instead of writing the rubber cheque, you'd better stop sending oil, steel and other arms to Japan."

Mao renounced the American suggestion so as to grasp the banner of nationalism to compete with the KMT. Although Mao's statement was quite narrow-minded but workable. One privilege Mao enjoyed as a communist leader who was representing a major non-governmental and oppositionist force engaged in a nationalist war. He was fairly free to point at various world aspects that he felt suitable for CCP interests without having any practical and theoretical responsibility. When his points or predictions conflicted with the reality, he had political room to make changes.

Two indiscreet remarks typified this position in 1941. In mid-May, Mao denounced the U.S. and British "success" of their second Munich if war resulted between the USSR and Germany. He anticipated that "the peaceful policy of the Soviet Union is a brake for the whole world" which found itself facing a full-scale war. His words remained fresh in the reader's minds when Hitler launched an all-out invasion of the Soviet Union on June 22, 1941. Again in mid-June, Mao teased the KMT for putting hope on war between the U.S. and Japan, "There is no single trace on today's agenda indicating a war between Japan and the United States." These words contradicted his long-held belief that the U.S. and Japan must fight in some foreseeable time. In fact, Japan bombed Pearl Harbor on December 7, 1941.

These two wars, the USSR versus Germany and the U.S. versus Japan, became the cornerstone of modern history. They changed Mao's vision of the world, and for the first time, engaged Mao and the CCP in the main stream of word politics. Immediately after the German attack on Soviet, Mao drafted a document for the Central Committee, appealing for an anti-fascist international united front, "Unite Britain, the U.S., and all the peoples in other countries, who are oppose to German-Italian-Japanese fascism, to counterattack our common enemy." Three days later, Mao returned to his former two front world, the fascist and anti-fascist. This remained the basic line for the CCP in dealing with international politics until the mid-1940's.

On the July 6, Mao telegraphed Zhou Enlai, (1) the current situation of the Soviet Union appeared stable, and the Japanese seemed unwilling to attack the Soviet, but pinned down Britain and the U.S.; (2) people's attitude toward fascism distinguished them as good or bad, "Do not worry whether they are imperialist countries or not;" (3) the main strategy of dealing with Britain and the U.S. was to draw them to the Soviet side, and reduce criticism of them. The next day, the CCP

Center published a declaration for the fourth anniversary of Anti-Japanese war where Mao made similar points as in his telegram.

Mid-July to mid-August was critical period for the birth of the international anti-fascist united front. Great Britain and Soviet Russia concluded a mutual aid treaty on July 12, 1941; Roosevelt and Churchill met from August 8 to 13. They jointly initiated a Britain-U.S.-U.S.S.R. conference to be held in Moscow September 29 to October 1. After the meeting, Roosevelt and Churchill issued a joint declaration of peace, later known as The Atlantic Charter. Mao and the CCP Center made quickly response to the Britain-Soviet treaty. Mao telegraphed Zhou Enlai:

> The Britain-Soviet pact will become a pivot of world politics. The U.S. has, in the sense of politics, to follow this line, and will no longer be able to manipulate everything; the Britain-Soviet pact will have an impact on Japan, increasing its misgivings; also, the pact has influence on China, it will impel positive changes for relations between China and the U.S.S.R., and the CCP and the KMT.[146]

While directing his followers actively to contact British and Americans in China, Mao maintained a discriminating voice about the U.S., even after the Roosevelt-Churchill meeting. On August 18, Mao gave his opinion on the meeting and the joint declaration to the Politburo. The declaration declared the determination of the U.S. for participating in a counter-aggressive war; it was good for Britain, the U.S., the U.S.S.R. and China. It left no room for peace with Germany, but had some margin for accommodating Japan. The next day, Mao's speech became an official statement of the Central Committee:

> ...(The Joint Declaration and the proposal of a Moscow conference) is a vital event with world historical significance. From then on, a new stage of world history has been opened up....The Declaration did mention Japan, the fourth article implies the possibility of trade with Japan and material supply to Japan, the seventh article implies permitting Japanese immigration. This is still evidence indicating an effort to rope in the group of Japanese who suggest maintaining the current situation. It reflects the willingness of compromise with Japan; this is one side. But, the second article of the Declaration opposes forcefully changes to territory. The third article holds to restoring nations who were divested of their powers and rights. More important,

the eighth article acknowledges the necessity of disarmament of all the aggressive nations. These are all anti-Japanese activity.[147]

Apparently the Central Committee statement repeated Mao's speech but highlighted the significance of the Joint Declaration and the upcoming Moscow conference. Meanwhile it specified Mao's dual assessment of the Declaration on the issue of Japan.

During October and November, Mao and the CCP focused on important current changes in the international political scene, referring to the changed leadership of the Japanese government, (Prince Fumumaro Konoye had been replaced by General Hideki Tojo on October 17) and the crisis of Moscow undergoing a siege by Germany. After the resignation of the Konoye cabinet, Mao postponed a discussion within the Politburo. He suggested a "wait and see" attitude.

Several days later, on October 20, he gave his analysis on what was occurring in Soviet Russia and Japan. Mao believed "the current situation seemed to have reached a critical time of transformation." The new Tojo cabinet should be regarded as a direct war-preparation military cabinet. It might take either a northward policy or a southward strategy; however, neither would happen right away. Moscow was not out of danger but Germany's offensive may have run its course. The next couple of weeks would be very critical. The cooperation of the U.S., Britain, the Soviet Union and China was definitely going to win the struggle with fascism.[148]

Based on this assessment, at the "Eastern Anti-Fascism Conference" held in Yanan at the end of October, Mao said:

Now, we have three united fronts, one is China's anti-Japanese national united front; one is the "A B C D" line in the East; one is the joint action of Britain,the United States, and the Soviet Union,...[149]

In spite of the accepting the "ABCD Line" (referring to America, Britain, China and the Dutch), Mao was not satisfied about the American's action on the western front. He thought that the U.S. ought to declare war on Germany, the sooner the better. On the eastern front, he warned the U.S. not to listen to Japanese but to use her strength, together with Britain and China, to punish Japan.

After Pearl Harbor, the Politburo held a two-day conference to discuss the Pacific war. Mao expressed his understanding of the current situation. This became the guideline for the CCP to adopt new strategies, policies, and a public statement. Mao listed six advantages to the U.S.-Japanese war for the Soviet Union and China, particularly the Chinese Communist Party. First, the Japanese would be unable to launch a large scale military offensive in northern and central China. Second, the KMT attack on the CCP border region would be reduced. Third, it was a vital blow to pro-Japanese and pro-German forces. Fourth, Chinese democratic politics would be more promising. Fifth, Soviet Russia was able to move part of its military force from east to west. Sixth, there was a possibility for a second war front in Europe. Mao made his predication about the world war:

> At the initial stage, the prospect of a U.S.-Japanese war will be to the advantage of the Japanese; the war will be prolonged. It will take two to three years for Britain and the U.S. to prepare for the war, so that they will have a decisive engagement. Britain and the U.S. may concentrate their strength on beating Germany first, then, their forces will go eastward to defeat Japan.[150]

A similar statement was issued by the CCP on the second day of the meeting. Mao drafted it, once again using a two-division approach: on one side, were nations and states carrying on a just war to protect independence, freedom and democracy. On the other side, were nations and states launching an unjust and plundering war.

To adapt CCP moves to the new world politics, Mao directed active contact with the British and Americans; however, this had no significant result. Mao stressed the importance of the overseas Chinese in Nan Yang (Southeast Asia) and demanded his comrades strengthen their forces. Moreover, Mao took advantage of the Pacific war, instructing all party members and troops to work hard to regain CCP vitality in the coming year, 1942, because the CCP and its border regions had suffered heavy losses from the domestic politics of 1941.

From 1936 to 1941, Mao emerged as the political and military chief of the Chinese communist party. He championed himself as a Marxist-Leninist authoritative source within the CCP, with the help of Chinese red scholars, such as Chen Bodai, Ai Shiqi, Zhang Ruxing, and others. Meanwhile, through the extensive reading of Marxist literature written by Soviet scholars, and combining conceptual theory with his own personal understanding, experience, and characteristics, Mao developed a world outlook which had been developing since his youth and long-time revolutionary career. With his stabilized political position in the CCP, Mao's theory was praised by party leaders as a Sincized Marxism-Leninism. Mao was now ready to begin a two-pronged campaign: to purge alien party elements and to build a Mao-style ideology in the Chinese Communist Party.

Therefore, in addition to his responses toward international politics, as discussed in this chapter, Mao carried out CCP informal foreign affairs and foreign policies. He also developed a theoretical framework for his world view that became his justified source for interpreting Marxism and Chinese history, politics and culture in the CCP. Mao's practice of foreign relations will be specified in Chapter 7 and his theoretical world view will be discussed in Chapter 9.

PART TWO

MAO'S PERCEPTIONS OF THE WORLD

After the chronological review of Mao's speeches, writings and actions in the first half of his life, one needs to go farther for a thematic exploration of his world view. Logically, Mao's perceptions of the world will provide the basic framework of his world view, reflecting his feelings and understandings when stimulated by a changing world.

Chapter 4

The World and Its Connection With China

Up to the mid-19th century, China was self-imaged as a world center. The concept of Sino-centralism was typically demonstrated by the tribute system with her neighbors, and calling "barbarian" peoples in remote parts of the world. Generally, it was a cultural-oriented self-image and perception of others. The self-image and perception were misled by an old-fashioned tradition, especially in the 19th century. The Sino-centric image was smashed by the reality of world politics in modern history. Anyone encountering harsh reality would give up the ridiculous self-image and misperception of others. This was doubly true for those intellectuals in the May Fourth era. Mao was one of the May Fourth generation of Chinese intellectuals. He definitely had no Sino-centric perception of the world. Although he, like many other Chinese intellectuals, had a strong nationalist mentality, it was a result of national crisis rather than national arrogance.

Stimulated by such a historical environment, Mao's perception of the world shared the common ground of Chinese intellectuals of his generation. Mao mainly held political, economic and ideological perspectives, and stressed world society, world system, world order. However, Mao had his own frame of vision, which was the result of his reactions to the changing world.

(I) Mao's Approach to the World as a Whole

China was a newcomer to the international community after World War I.[151] Why one of the world's oldest nations had to be one of the latecomers of world society was due not only to the long-time self-restricted tribute system but also to the unequal treaty system, which replaced the tribute system after the mid-19th century.

From a Chinese nationalist perspective, the latter played an even more negative role, since the tribute system had gone forever. The situation did not improve substantially after China was aware of her inferior position in the international community at the end of World War I, especially at the Paris Conference in 1919. The awareness came despite the fact that the Conference symbolized a beginning of China's membership in world society in the sense of modern world politics and history.

Thereafter, to be an equal member of the international community was one of the primary goals pursued by Chinese, especially young Chinese intellectuals including Mao. The process of setting, routing, and reaching the goal had very much to do with their new perception of the world. Mao shared the principal points with the mainstream of Chinese intellectuals on the one hand, while he developed his own pattern of perceiving the world on the other hand.

The new perception of the world in early 20th century China was just common sense. The world as a whole is an all-nation-embraced society; everything in world society is interrelated, and every force in world society interacts. China is only a part of the world; She is a weak and passive member of world society. Despite the simplicity of these points, they were a revolutionary reversal of the notorious Sino-centric self-image. Thanks to the changes in Chinese world views since the second half of the 19th century, Mao had no psychological and contextual obstacle to receiving these basic ideas as his point of departure to further his perception of the outside world. However, some patterns of his perception of the world were distinctive.

(1) Being a world's inhabitant   In 1915, at age of 22, Mao wrote to his friend referring to himself as "an inhabitant of the world." He also realized that one can "study how to be an inhabitant of the world," and identified learning as "a matter of world view and of international relations."[152] Here, Mao extended the traditional Chinese view that treated history as a reference for current usage, especially in the political realm. The diversification of the world, for Mao, functioned as valuable experiences and lessons. In his writings and speeches, Mao was never hesitant to cite history, culture, and thinking from various nations, particularly world powers, no matter how negative his feelings toward the particular country under a particular circumstance at a particular time.

A striking later change was that Mao showed little interest in political institutions, values, and laws of those world powers after he became a career revolutionary and communist leader, while these used to be exciting foreign aspects for young Mao.

(2) The East and the West: A negative-effect rule The terms "the East" and "the West" employed here go beyond geographical destination. They are political in their connotation, therefore, Japan is treated as a power of the West. In his early days, Mao, like many young intellectuals in the May Fourth era, mainly appreciated western cultures. But in regard to the politics of the East and West, Mao was not a pro-Westerner. Instead he was a cool-eyed observer and an interest-oriented realist.

Although he did not speak out in this way, one can find that his commentaries on current world politics showed a rule of negative effect, especially when he was analyzing world politics in the 1930's, a decade of growing worldwide crises. The rule tells people that political tension or relaxation in the East and West go in opposite direction. For instance, when Mao observed a pending World War II among Western imperialists in 1930, he welcomed the Western "tension," because the possible war would be "an extraordinary benefit for the Chinese revolution" which he was conducting under very difficult conditions.[153] The eruption of World War II was, in essence, a great relaxation for China, especially after Pearl Harbor. Mao soon issued a directive to his communist cohorts, an inner-party order to take advantage of the Pacific War to extend the Communist sphere. The crisis in the Western world eased the situation in China, including the CCP controlled area.

(3) The outside world--a dominant factor In the period we are discussing, Mao was certainly an internationalist rather than an isolationist. This is particularly true when one considers Mao's perception of world politics and its impact on China.

In 1920, Mao directly integrated China's problem into the world problem. He took an attitude of cosmopolitanism or worldism in discussing an updated goal of the New People's Society (Xin Min Xue Hui) with his fellows in the Society. In the late 1920's Mao shaped his famous "semi-colonialism" theory to identify the nature of China's society and worked out his type of revolution. The implication of the theory is a proposition--"China's internal affairs were dominated by the outside world." Later in the Yanan era, Mao further developed his theory of semi-colonialism through his assessment of modern Chinese history. He wrote in the article entitled "Chinese Revolution and Chinese Communist Party":

> Chinese society remained feudal for 3,000 years. But is it still completely feudal today? No, China has changed. After the Opium War of 1840 China gradually changed into a semi-colonial and semi-feudal society. Since the Incident of September 18, 1931, when the Japanese imperialists started their armed aggression, China has changed farther into a colonial, semi-colonial and semi-feudal society.[154]

However, Mao could recognize but not accept the domination of foreign forces. A primary mission of his revolution was to achieve a Chinese self-determined fate for the Chinese nation, particularly by the CCP led by himself. Therefore he never ignored the international perspective when he looked at domestic matters.

(4) **China-World-China: A new type of Sino-centricism** As an important member of the May Fourth generation, Mao certainly had no connection with the Sino-centric world view in the full sense of its traditional meaning. But as a Chinese revolutionary, later a Chinese communist, sharing a strong nationalist mentality with many people, he treated China as the means and ends for his revolutionary project, or from another perspective, for his struggle for power. When dealing with international affairs, Mao always took China as his starting and ending points.

For instance, one of the reasons why Mao delayed (due to the delay Mao no longer had a chance to do so) his going abroad to study was his belief that it would be worthwhile spending longer time learning more of Chinese civilization. He described such knowledge as a "useful frame of reference" for perceiving the world, not only for understanding the world but also for devoting oneself to the world. Therefore, Mao continued his point "if we want to contribute our bit to the world today, we naturally cannot do so outside this domain of `China.'"[155]

Clearly, Mao believed that only by starting from China could he do something significant in the world. This belief did not contradict his perceptions of the world as we introduced them above. Taking world history and politics as a reference, Mao opened his mind to guide his revolution and power struggle. Using the negative-effect rule, Mao initiated his skill of balancing powers for maximized benefits. Admitting the outside world as a dominating factor in China's internal politics, Mao developed his theory for a Chinese revolution, and set a permanent target for Chinese nationalism. From Chinese revolutionary and nationalist perspectives, Mao thought that it was time for China to be the revolutionary center for worldwide socialism and a nationalist headquarters for the anti-imperialist enterprise.

One might label Mao's China-related concern, strategy, and ambitions with the old concept--"Sino-centric". However, it is generally a borrowed term. In essence, Mao's new type of Sino-centricism is an outward prism with a basic sense of the modern world.[156] Its major contents include the interests, strategies, and goals of the Chinese revolution and Chinese nationalism. Therefore, we can say it is functional or operational, unlike the traditional one that was theoretical.

(II) Mao's Viewpoints of the Existing World Order

Wearing the lens presented above, Mao framed his sense and understanding about world order. In political science, world order means the world is shaped in a certain order, often in the long cycle of global politics, dominated by a predominant impulse that has expressed "a will to power, the urge to control and to dominate, to imprint pattern on events."[157] It is inevitable that people may hold diverse perceptions or misperceptions on world order while taking different stands. That was what Mao did from the late 1910's to the early 1940's.

The effort to establish a certain kind of world order promoted by the great powers could be traced back to the two Hague Peace Conferences held in 1899 and 1907.[158] But the world order could not be considered erected, because of disputes among the major powers, especially between Britain and Germany. Less than a decade after the second Hague Peace Conference, the world was forced into an unprecedented war. With the defeat of Germany and the emergence of

America, which appeared to be, instead of Britain, the new leading force on the world political stage, another effort at a new world order was called for. From President Woodrow Wilson's Fourteen Points (January 8, 1918), the Paris Peace Conference (January 18, 1919), the Treaty of Versailles (June 28, 1919), and the League of Nations (January 10, 1920), to the Washington Conference (November 12, 1921-February 6, 1922) and several treaties signed at the conference, such as the Nine-Power Treaty (February 6, 1922) which is mainly a China-related pact, a new world order known as the Versailles-Washington system was taking shape.

What did it mean to China and to Mao as well? China, for the first time, appeared in world society as a nation-state in the modern sense of world politics, but suffered from her internal disintegration and backwardness, in addition to external oppression and greedy demands. Therefore, in such a new cycle of global politics, China had little say even in matters relevant to her, despite an assertive diplomacy for sovereign rights adopted by China's northern government. Given such a circumstance, officially China was understandably unhappy with the process of shaping the new world order. The non-official Chinese reactions to the settlement of China-related issues were extremely negative.

(1) Mao's attitude toward the Versailles-Washington system
Mao was a radical young intellectual and soon became a career revolutionary during the emergence of the Versailles-Washington system. On the one hand, he positively received Wilson's Fourteen Points, although no source available indicates their influence directly. However, during his first visit to Beijing, Mao organized a Problem Study Society which was apparently influenced by Hu Shi's idea, "More study of problems. Less talk about *isms*." In the "Statutes of the Problem Study Society" written by Mao and published in *Beijing Daxue Rikan* (*Beijing University Daily*) on September 1, 1919, Mao catalogued seventy-one problems that he thought were worth studying. About forty-seven of them were international issues and one can easily find that Mao was interested in the issues raised by Wilson in his famous Fourteen Points. These include limiting military armaments, freedom of the seas, the League of Nations, and Russia.[159] Moreover, on several occasions, Mao attacked secret treaties, also a main target of Wilson's criticism. On the other hand, Mao strongly discredited the Paris Peace Conference and the Versailles Treaty. He told people "do

not even count on this peace treaty `lasting five years'."[160] He quoted the words of General Jan Christiaan Smuts, a treaty signer representing south Africa in the delegation acting for the British Crown, "The promise of a new life, the victory of the great human ideals, ...the fulfillment of [the people's] aspirations toward a new international order, are not written in this treaty...."[161] Here, Mao accepted a moral and socially valuable base for an ideal world order. But he realized that a new international order based on not only political, but also economic power was emerging.[162]

One can say that in his youth Mao had some positive comments on what the U.S. recommended. He once saw the birth of the League of Nations as one of the great reforms people had experienced since the European Renaissance.[163] Later, after he became a career revolutionary, Mao's perception of the new world order was generally negative.

A few months after the founding of the CCP, following the advice of the CCP center, Mao organized a mass rally of 10,000 and demonstrated in Changsha against the ongoing Washington Conference. The rally charged the Washington Conference as "a conference of sharing the booty" and "a peace among the tigers."[164]

In 1923, Mao mentioned the Washington Conference twice. In an article "External force, the Warlords and the Revolution," he emphasized the strategic aspect of the world powers. He then expressed three related points about the Washington Conference. First, it was a new move for invading China. Second, at present and for the near future, international capitalism needed to adopt coordinationism (*Xietiao Zhuyi*) by accepting America's "Open Door" policy. Third, the coordination would break up eventually.[165]

In another article, "The British and Liang Ruhao," Mao took up concrete issues such as the economy and national sovereignty. He kept asking with nationalist passion, "My fellow countrymen who superstitiously believe in the Washington Conference: what has the Washington Conference given us?"[166]

Mao's criticism of the Washington Conference turned a little softer and relatively more objective in the mid-1930's. On December 27, 1935, just after he became head of the CCP, Mao traced the history of Japanese aggression in China and then admitted the Washington Conference as another block in the way of Japan monopolizing China. He wrote:

In 1922 at the Washington Nine-Power Conference called by the United States, a treaty was signed which once again placed China under the joint domination of several imperialist powers. But before long, the situation changed again.[167]

Because Mao always had the Chinese issue as his core concern, his commentaries on the Washington Conference lacked a broad sense of international politics. But he did provide some ways to approach the issue of world order, such as focusing on power politics--the competition among the powers, extension of the powers and relations between the powers--as well as a nationalistic perspective in asking "what has the world order given us?".

His other comment on the Nine-Power Treaty explored a new aspect of world order established at the Washington Conference, the moral aspect. He did not want to recognize this aspect in the early 1920's and when he did admit it, he showed little interest in the mid-1930's. For instance, in response to American writer Agnes Smedley's question, Mao talked about the Treaty again:

These treaties, from today's viewpoint, expressed indeed a desire for peace, that is why those aggressive countries opposed them. But these treaties, for these aggressive countries like Japan, are merely a moral force of sanction, ...therefore, [the treaties] have little significance in *realpolitik*. To stop Japanese attacking China, it is necessary to have a new kind of treaty,...[168]

In other words, the Washington system was out of date.

Actually, Mao started talking about a new cycle of world politics in his Jianxi period. In Mao's philosophy, which we will discuss later, a balance of the world powers is a short-term phenomenon and will yield to unbalance sooner or later. Then another contest among the various political forces will take place. As a result of the contest, a new but still temporary world order will be generated. As he asserted in 1919, soon after the signing of Versailles Treaties, "'this grayish-yellow thick volume' would not be as stable and solid as the Alps." In 1923 Mao also anticipated that coordination based on America's "open door" policy would break up eventually. His prediction was realized in late 1920's and early 1930's by the challenges of German and Japanese to the old Versailles-Washington system in the West and the East respectively, and to the whole world with their alliance.

Comparing Mao's stand toward an international order between the two sets of decades (the 1910's-1920's and the 1920's-1930's), one finds that, ten years later, Mao no longer took those idealistic and moral criteria into account. Yet he put more emphasis on world economic and political factors. While his focus was consistently on motivations and moves of the world powers, his commitment to communist revolution served as a critical guideline for him to perceive the world situation. It even shaded his nationalistic emotion to some extent. The changes and continuities of Mao's approach to the world order had great significance in his later life.

(2) Mao's analysis of the world situation from the 1930's to the *Atlantic Charter* The worldwide economic crises occurring in the late 1920's and the 1930's played a great role in speeding up the collapse of the world order that was actually built up less than a decade before. Although hidden in deep mountains, Mao noticed the "industrial panic due to overproduction" spreading over the whole world (1930). He suggested that the panic of world capitalism was the end of a short-term stability for capitalism after World War I (1933). Therefore, Mao believed that the most dire of economic crises had given birth to a war craze (1934).

In view of the contest among the world powers, as early as late 1928 Mao anticipated an inevitable world war, thinking it was only a matter of time. At that time, he referred to the interest conflicts between the U.S. and Japan in China. In early 1932 Mao saw further tension within imperialism. What the Japanese did in Manchuria and Shanghai was evidence of redividing the world. It would certainly result in an imperialist war. In late 1935 Mao reiterated his prediction of a pending war because of the contradictions among the imperialists in the East and in the West as well. He specified that the war would be a Pacific war between Japan and other powers, particularly, the United States.

Mao admitted that the focal point of international politics was in Europe (1938). Yet, his attention was mainly on the East, especially on China-related problems. He thought China was one of the two major foci of current world politics (1928). He saw the political order of the East as a reflection of the world order. It is well known that the Washington system was, to a great extent, a victory for the U.S. "Open Door" policy, especially in China, and for checking the growth of the

Japanese navy. Japan made its commitment to world order at the Washington Conference, in which it was not entirely a loser in China-related issues. But the "Open Door" was a virtual contradiction of Japan's fixed goal to monopolize or dominate China. Mao, as a Chinese nationalist and communist, could accept neither of these two China policies.

Nevertheless, Mao made clear that the conflict between the world powers, particularly between the United States and Japan, would do some good, either for the whole Chinese nation or for the Communist Party. Departing from this point, when he analyzed the political order of the East, he usually pointed out, without value assessment, the confrontation and differentiation between the so called "New Order in East Asia" promoted by the Japanese and the "Open Door" policy endorsed at the Washington Conference (April 8, 1939). Mao always criticized any attempts to minimize or ease the tension between the powers in the Far East and the Pacific. His ultimate goal was to build, through the Sino-Japanese war and a pending Pacific war, a strong political force that had no dependence on any foreign power, even Soviet Russia. That was why Mao was reluctant to stop criticizing the pro-British-American group and political tendency in China at the turn of 1940 and 1941.[169]

Holding an independent attitude, Mao was an active advocate since the mid-1930's of an anti-fascist united front in the Pacific area. Therefore, he looked at the joint declaration of peace aims issued by Roosevelt and Churchill on August 14, 1941, as a "political fulfillment" of the united front (August 19, 1941). Unfortunately, Mao had not foreseen that the document, later known as the *Atlantic Charter*, was the base for a new world order after World War II, although Mao did use such words as "a new stage of world history" and "an international base for..." to praise the document. A more logical explanation of Mao's shortsightedness might be that he disagreed with or even disliked many principles of international relations in the Charter, which eventually became a blueprint for the United Nations Charter. Mao, as a Chinese communist leader and a nationalist revolutionary, had his own principles to classify international relations and world politics.

(III) Mao's Trifocal Vision of the World System

There were three pairs of refractive lenses comprising Mao's conceptual viewing of the world system. First, colonialism and imperialism served as a major clue for Mao, explaining internal and external, historical and current politics. The conceptions stemmed from an interpretation of modern Chinese history and Leninist theory, but were mainly from a nationalistic perspective. Second, capitalism and socialism came from Marxist-Leninist viewpoint of international system. Mao used them to fit his ideal and committed ideology. Third, fascism and democrats reflected, to a great extent, international politics in the 1930's and early 1940's. Mao adopted them in a practical sense and showed himself as a realist in the changing international relations.

(1) Mao saw world politics dominated by colonialism and imperialism   In accord with his view of the outside world as the dominant element, Mao applied world colonialism and imperialism to explain current politics and modern history, particularly China's current politics and modern Chinese history. In line with this approach, anti-imperialism was a keynote of the Chinese nationalist revolution and Mao's revolution as well. Semi-colonialism played an extremely important role in Maoist analysis and the strategy of his enterprise.

In retrospect, the opening shot of anti-imperialism was fired in 1901 by Liang Qichao, a leading intellectual in China's course of entering the modern world. Liang's article, "On the Development of Imperialism and the Future of the World in the Twentieth Century," represented the voice of China's new intellectuals, determined to renovate the country to match the power of the West. In his youth, Mao was certainly familiar and agreed with this voice. But he paid greater attention to Western culture. Except for Japan because of the "Twenty-one Demands," in Mao's eyes the Western powers were positive, even attractive in many ways, Mao favorably cited Western history, military organization, institutions, and philosophy. Not surprisingly, Mao started to join the national-wide anti-imperialism chorus in the May Fourth era, which was stimulated by Chinese anger with the Paris Peace Conference.

In the early 1920's, imperialism and colonialism were, for a majority of Chinese revolutionaries including Mao, the cause of notorious realities: economic exploitation and political oppression on the world powers' side, meanwhile, economic backwardness and political disintegration on the weak nations' side. At that time,[170] Mao seemed not to use the concept of imperialism in entirely Leninist way.[171] It was more a nationalist revolutionary's conception for striking back at the external force that had historically misused China and it reflected the international *realpolitik* at the Washington Conference.

After the breakdown of the First United Front between the Chinese Nationalists and Communists, Mao started to develop his own revolutionary theory and strategy. Therefore, imperialism became a useful notion to describe China's reality. Opposite to the historical sequence of world colonialism and imperialism, in China, imperialism came first in the context of the worldwide transitional period from old colonialism to new imperialism. Then imperialist countries sought and contested for more privileges in China. As a result, semi-colonialism as a conceptual description of China's political, economic, and territorial disintegration appeared in Chinese nationalist thinking on the connection of internal and external politics.

The term semi-colonialism was even more important for Mao's revolutionary theory and strategy.[172] To describe the situation and competition between Japan and other powers in the Far East and Pacific, Mao drew a colonial and semi-colonial map of China's miserable reality in 1933. Japan had already set up a Manchu. Guo (Manchu State) by gunfire; it wanted a Mongol Guo too. Britain was planing to build a Tibet Guo in western China. France was invading Yunnan and Guizhou. The US was trying to carve up provinces along Yangtze River.[173] While at this point Mao's concept of imperialism and colonialism still mainly served to interpret China's internal politics, his approach showed it was also external domination.

In Yanan, Mao focused his view of imperialism on a larger context--modern history and international politics. His view of imperialism was not limited to air nationalistic feeling or to narrat existing realities. Partly because of his changed personal political position, and partly because of his effort to be a theoretical authority for the Chinese communists, Mao made his world picture by applying a more theoretical and Leninist concept of imperialism.

For instance, Mao believed that imperialism framed the world picture as a whole. He declared that "ever since the monster of imperialism came into being, the affairs of the world have become so closely interwoven that it is impossible to separate them" (December

1935). Mao traced the procedure of imperialist intervention in China since the middle of the 19th century. He thought the invasion of imperialism had a dual consequence. It reinforced the disintegration of Chinese feudal society, which resulted in the birth of capitalist elements. At the same time, it jeopardized China's independence, which produced a colonial and semi-colonial society (December 1939). Mao affirmed that imperialism was the source of war.

Based on this Leninist view, he described the war since the beginning of the 1930's in Manchuria as another imperialist war after World War I, which was regarded as the first imperialist war according to Leninism. The only goal of the war was to re-divide the world, as Mao indicated in his argument on the second imperialist war. A theoretical work, "On Imperialist War," was written between late 1939 and the first half of 1940. However, it was soon viewed as inappropriate because of developments in world politics and the war. Mao and the CCP had to keep this analysis out of the limelight. Mao's "On Imperialist War" would be considered as important as his "On Protracted War," if no further actions had been taken by fascism after 1940.[174] In spite of the unfortunate fate of his argument in "On Imperialist War," Mao's view of colonialism and imperialism served as a crucial reference in understanding world power politics and its impacts on China.

(2) **Mao divided the world into two basic camps: socialist and capitalist.** Although the two-camp division was a regular "Cold War" frame of world politics in the 1950's, Mao used the concept to view the world as early as in the 1920's. However, it had no operational significance for diplomacy and foreign policy then as it did later. For Mao, socialism and capitalism were two terms that explained ideological, economic, and social aspects of the world system. They differed from colonialism and imperialism that were oriented toward foreign policy and military force. Also differing from his concept of colonialism and imperialism that were mainly viewed from a nationalistic perspective, socialism and capitalism were a pair of concepts that reflected Mao's long-time love and hate and his ideological commitment to Marxism-Leninism.

Mao was influenced by socialism, though not a Marxist brand of socialism, as early as age seventeen or eighteen, just before the famous 1911 revolution in China. He recalled that he first learned the term socialism in a newspaper of which he was an avid reader. He even "wrote enthusiastically" to his classmates on the subject after he read some pamphlets about socialism and its principles. Although only one of his classmates responded in agreement, it apparently revealed Mao's ideal then of a social system.[175]

In contrast to his attitude toward socialism, Mao treated capitalism as one of the "four evil demons" in the world with negative role similar to the Chinese traditional "three bonds" on individuals. Mao saw capitalism as a great crime to suppress the individual.[176] In spite of the fact that his understanding of capitalism then was far from the commonly accepted definition and had no Marxist color at all, Mao showed his hatred for capitalism. It would remain a lifetime enemy but its definition would change from time to time.

To Chinese revolutionaries like Mao the Russian revolution offered an actual socialist revolution and society as well as an ideological system. He wrote:

> Following the change in the political structure of the Russian government, socialism has gradually been transported into East Asia. Although there are many different factions, the flow of this tide cannot be stopped.[177]

It was very important for Mao to realize these two critical points, namely, the eastward flow of socialism and the existence of different socialist factions. From here Mao made his commitment to a Chinese type of socialist revolution and Marxist-Leninist brand of socialism. In many cases, the socialism was identical with the term communism.

In the 1920's and 1930's, Mao used his love and hate for socialism and capitalism to define the world. The world consisted of two basic camps: a counter-revolutionary one led by the big bourgeoisie and a revolutionary one led by the proletariat (October 28, 1925).[178] There was the red banner of revolution held aloft by the Third International and the white banner of counter-revolution held aloft by the League of Nations (March 1926).[179] If revolution and counter-revolution are the political attitudes of the two camps and the proletariat and big bourgeoisie are the class bases of the two camps, the penetration of world capitalism into China's traditional economy and society in modern history was a manifestation of the economic and social significance of world capitalism. Mao offered his analysis on this aspect of world capitalism in the First Congress of Peasant

Representative of Hunan Province (December 1926).[180] Thus far, Mao had generally identified his understanding of socialism and capitalism with the Marxist-Leninist analysis.

In 1930 Mao talked about worldwide class struggle in an open-letter to the soldiers of the KMT armed forces. He wrote that "Today the whole world has split into two battle lines, one is the imperialists and capitalists' line,...one is the proletarians' line,....".[181] In 1932, Mao declared "The confrontation and conflict of two different systems has diametrically reached an unprecedented point," referring to the contradiction between the socialist and capitalist systems in justification of the CCP effort at a soviet system in Jianxi.[182] In 1934, Mao reported on the confrontation between the two worlds--socialist and capitalist--by comparing the economic achievement of Soviet Russia with the economic crisis of the capitalist countries.[183] Except for the time when Mao was advocating a united front, the two-camp image continued throughout Mao's speeches and writings in most of the 1930's.

In early 1940, Mao's analysis of the division between socialism (or communism) and capitalism appeared very theoretical and systematic with a Marxist-Leninist-Stalinist tone. In his very important article, "On New Democracy," by citing both modern Chinese and world history Mao affirmed that socialism (communism) is a more advanced stage of human history, like a sunrise, while capitalism is a fading phenomenon like a sunset, although it had some historical functions. Given the results of World War I and the Russian Revolution, Mao believed that everything in the world was tied to each other. Any revolution in a colony or semi-colony was connected with the Russian socialist revolution.

He distinguished two world revolutions: the old one and the new one, demarcated by the First World War and the Revolution of 1917. In view of these factors, Mao concluded "The world today is in a new era of wars and revolutions, an era in which capitalism is unquestionably dying and socialism is unquestionably prospering." Furthermore, Mao described communism as "at once a complete system of proletarian ideology and a new social system. It is different from any other ideology or social system, and is the most complete, progressive, revolutionary, and rational system in human history....The whole world today depends on communism for its salvation, and China is no exception."[184] Less than a year later, Mao stored away some of his most ideological analyses. Some were entirely hidden like the theory of imperialist war, referring to the current world war. Some were temporarily restrained, as with his theory on socialism and capitalism in the article "On New Democracy." The reason was the birth of an international united front against fascism, a common enemy for all human beings. No doubt, this reflected a non-ideological feature of Mao's way to approach the world, which will be discussed later.

The context in which Mao used the two-camp division to frame the world raised two interesting facts. On the one hand, Mao showed great esteem for Soviet Russia as the leading or representative force of the socialist camp. Ironically, on the other hand, Mao was at the same time building his own style Marxism and developing his dissenting voice toward Moscow. This phenomenon reflected Mao's attitude toward the Soviet Union and The Third International (the Comintern), which will be discussed in the next chapter. Thus the two-camp division of the world was merely a part of Mao's perception of the world in certain situations. In addition to nationalistic and ideologically dominated views of the world, Mao had other views on other bases, such as pragmatism.

(3) Mao accepted the conceptions of fascism and democracy as an alternative description of world politics Compared with the above mentioned two pairs of concepts Mao adopted for perceiving the world, this pair of concepts was realistic and practical one. However, it still had some nationalistic and ideological flavors. Examining the thread of Mao's application of the two concepts, one can find how the realist and practical considerations interweave with nationalistic passion and ideological faith in Mao's way of approaching the complicated and ever changing world.

Fascism was a form of totalitarian dictatorship that flourished between the two World Wars. Fascist movements often grew out of socialist origins, but they were basically anti-Communist. However, fascism was not a uniform political movement; it differed in different times and places. In accord with the initiation of a new united front in the mid-1930's, domestic and international, Mao began to use the conception of fascism and democracy to draw a line between the great powers of the world. These two concepts became an alternate approach for him to perceive the world as a whole.

Mao's typical elucidation of democracy appeared in his theory *On*

New Democracy. He identified a democratic revolution as a less advanced but necessary stage with reference to a communist-led revolution. It includes two major stages: a new democracy one and a socialist one. To explain the new democratic revolution, Mao differentiated the current revolution led by the CCP from the previous one led by the Chinese bourgeoisie. He announced that the new democratic revolution, although still having some aspects of the bourgeois one, was part of the worldwide proletarian revolution. Here three points were of importance: (a) the class attribution of democracy was bourgeois; (b) democracy was a progressive trend in the current world; and (c) democracy, while a domestic system, was relevant to international politics.

In terms of international politics, Mao's concept of democracy was no more than a label for cataloging political identity. For a particular nation-state, democracy was basically an external identification, not an internal entity. To judge if a nation-state was democratic or not, Mao concentrated on its class attribute and international relations rather than examining its philosophical base and internal system. Mao did not favor democracy very much because of its class attribute in his analysis in *New Democracy*. Yet he held a generally positive attitude toward it when his focus was centered on international relations. In short, Mao used the conception of democracy to label those countries who stood opposed to the fascist countries, in a generally positive but not a really favorable manner.

From the end of 1935 to September 1939, prior to the European War, Mao's thinking on world affairs centered on inviting as much outside sympathy and assistance as possible for the CCP and China's anti-Japanese struggle. Accordingly, he stopped the public use of two pairs of concepts, namely, colonialism and imperialism, and socialism and capitalism, during this period. Instead, the conceptions of fascism and democrats substituted as a general keynote in depicting the world situation. To some extent, the new pair of concepts altered Mao's ideological orientation on international relations. However, as regards nationalistic considerations, this did not conflict with political reality and remained a stable factor in his global view.

1939 was a year for Mao to turn his realistic and practical approach back to ideology. At first, Mao responded to Roosevelt's "Declaration of Protecting Democracy," perhaps referring to a famous speech made in Chicago in October 1937. By adopting the term "democratic country," Mao brought the United States, Britain and France into this category indicating his dual but mainly positive, feeling toward those countries. Later, in another talk with Snow, he put China into this group too in the sense of foreign policy that he emphasized intentionally. In a stronger voice, Mao later in 1939 was ideological again because of the outbreak of the European War which Mao called "the second stage of the Second Imperialist War." In his argument on the imperialist war, he announced that the distinction between fascist and democratic countries became meaningless due to the new stage of the imperialist war. Then he suggested a new way to draw lines for the world's political map using the different attitudes toward unjust war and people's liberation war. The former meant the ongoing war between world imperialists; the latter indicated a class struggle or nationalistic fight carried on by oppressed nations and peoples (September 1939).

The concepts of imperialism, capitalism, socialism appeared once again in Mao's view of world politics, only to be replaced by the realistic and practical view of world politics in mid-1941, after Germany's attack on the Soviet Union, and again at the end of 1941 with outbreak of the Pacific War. Mao reapplied the idea of the conflict of two camps, namely, the fascist camp and anti-fascist camp, in accord with the dramatic and rapid change in the world political situation.

In sum, the evolution of Mao's perception of world order was virtually a three-stage process. As a radical youth, Mao carried a strong nationalist passion. He was interested in many new ideas including international morality, when he was talking about the political settlement among the world powers after the World War I. Then Mao became a career revolutionary and was an important figure of China's revolution in the early 20's. He started to look at the newly established world order through the prism of political-power theory and nationalist emotion. Mao continued to take these two basic dimensions, plus communist ideology and his own political destination, in his Jiangxi and Yanan period. Therefore, the two major stages of the international affairs during the period we are discussing, namely from the stage after World War I to the stage of World War II, provided Mao with a great international political panorama to picture the world from various angles. Except for some similarities at the realistic level, Mao's perception of the world offered diverse viewpoints and approaches about world order and international relations. In spite of the fact that Mao's thinking was not very influential on China's international relations, not to mention the world political stage. Later it provided another perspective for understanding the world, and would have an extremely important impact on China's politics, its internal and external policies, as well as on international relations and world order.

The connection between the world and China was, to a great extent, manifested through relations between the Great Powers and China. During the first half of the 20th century there was two-way access to link those powers and China. On the one hand, the "China question,""China affairs," or "China problem" was one of the hot points for the Great Powers's political and economic rivalries in the world, particularly in Far East. On the other hand, China and the mainstream of Chinese intellectuals were struggling with a twofold task: to modernize China and to maintain national identity. Both goals had very much to do, either positively or negatively, with the world powers. This is especially true in Mao's case, as he was an enthusiastic student of those great powers in his youth, an energetic nationalist in his initial stage of revolutionary career, and an ambitious communist leader in the most recent period we are discussing.

Having examined Mao's image of the world as a whole, Mao's explicit or implicit value references for each of the great powers, namely, the Soviet Union, the United States, Japan, the United Kingdom, France and Germany, will be given in order to further reconstruct Mao's perceptions and images.

Chapter 5

Mao and Soviet Russia:
Relations, Attitudes and Images

Relation with Russia, one of China's most important neighbors, was a very problematic and complex issue for Chinese and for Chinese Communists as well. The geographical and historical settings of the relationship between the two nations were not favorable. Geographical closeness and over 5,000 miles of common border, the longest boundary line between any two countries in the world, could cause endless frontier disputes reflecting divergent national interests and external policies toward the other side. Perhaps with that consideration, a famous Chinese statesman, Lin Zexu, made a prophetic statement not long after the Opium War (1839-1842). He said that "the country which will eventually be a great menace to China is Russia." Historically, Chinese and Russians began directly contacting each other through the medium of the Mongols. This shaded the Russian image of Chinese with an alleged fear of "yellow peril." Actually, things went the opposite way with respect to bilateral relations. Since the first conflict and the Nerchinsk Treaty between China and Russia in 1689, which was considered an equal treaty between the two and the first between China and a European power,[185] Russia had always held an offensive posture toward China. In the second half of the 19th century, Russia joined other western powers to seek benefits in China. From 1858 to 1917, Russia seized the Amur and Ussuri regions, penetrated into Manchuria and Xinjiang, and made Outer Mongolia a Russian protectorate.

The heritage of Sino-Russian relations became a gulf that could be hardly bridged, given the tradition of Chinese political culture that maintains a no-confidence attitude toward a strong or giant neighbor and takes fresh lessons from history seriously. Not until the Russian Revolution in 1917 was the gulf overcome to a large extent, at least temporarily in the relations between Moscow and the CCP. The Russian Revolution did not permanently eliminate the gap caused by historical and natural heritage, as evidenced in the dispute between two countries during the 1960's and 70's. However Lenin's revolution made many substantial changes in the nature of Sino-Russian relations as well as in the means of the bilateral connection.[186]

One of the most significant changes after the October Revolution was that political and ideological elements were deeply involved in Sino-Russian relations. For many Chinese intellectuals who dominated China's politics, including its foreign policies, in most of the 20th century, the newly born Soviet Union was a model of political and social revolution. The doctrine of Marxism-Leninism legitimized the Chinese revolutionaries. The Soviet Communist Party and its agent, the Comintern, had the authority to participate in China's various internal and external affairs. The political and ideological elements were clearly manifest in relations between the Soviet Russia and the KMT from 1924 to early 1927 and even more apparent in relations between Soviet Russia and the CCP ever since the birth of the CCP. However, the influence of the political and ideological factors did not function the same way or at the same level.

Another great difference between the transition period and the post-Revolution era in Sino-Russian relations was that there were always more than one threads connecting them afterward. For instance from 1917 to 1924, examined by Allen S. Whiting, there were several Soviet policies on China: basically, a revolutionary China policy represented by the Profintern (the Red International of Trade Unions) and a diplomatic China policy advanced by the Narkomindel (the People's Commissariat for Foreign Affairs). The former focused on Asian revolutionary prospects and tried to win "friends in the bourgeois-led movements for independence." The latter aimed at "establishing Soviet Russia's place in the Far East regardless of the means required."[187]

After 1932, the year of re-establishing diplomatic relations with the KMT government, the Soviet China policy again became a two-sided coin. On one side, it was developing a "friendly" relationship with the KMT government in order to have an ally to assure Soviet security in facing the threat from Japan. On the other side, Soviet Russia was pursuing a communist drive in China via the Comintern although at a reduced effort compared with the 1920's. In short, the revolutionary and the diplomatic activities were two basic forms of Sino-Russian relations until 1949. The two sometimes worked separately and at cross-purposes, and sometimes remained distinct but parallel. The peculiar nature of Sino-Russian relations was a true reflection of the complicated political environment, domestic and international, for both countries.

Thus three fundamental factors, namely, the historical heritage including geographical concerns, the political and ideological influence, and the co-existing two fronts of bilateral connections, framed relations with Russia for Mao and the CCP. They also framed Mao's image of and attitude toward Soviet Russia.

Along with Japan, another worrying and troublesome neighbor, Russia was one of the two major threats to the territorial integrity of China in the 1910's. Mao realized this point clearly. In his couplets that mourned the death of his fellow student in May 1915, he wrote:

Repeatedly the barbarians have engaged in trickery./ From a thousand *li* they come again   across Dragon Mountain....[188]

The feelings I hold in my breast are like fire,/ Learning against the rocks,/I give vent to song./ The mountain ridge is green and luxuriant,/ We pledged to try long swords;/ The eastern sea holds island salvages,/ In the northern mountains hate-filled enemies abound./ Together we denounced the licentious,/ But how shall we purge the evils in ourselves?[189]

Here, "the barbarians" was an expression of censure common in China; it no longer reflected a Sino-centric world view. Specifically, Mao was referring to Japan and Russia.

Russia's interests in China, particularly in northern Manchuria, western Inner Mongolia, and Outer Mongolia, had been established and developed since the turn of the century. However, Russia's prestige and influence abroad were diminished badly after the outbreak of the World War I because of its poor showing against Germany. Moreover, Russia was anxious about Japanese expansion in the Far East, especially in China. To protect its sphere of interest in this region, Russia concentrated its diplomatic efforts in the Far East during the war by proposing a guarantee of their respective Far Eastern possessions among the interested powers. She was most eager to secure Japan's good will. As a result, two conventions, one public and one secret, were concluded on July 3, 1916. The pawn in the international chess game of high politics was China's interests in her own territory. China was not informed of the terms of the public convention immediately after its conclusion, not to mention the secret one. Having read the urgent telegram sent back to Beijing by the Chinese ambassador, which was published in the *Dagongbao*, Mao made his response on the "Russo-Japanese Agreement" in a letter to his friend:

> This agreement has already been concluded. In addition to both countries agreeing to respect each other's rights in Manchuria and Mongolia, Russia has given up its railroad line between Changchun and Bingjiang and navigation rights on the Sungari river, and Japan has agreed to assist Russia with weapons, ammunition, and other war materials. Until now, only a small part of this news has been published; the most important of it is being kept a secret.[190]

Mao was right. The secret convention of the treaty was not released until the collapse of the Tsarist Government in October 1917. On July 28, 1919, in an short essay on a rumored "Secret Treaty Between Japan and Germany," Mao denounced any secret treaty in general and attacked the Russo-Japanese secret treaty in particular,

> What kind of thing is a secret treaty?...The secret treaty between Japan and Russia was publicized by the Lenin government and not only failed to be concluded, but caused a great loss of face.[191]

The ending of Tsarist imperialism did not end the hostility of Chinese caused by what Russia had done since the second half of the 19th century. It also did not terminate China's suspicion of Russia due to ever possible confrontation and conflict of respective interests, security, and external policies in Northeast Asia or in extended regions. The existence of these elements was demonstrated repeatedly in later Sino-Soviet disputes. Nevertheless, Lenin's revolution gave birth to a new Russian government and a new type of Sino-Russian relations as well.

The most prominent change in the relationship after the October Revolution was the fundamental transformation in the Chinese image of Russia in four ways. First, the Russian Revolution became the fashion among China's influential intellectuals who were looking for a model of political and social revolution, since they had shouldered the mission of strengthening China. Second, although it had been extremely weakened at the time, Soviet Russia was also the first world power who adopted a fair and equal attitude toward China through offering to grant everything that the Versailles Peace conference had just appeared to reject.[192] Third, the Marxism-Leninism that was the dominant ideology in Soviet Russia gained momentum in China owing to the success of the revolution. However, the most influential doctrines accepted by Chinese radical intellectuals were only some of its elements, such as socialism, the importance of the masses, class struggle, and violent revolution. Fourth, Soviet Russia's promotion of its style of revolution, usually via the Comintern, had a crucial impact on China's domestic politics in the early 1920's. As is well known, the reformed KMT and the newly born CCP were the twin products of the missions of Soviet or Comintern representatives to China.

Mao was convinced by the Leninist Revolution, converted himself to Marxism-Leninism, and committed himself to the Soviet Russian type of revolution. In 1919, the Bolsheviks began to attract Mao's attention:

> Each of us should examine very carefully what kind of thing this extremist party really is....In the twinkling of an eye, the extremist party, to everyone's amazement, has spread throughout the country, to the point that there is no place to hide from them.[193]

Mao followed his own advice seriously. Russia, socialism and Marxism were his major study tasks in 1919, 1920, and 1921. The conclusion of such intensive study was to abandon the term "extremist" (*guoji*), which was commonly applied to the Bolsheviks at that time, and to further his enthusiasm. On July 28, 1919, three days after the issuing of the Karakhan Manifesto, Mao quoted favorably what Lenin's government had done in discarding the China-related unequal treaties. He also expressed his negative view about the treaty system of the world powers. At the end of 1919, when Mao was advocating a "New Village" social reform, he considered Soviet Russia "the exemplar of a social revolution," and a "model country." In March 1920, Mao set his destination of studying abroad on Russia because, for him, Soviet Russia was "the number one civilized country in the world." In September 1920, when Mao was promoting an autonomous movement in Hunan, he declared, "Russia's flag has turned red, and it has truly become an international world for the common people." Mao even analyzed Lenin's efficient path to power:

> Lenin depended on millions of party members to start an unprecedented course of popular revolution that made a clean sweep of the reactionary parties and washed away the upper and middle classes. He had the ideology (Bolshevism), and the opportunity (the defeat of Russia). He was prepared, and had a truly reliable mass party that rose up at the first call and carried out orders as smoothly as flowing water. The class of toiling peasants, constituting some 80 to 90 percent of the whole population, also responded immediately. Here lay the reasons for the success of the Russian Revolution.[194]

Technically, Mao grasped Lenin's revolutionary path and praised it objectively, but he was not ready to apply it to China while he was developing a Hunan Autonomous Movement. He said:

> I would give my support [to the Leninist way] if there were a thorough and general revolution in China, but this is not possible (I will not go into the reasons right now). Therefore, in the case of China, we cannot start with the whole, but must start with its parts.[195]

This reveals a basic attitude of Mao toward other's experience: he would appreciate it sincerely yet he might deny it as a universal path. The key for evaluating other's experience was to see whether it fit China's reality and condition as perceived by him. Soon after Mao realized that his effort for a Hunan Republic was in vain, he changed his position to support Soviet Russia's revolutionary way in principle, at the turning point of 1920 and 1921. Mao continued to hold this revolutionary banner as a symbol during all his life. However, his basic attitude remained unchanged and was a conspicuous feature in his whole life.

Marxist-Leninist ideology was another new element in Sino-Russian relations after the Russian Revolution. Mao's attitude toward the new ideology passed through several stages. His initial faith in Marxism-Leninism derived from reading a few available Marxist books and very limited information on the Russian Revolution. Through reading, Mao was moved by such basic Marxist-Leninist ideas as the socialist ideal, the confrontation between socialism and capitalism, class analysis and class struggle, and the importance of a popular mass base. Examining what Mao learned and believed in his youth, one can easily find the roots or channels for his accepting these ideas. Mao began to dream of visiting Soviet Russia. He regarded it as the first and unique model of the social revolution that fit his ideal. More important, Mao appreciated the basic practical factors of Lenin's revolutionary path, such as ideology, political party, and popular mass base. After Mao converted to the communist movement, Marxist-Leninist ideas, the Russian experience, and Mao's long time aspirations were perfectly combined. Soviet Russia was identical with the Marxist ideology that fit his revolutionary ideal. One might call this the idealist stage. The keynote was the belief in high principles that directed Mao's attitude toward and image of Soviet Russia.

The situation became more and more complicated with the establishment of real relations between the revolutionary Chinese and Russians (some were from other countries but represented Moscow). These persons were sent to China carrying the instructions and directives for China's revolution. Personally Mao had no direct relations with those Russian advisors and received no recognition from them. As we noticed earlier Mao used a derogatory term, "foreign devil," for these persons when he talked with Zhang Guotao in 1926. Practically, Mao found they had no knowledge of China and did little thing good for its revolution. Therefore he blamed Borodin and Roy, the two major envoys of the Comintern in the mid-1920's, when he later recalled this particular period to Snow. Theoretically, Mao accumulated his experience in worker and peasant movements and in the CCP and KMT affairs. He contributed several essays that reflected China's societal conditions and combined first-hand observance with Marxist ideology, particularly, the concepts of popular mass movement and class analysis in society. This was the stage where Mao began to lose his confidence in the representatives of Soviet Russia and the Comintern. After that, Soviet Russia had two meanings: a symbol of communist revolution and a headquarters controlling revolutions outside Russia. Accordingly, Mao's attitude toward Soviet Russia was split into two: staying firmly with the former while deeply suspecting the latter.

The dual meanings of Soviet Russia and Mao's dual attitude toward Soviet Russia continued to develop in the Jiangxi period. On the one hand, Mao publicly showed a pro-Soviet attitude with a heavy ideological tone. Mao borrowed the term "soviet" to name his red border area and the government in this region. Apparently it was a revolutionary experiment with the Soviet Russian pattern in mind. Mao complimented the achievements of Soviet Russia on every possible occasion. He looked to it as a model of the socialist system and the leader of the socialist world. As noted in chapter four, two camps--socialist and capitalist--were the picture of world politics Mao depicted in a strong ideological mood. Mao's speech on the Chinese Eastern Railway incident illustrated the significance of ideology on Sino-Russian relations. Setting aside his nationalist mood, Mao wrote:

> The Soviet Union has become our (workers, peasants, and soldiers) big brother. It is leading a thousand-million poor to overthrow the imperialists and warlords. This caused a terrible panic among imperialists. They have to ally together attacking the Soviet Union, ... Chiang Kai-shek boldly assaulted the Soviet Union. He responded loyally at the imperialists' instigation, so that there has been created the storm of the Chinese Eastern Railway for several months. It was clearly the start of the imperialists' attack on the Soviet Union.[196]

On the other hand, the Jiangxi period is well known for Mao's fighting the "Russian returned students" and the representatives of the Comintern, specifically, Pavel Mif and Li De (Otto Braun). The two Moscow-sent foreigners were involved in the Chinese communist revolution at this time, but both were proved to be Moscow's mistake. Li De, a graduate from the famous Frunze Military Academy in Moscow, was a military advisor. He suffered from being ignorant of everything in China. According to Dick Wilson, he was no more than "an idealistic and puritanical young German [who] goes to China without any language or culture training, to tell his Chinese comrades how to make a Marxist revolution,"[197] Mif's role or reputation was even worse than that of Li De. Mif was Stalin's appointee to the Far Eastern Department of the Comintern in the late 1920's. Although he had been on the China Commission of the Comintern as early as 1925, and was a teacher and head at Sun Yat-sen University in Moscow, he barely knew China on a realistic basis. He especially had little knowledge about what was happening in the Jiangxi Soviet. "Mif's account of Red Jiangxi, however, was brief, general, and based on sparse documentation."[198] The worst thing he did was to support his Chinese disciples who had studied in Moscow in an attempt to take over the leadership of the CCP in 1932. Known as "Stalin's China Section" or "Twenty-eight and a half Bolsheviks," led by Wang Ming (Chen Shaoyu), they dominated CCP affairs until the Zunyi Conference in January 1935. Mao's struggle with these persons directly and with Comintern headquarters indirectly had multiple causes. These included a personal "love-hate" ambivalence, organizational rebellion, and ideological divergence.

The separation of Moscow from Marxist-Leninist ideology was another big step in the evolution of Mao's attitude toward Soviet Russia. If the outcome of such a situation can be deduced by abstract logic, then Moscow might, in essence, remain only of symbolic significance. Even that could not be maintained forever, because the source of keeping it a revolutionary symbol was what it used to be, rather than what it was and would be. However this was not yet the case in post-Jiangxi days. In fact, the tendency to downplay Soviet Russia's reputation among Chinese communists, particularly in Mao's faction, was deliberately ceased. To be specific, the attacks proposed by Mao and the CCP on "Russian returned students" and their errors never targeted Moscow explicitly and overtly until the latter 1950's.[199]

Several factors explain this delay. Firstly, Mao needed an endorsement from Moscow to legitimize his taking over the CCP leadership during the Long March. Secondly, Mao was looking for any possible support, spiritual or material, after the CCP and the Red Army arrived in northwest China, a very weakened force reaching a remote, poor, isolated place. The Soviet Union was naturally the number one possibility to offer such a support. Thirdly, Mao had never given up his ideal and faith that was formulated as a Chinese communist dream since he converted to Marxism-Leninism and became committed to the Russian type of revolution. Therefore, the October Revolution would not fade in the symbolic sense. Anything happening in Soviet Russia that was irrelevant to China, especially to the CCP, would be treated positively, at least moderately. Fourthly, Mao realized his weakness in pure, orthodox Marxist theory yet he sought to clothe his thinking about China's revolution in authoritative language. To create a sinicized Marxism, he had to first absorb the ideological resource available and then produce his own brand of Marxism. Moscow was the only source of Marxist-Leninist theory, either first or second hand. Thus Moscow still had an ideological significance and impact on Mao's faith, although he would not automatically link Moscow with true Marxism in general or sinicized Marxism in particular.

One may divide Marxist-Leninist ideology into two levels, the political ideal and the revolutionary operation. On the former level, at least during this period, Mao's commitment to Marxism-Leninism was identical with his appreciation for the Soviet brand of socialism. On the latter level, Mao ran the Chinese revolution on his own path that he created and became a paradigm of China's revolution. The paradigm included emphasis on China's national condition, means to mobilize the masses, especially the peasantry, strategies and tactics for armed struggle, particularly for guerrilla war, and patterns for party and governmental organization and operation. These Maoist practices served as a solid foundation of his revolutionary theory that he refined and theorized in Yanan. Known as Sinicized Marxism or Mao Zedong Thought, it became the CCP ideology. However, it was contradictory to the instructions of Moscow delivered through the representatives of the Comintern and Russian returned students.

Last, but not least, the co-existence of two or more fronts in relations between the Russians and the Chinese made the relationship even more complicated.[200] As noted, multiple connections between the Russians and their respective Chinese counterparts lasted from 1917 to 1927. The Soviet Government, the Soviet Communist Party, the Comintern, and Russian commercial agencies had established and developed their diplomatic, revolutionary, and economical interests in different parts of China dealing with different groups of Chinese. In North China and Manchuria they delt with the Beijing government that was controlled by various warlords. In South China, they set connections with the Guangdong government, the KMT, and the CCP. In China's peripheral regions, such as Outer Mongolia and Xinjiang they maitained links with local governors. After several years of withholding official relations, mainly because of the rift and then of the First United Front of the Chinese Nationalists and Communists, Soviet Russia restored formal diplomatic relations with the Chinese Government in Nanjing (1932). Meanwhile Russia never stopped its commands to the CCP through underground paths. In addition, the diverse perceptions existing within Moscow and the factions in the Soviet Communist Party and in the Comintern confused people trying to understand an already complicated episode in Sino-Soviet relations. Seeking national interests and promoting the Soviet brand of revolution were two different goals motivating Russian activities in dealing with Chinese. Before 1927 emphasis was on the latter. The course of Russian advice to the Chinese communist movement had seriously undermined Moscow's credibility for commanding the CCP. This is particularly true when the party came under the leadership of Mao, although Mao made no public comments on Russia's "policy of double dealings" during this period, given his position then.

While Moscow maintained its multiple lines to deal with diverse Chinese political forces, mainly the KMT and the CCP, Russia's national interests became a major concern from the early 1930's on. The growing threat from the international environment prompted an important shift of Russian emphasis in relations. In response to Moscow's dual activities with the CCP and the KMT, Mao, now a leader of Chinese communist forces, took a pragmatic approach. He also placed interests--China's national interests, especially, the CCP's interests and his personal interests on center stage.

Mao's conversation with Snow of July 23, 1936 illuminated the nature of the relationship between the Comintern and the CCP. Snow asked the hypothetical question "Would the economic and political relationship between Soviet China and Soviet Russia be maintained within the Third International or a similar organization, or would there probably be some kind of actual merger of governments" if the CCP won victory? Mao answered directly that the CCP "will have to speak for the whole nation. It cannot speak for the Russian people or rule for the Third International, but only in the interests of the Chinese masses." There is a possibility of coincidence of interests for both the Chinese and Russian masses, "But of course this basis of common benefit will be tremendously broadened."[201] When Mao spoke as a Chinese communist leader, he saw the problem of dealing with very aggressive Japan a common and urgent issue for both Chinese and Russians.

In fact, the problem began earlier. The rising tide of Hitlerite military strength in Germany and Japanese conquest in Asia threatened to put Soviet Russia in a vice. Struggling for escape or delay from the showdown with superior fascist forces, Moscow's tactics had gone through intricate convolutions in the Far East, from appeasement of Japan at one extreme to undeclared war with Japanese troops at the other. During the decade of the 1930's, Stalin surrendered the Russian position in Manchuria, fought an undeclared war to keep Outer Mongolia under his wing and created a new Soviet satellite in China, the province of Xinjiang.[202]

Although these Russian moves could not coincide with China's national interests, they might have been of something benefit for the CCP from the perspective of communist revolution. No doubt common interests existed as long as the Japanese threat remained for both nations. Therefore, Mao responded to the Comintern call to build an anti-fascist united front in 1936 and welcomed the non-aggression pact of 1937 between the Chinese and Soviet governments. In 1939, after the Soviet-German pact, Mao made his strong, although somehow undistributed, argument supporting Stalin's decision. One of the major reasons for Mao to be positive was that he believed that the Pact had shocked the Japanese.

Nevertheless, these instances do not show that all of Mao's positive attitudes toward Moscow's China-related moves were determined by China's national interests. As mentioned in Chapter 3, Mao took a peculiarly positive position publicly toward the Soviet-Japanese pact in 1941. The pact upset the majority of Chinese nationalists because it would encourage Japanese moves westward in China and southward in the Pacific region. Mao's speaking highly of Stalin's decision in this case could be explained various ways except by China's national interests as a whole. In essence, realizing the CCP's minor role in national affairs, Mao did not think it was the time for the CCP to bargain or discuss China's national interests as a whole with Russia.

Mao purposely linked his revolution with national interests upon his arrival in Yanan. Thus, there was no trouble in principle for him to make CCP interests superior to everything else.[203] He told Snow that his question about the nature of the future relationship between the CCP when it assumed power over the whole nation and Moscow was "a purely hypothetical question." Given the position of the CCP at that time however, a big principle underlay Mao's answer to Snow's question: securing the independence of the CCP with her distinctive interests. He assertively rejected the image of the CCP's being ruled by the Comintern:

> ...Although the Communist Party of China is a member of the Comintern, still this is no sense means that Soviet China is ruled by Moscow or by the Comintern. We are certainly not fighting for an emancipated China in order to turn the country over to Moscow![204]

Mao's flat denial of the alleged "command of Moscow," which was a common allegation of CCP dependency on Soviet Russia, pledged future equality in the relationship. Mao ensured the outside world that China and the CCP, even in an assumed world union of communist regimes, would *never* be at the "command" of Moscow.[205]

A tactic of double dealing was applied for maximizing CCP interests: trying to gain Moscow's every possible support, while standing firmly for self-reliance; going the CCP way designed by Mao, while avoiding any open dispute with Moscow. After Mao took over the CCP center, it sent a senior party member, Chen Yun, to Moscow at the half way point of the Long March. Upon arriving in Yanan, one of the several major tasks Mao scheduled in 1936 was to open a path for reaching Soviet Russia in order to gain material aid. From 1936 to 1941, Mao emphasized repeatedly and publicly Soviet Russia's support for China's anti-Japanese course. These efforts did not receive sufficient and substantial recompense as expected. Chen Yun's mission was undermined by the Comintern's loyal follower, Wang Ming.

From spring 1936, badly needing material and technical aid from the Soviet Union, Mao kept trying to reach Moscow by sending his representatives there or by extending the sphere of the CCP controlled territory in northwest China. After futilely trying different routes through Outer Mongolia, the CCP eventually learned of the close relationship between Moscow and General Sheng Shichai, the ruler of Xinjiang. From then on, Xinjiang became a transfer station between Yanan and Moscow until the early 1940's. However it was not the material supply line as Mao expected it would be.[206] Xinjiang's role of either pivot or pawn in China-related politics contained new implications--a delicate relationship between the two major communist forces in the world.[207] Moreover, Xinjiang manifested a potential conflict of interests between the two communist parties. The case of Sheng Shicai's application to joining the communist party served as a dramatic proof.[208] The worst case was that Mao had to order Zhou

Enlai to complain of continuing Russian arms to the KMT in January 1940 when they might be used to attack the CCP military force.

Mao's effort to win Russian support was not completely fruitless. He did gain an extremely important endorsement from Moscow for his winning power within the CCP, although full recognition came too slowly. Before 1935 Moscow's information about the CCP, especially the Jiangxi Soviet led by Mao, was poor. There was even a formal obituary of Mao printed in the official organ of the Comintern, the *International Press Correspondence* or *Imprecorr*.[209] However, lack of personal relations and diverse opinions on China's revolutionary strategy and tactics were even more basic reasons accounting for Mao's unfavorable position in Moscow. After Mao became the *de facto* head of the CCP, the situation underwent substantial change. In 1935, the official journal of the Comintern published a long article introducing Mao, in which he was called "a leader of the Chinese people,""revolutionary commander","statesman" and "an expert who knows popular mass psychology profoundly". This is considered Mao's first biography in the world, although it was full of factual errors. It was two years before Snow's *Red Star Over China*.[210]

The recognition of Mao's leading position legitimized his unusual action at the Zunyi Conference. More important, it gave Mao strong support in his fight with another senior leader of the CCP, Zhang Guotao. The official affirmation of Mao's line came to Yanan at the beginning of 1936. On the New Years Day he telegraphed Zu De telling him, according to the person sent by the Comintern, that

> It is said that the Chinese Party holds a very high position in the International, she is titled the number one party besides the party of Soviet Union. The Chinese party has fulfilled her task of Bolshevization. All the Soviet Union and all the world are praising our Long March.[211]

On the 24th of the same month, another Chinese representative of the Comintern told Zhang Guotao that "the International has approved the Center of the Chinese Party's line completely."

Two and a half years later, Mao won another competition over a tougher rival--Wang Ming, the head of the "Russian Returned Students" and a long-time favorite of Moscow previously, had unique personal connections with influential persons there. In a two-week meeting of the Politburo, Wang Jiaxiang, a senior party leader who just came back from Moscow, transmitted a directive of the Comintern fully affirming the CCP political line, particularly the strategy of the Second United Front that was a major point of dispute between Mao and Wang. Meanwhile, the Comintern required all the leaders of the CCP to solve the problem of unified leadership under Mao.[212] This was a final blow for Wang Ming's political career in the CCP. The factional dust settled down after that. Mao established sole and exclusive leadership within the party. In view of this, Mao admitted that the directive of the Comintern offered a guarantee for the success of the Conference. In return, Mao spoke highly of the Soviet Union and Stalin in this period. The most noticeable instance was in 1940. Mao made his early expression of "lean to one side" policy: "Once the conflict between the socialist Soviet Union and the imperialist powers grows sharper, China will have to take her stand on one side or the other. This is an inevitable trend." There was no way to be neutral.[213]

The mutual recognition and respect between Yanan and Moscow certainly had political and ideological bases. Yet it was more the result of a mutually realistic attitude. With the same realism, the divergence on interests between the two appeared implicitly or explicitly at any given time. This was especially true in 1941, the time of increasing crisis in the United Front between the CCP and the KMT and also of an unprecedented war facing the Soviet Union. At the time of the New Fourth Army incident, for instance, Moscow kept its relations with Chiang Kai-shek. Its reaction to the incident was cautious and conciliatory rather than angry and sharp. The behavior of both sides was understandable. For Mao to keep his own communist forces was crucial in what he deemed to be the inevitable struggle in future. For Stalin to maintain good relations with the KMT in order to keep the KMT force in action against the Japanese was the most profitable option. Interestingly, Mao revealed this difference with Moscow in a mild way after the crisis turned in favor of the CCP. On February 7, 1941, Mao intentionally added two paragraphs exposing the conflict:

The entire stand of the CCP...was endorsed unanimously by the whole party,...Chiang, He, Bai [He and Bai were both high officials in the KMT and relevant to this event] believed originally that we would be scared, they thought since the Soviet Union does not want to break the relationship, the CCP would not dare to take a tough line. Now they saw the situation is going in this way, then became flustered, as it is beyond their expectation,[214]

Another example of interest-orientated differences between Moscow and Yanan came with the German attack on the Soviet Union. This turning point on the world political scene gave China and the CCP an opportunity to relax because it brought most of the major powers against Germany and Japan. Now it was the time for Moscow to invite help from the CCP. On July 15, 1941, Mao gave Zhou Enlai his opinion on assisting Russia militarily:

> We have determined on doing our best to help the Soviet Red Army to win the war under current conditions....We will employ a long-time struggle strategy for holding out against the Japanese, that is, to solidify the base areas behind the enemy; to carry an extensive guerrilla war; but not to risk everything on a single venture.[215]

Thus, Mao reciprocated Russian lip service. Three days later, Mao told Liu Shaoqi, "A big move must sap our vitality, it will be no good for either the Soviet or ourselves....The overall situation will be determined by the victory battle of the Soviet Union."[216] Over a month later, the Ministry of National Defence of the Soviet Union formally asked the Eighth Route Army to send troops to South Manchuria in case the war between Russia and Japan happened. Mao replied in a telegram that was approved by the Center of the CCP on September 7, 1941. The contents of the talegram remain unknown so far, but one can guess the ambiguous response Mao gave. The next year, in May 1942, when the war worsened, Mao denied a similar but urgent request from the Soviet Union Supreme Command. This event sowed a far-reaching bad seed in the shared soil of friendship between the two.[217]

The Soviet relationship had very special meanings for Mao from his early revolutionary career to his leadership of the Chinese Communist Party. Being connected with many vital matters, the relationship was wholly different from Mao's views on outside powers who had little or no direct relevance for daily life in the CCP. Nevertheless, it is important to see Mao's views on the United States, Japan, Great Britain, France, and Germany. They reveal a dimension of Chinese nationalistic feelings and also foreshadowed later CCP attitudes toward the powers.

Chapter 6

Mao and Other Great Powers: Relations, Attitudes and Images

(I) Mao and The United States

The term "a special relationship" was used for describing the Sino-US relationship in Michael Hunt's research on the issue.[218] Compared to other world powers that were generally perceived by Chinese as threatening and evil, the United States was physically the "farthest west" and seemed too far away to indulge in open territorial ambitions in China. Geographical distance gives a secure feeling for external relations in Chinese traditional political culture. Moreover, Americans behaved differently in the mid-19th century. Lin Zexu, the principal Chinese official at Canton around the time of Opium War, called the American merchants "good barbarians," as they were more respectful of Chinese regulations and less aggressive than the British merchants. In 1861, Zeng Guofan, the most prominent official and Confucian scholar, compared the four "western barbarians" whom China most confronted. The English are the most crafty, the French next. The Russians are stronger than either the English or the French. The Americans are of pure-minded and honest disposition and long recognized as respectful and compliant toward China.[219] Although there existed some opposite impressions of Americans, the positive feelings prevailed among the majority of Chinese.

Coming to the 20th century, the U.S. and Japan were the two latecomers on the scene of power politics in the world, particularly in the Asia-Pacific region. Nascent American public opinion of China in the first years of the new century was negative because of U.S. participation in suppressing the Boxer Rebellion. However, in the 1910's the majority of Chinese felt that the U.S. "Open Door" policy was rather mild compared to what the Japanese were doing in China. Moreover the U.S. was the only possible, available, and effective force to check Japanese ambitions in the region. Naturally, many Chinese, especially leading politicians and intellectuals, turned to the U.S., not only to seek help in foreign affairs, but also to learn from the achievements of Americans in various fields. By 1914, as Hunt's research noted, the "special relationship" between China and the US had been formulated.

As a result, "America is a model of western civilization" and "America is the checking force on Japan's aggressive way" were the two existing Chinese images that Mao encountered and resonated to for his view on the U.S. in his youth. A few years later, a Marxist-Leninist ideological perspective was added to the image of the United States for quite a few Chinese revolutionaries, including Mao. Therefore, the image of "America is an imperialist competing with the others in China" plus the previous two concepts constructed a triple-faceted frame for Mao's picture of America.[220]

(1) **America as a model of western civilization** This image was generally in Mao's mind as a youth, and had some impact in his later days. As he told Snow, he heard about America for the first time in his teens. Since then, he admired Washington as one of the great heroes of the world. Washington's history of winning an eight-year difficult war and building up the American nation must have impressed Mao very much.[221] At 23, Mao paid his respects to another US president, Theodore Roosevelt, because of his personality as a politician and statesman. Mao wrote to his closest friend, "I still remember the story about his going to somewhere to make a speech and being stabbed by an enemy. Although his blood and guts were spilling out, he calmly finished his speech before attending to his wounds. I cannot help admiring his bravery and fortitude. I hear that he has reached the fullness of his years, yet his courageous and dauntless spirit has not declined."[222]

Admiration of a currently active U.S. politician reflected of Mao's recognition of American values at that time. Liberalism, individualism, and pragmatism were interrelated, typically western, and particularly American values. Mao's early activities and thinking were conspicuously marked by these values. For him, liberalism meant independence, self-rule of the people, and free status as a nation. In 1920, He advocated an independent, autonomous, republican Hunan province, his home town, and tried to lead people into a "position similar to that of one of the states on the North American continent a hundred years ago."[223] Mao realized that it would not be easy to make Hunan liberal unless, as he wrote to his teacher, "The whole situation changes in the future, and our status becomes like an American or German state."[224] To promote his goal, Mao adopted the spirit of the Monroe Doctrine and called his suggestion as the Hunan Monroe Doctrine.

Individualism, at the core of Western values, attracted Mao most in 1917 and 1918. Stuart Schram, the editor of Mao's writings (1912-1949), counts the terms "individual" and "individualism" occurring in nearly a third of Mao's notes on the work of German philosopher Paulsen, as against less than five percent of the pages for 1912-16 and 1919-1920, and "the will" on a fourth of the pages, as compared to two or three percent for the earlier and later periods. Throughout his commentaries, Mao made the basic point about the primacy of the individual *vis-à-vis* the group repeatedly in different ways.[225]

Mao's acceptance of pragmatism has amply evident in the first chapter of this study. However, he was never enamored of Western culture, and he did not entirely abandon Chinese culture in his youth as did many radicals. After Mao converted to Marxism, liberalism, individualism, and pragmatism that used to have important influences were largely discarded in words. Nevertheless, their impact did not totally disappear in Mao's behavior.

(2) America as a Pacific power versus Japan According to Akira Iriye, this Chinese image of the U.S. was initiated by late Qing officials such as Yuan Shikai and Tang Shaoyi. It grew during the First World War, when a distinctly idealistic "Wilsonian" approach to foreign policy was emerging in the Asia-Pacific region.[226] Mao's response was quick. In his letter to a friend in 1916, Mao anticipated a Pacific war with Japan on one side and the other side would be an alliance of China and the U.S.[227] Although the Chinese were disappointed by what the U.S. had done in Paris (1919) and in Washington (1921-1922), Hopes for American antagonism to Japan and American help to China reoccurred in the early 1930's. The

Chinese still believed that the U.S. would inevitably be involved in the Asia-Pacific region, moving from moral statements to economic steps and from political pronouncements to military actions. Mao shared this faith even after he became the CCP leader. However then his perception of the U.S. as a rival of Japan and a positive force for China in the Pacific blended analysis of the *realpolitik* of the region with Marxist-Leninist commentary on world politics.

Mao grasped the concept of interests as a crucial factor of world politics. In 1937, he said that "the interest of the U.S. in the Far East is mutually antagonistic to the continental policy of Japan. Therefore, America should not watch a fire from the other side of the river with respect to China's trouble."[228] Departing from the interest analysis, Mao saw all nations who had interests in the Pacific and China forming an anti-Japanese front because Japan's invasion of China also harmed these nations. Mao was an enthusiastic advocate particularly for a Sino-U.S. relationship in the mid and late 1930's. As is well known, from 1936 to 1939 he had personal contacts with many foreigners, mainly Americans, who visited the Communist base. Mao tried to have direct contact with American authorities. For instance, he co-signed a letter with Agnes Smedley to President Roosevelt asking medical assistance for China's anti-Japanese effort. His message was most likely passed to Roosevelt through Evans Carlson who had a personal arrangement with the president. However its delivery seems to have had no effect on relations between the two sides.

More often, Mao sent his understanding of American politics and foreign policy to Washington and Americans through visitors in Yanan. For instance, Mao commented on American isolationism when answering questions raised by T.A. Bisson. He pointed out that, "Many people in the United States are thinking and talking of isolationism today, but in fact America is not isolationist. ...[Because] Capitalism of the imperialists has a world nature. It must exist in relation to the whole world." Mao stated frankly, "In the position China is in, we not only need the help of America, we must also use the contradictions between American and Japanese imperialism." Then, he put the topic in practical terms: "Here, then, is a point China holds in common with the United States: in foreign policy there is the possibility that we may come together. We are different from Trotsky. Our united front is anti-Japanese, not anti-all-imperialists." Mao ended his talk with a commission for his guest, just as in many other such talks. He told

Bisson, "Please convey this message to the American people....that the joining of our two countries in a united struggle can lead to an entirely new world is the hope common to us."[229] In isolation, these words had little significance except as rhetoric, but Mao's long recognition of the U.S. as a Pacific power that could compete with and check Japan, prompted his strategic calculation under certain circumstances he thought being opportune. Thus what Mao said in 1937 can be seen together with similar words in his youth and in his later life.

(3) **America as an imperialist**   As noted before, a negative image of the U.S. existed in China since the middle of 19th century but it was never dominant. The concepts of capitalism and imperialism were always perceived as evil. However, owing to the painful history of modern China, they evoked an anti-foreign and nationalistic mood. These two factors, the bad image of the U.S. and anti-imperialist emotion, came together in the May Fourth movement. The increasing spread of Marxism-Leninism through the Russian Revolution added to the negative view of the U.S. As a result, a "love/hate" dichotomy became a pattern of Chinese attitudes toward America. Mao shared such an ambivalent set of images during the May Fourth period. On one side of the coin were American values: liberalism, individualism, pragmatism, and even Wilson's ideas of international affairs. On the other side was Mao's criticism of "the very civilized, very wealthy United States of America." He warned "some congressmen, who get a lot of votes because they have a lot of money, and get elected because they have a lot of votes,...that your `day of judgment' is at hand!"[230] Mao even teased Wilson's performance in Paris by saying that "Wilson in Paris was like an ant on a hot skillet....He did nothing except attend various kinds of meetings where he could not speak his mind."[231] Mao attacked America's industrial system too when he wrote "the United States is the first nation of the globe to be an industrial despotism, and it is from this that the evil system of the trusts has arisen. For the pleasure of a few, ten million must weep. The more industry develops, the greater will be the number of those who must weep."[232]

From 1921 to 1935, the slogan of anti-imperialism was a main component of CCP propaganda. In the first half (1921-1927), anti-imperialism combined nationalism and communism. This reflected the short-term alliance of the CCP and the KMT. The propaganda was successfully promoted by Mao between 1925 and 1926 while he was in charge of the Department of Propaganda in the KMT. Consequently the slogan became something that everyone knew and accepted all over the country. In such an environment, the original perceptual or conceptual dyad of Chinese toward the U.S. was doomed to be replaced by the emotions of anger and hostility.

Mao made great effort to dissuade the Chinese people, especially the middle class, from excluding the U.S. from the world's imperialists. He saw imperialism as one of the two causes--the other one was feudalism--of China's political chaos, economical backwardness, and diplomatic weakness. An example Mao gave of U.S. villainy was support of Cao Kun, well known for bribery during the presidential election in the early 1920's. Mao declared that "previously there was a group of merchants who had illusion about the United States, who believed that the U.S. was a good friend who helped China and who did not realize that the U.S. was a first-class hangman second to none at murdering people."[233] The disillusionment with the U.S. was also seen from economic, military and cultural perspectives.

After the opening conflict between the KMT and the CCP in 1927, Mao persisted in his communist propaganda of anti-imperialism while also paying attention to the contradiction between the U.S. and Japan in China and the Pacific region. However, the major CCP target was the KMT led by Chiang Kai-shek and supported by foreign imperialists, as Mao believed. Therefore, he often emphasized attacking American imperialism rather than utilizing American power in the Asia-Pacific area. In mid-1934 Mao responded to the North China incident declaring it was a further step in the Japanese invasion and he called for "fighting with Japan and all imperialists." He again appealed to people to "abandon any illusion of the League of Nations and the United States."[234]

The dichotomous perception of the US re-emerged among Chinese in the 1930's, though the patterns of the dichotomy varied, depending on the specific person and time. After Mao arrived at Yanan, he held no longer a "love/hate" pattern as in his youth. Instead as *the* Chinese communist leader Mao altered his attitude toward the United States from time to time for either realist or ideological reasons. A double meaning existed for "Beautiful Imperialist," a literal translation of an oft-used term, Mei Di, (American imperialism). For Mao, realistically the U.S. was a critical power that could be used to balance world and regional politics based on China's, especially the CCP, interests, therefore it is beautiful. Ideologically, the U.S. is a leading world power that will have primary contradictions with communism according to Marxist-Leninist theory, and therefore is still an imperialist. With this pattern in mind, Mao made every effort to invite America's attention, sympathy, and aid, if possible.

Although he did not reach his goal directly for the time being, Mao won some far-reaching significant reports from Americans who had conversations with him in Yanan. Meanwhile, he never stopped his communist rhetoric on the U.S. A typical example of this dual attitude appeared in two statements in September 1939. One is an interview with journalists in Yanan. In this public speech, Mao described a three-part division of the world capitalist camp. He treated the U.S. as part of the third group that had maintained democracy and normal economic life within the nation and had made some contributions to world peace. The other view came in an outline of a lecture to be given within the CCP. The outline was written only two weeks after the interview. Mao changed his mild tone about the U.S. into a fierce criticism:

> In every neutral state, like America, the communists should explore the imperialist policy of the capitalist government in front of the people. The policy means neutrality in name, backing the war in fact, moreover, to try make a big pile through the war. The American imperialist had already made a pile wearing the neutral mask during the two-year Sino-Japanese war. Now, he wants to make a pile in the new war....[235]

The reason for Mao's change of attitude toward the US was newly arrived information about America's tougher stand against Germany in Europe. Such a switch reflected Mao's strong ideological stand because his switch was in cooperation with Moscow, while having nothing directly to do with Chinese affairs. However, it needs to be noted that the time of ideological overflow was always a time of increasing political and even military tension between the CCP and her opponents, such as the KMT. Beside ideology, nationalism was associated with the use of imperialism to identify Western powers including the U.S. To Mao's vision of the international situation, particularly that of the Asia-Pacific region, America had replaced the British plotting a Far Eastern Munich after the European war started. As late as June 17, 1941, Mao was still rebuking the KMT lack of national confidence and national sense, because it "was infatuated with building up their national center within the New York Stock Market."[236] Only a few days later Germany launched its attack on the Soviet Union and changed the international political scene. Mao welcomed the Roosevelt-Churchill Declaration of August 14, 1941, but his suspicion of America's appeasement policy toward Japan existed until the outbreak of the Pacific war.

(II) Mao and Japan

At the beginning of the twentieth century, Japan became a puzzle for Chinese intellectuals who were questioning the true values of Eastern and Western cultures in the process of modernization. Japan also became *the* major threat for China's politicians and statesmen who were concerned about national security, sovereignty, international status, and other national interests. In a word, it was a watershed for Chinese perceptions of Japan and the Japanese. The new image differed entirely from the previous one held during the long-established Chinese domination of the relationship. The new stereotype of Japan and the Japanese, much more complex than the previous one, impacted on Sino-Japanese relations significantly. The attitude of Mao toward Japan was closely linked with this historical background and accorded with the majority of Chinese views.

(1) **The Twenty-One Demands as turning point from positive to negative attitude toward Japan in Chinese mood** The first Sino-Japanese war in 1894-1895 sounded the alarm for most Chinese officials and intellectuals to recognize the real distance between old China and the modern world. Yet, it did not initiate a bad image of Japan and the Japanese for the majority of Chinese. Westernization had the same meaning for modernization in both China and Japan. The two countries started toward modernization almost simultaneously but the results were vastly different. In the wake of Japan's success, Chinese started regarding Japan and the Japanese as a model to achieve Westernization. Japan was seen as an oriental filter for Chinese to perceive new ideas through an oriental nation and as a short cut for China to catch up with the modern world. It was also a refuge for Chinese radical reformers and revolutionaries to rally their force and restore their prestige. However some Chinese were alerted to the fact that Japan had stepped on the expansionist and imperialist

road and therefore it would be a major danger for China. Also some Chinese experienced Japanese political or racial discrimination while they were staying Japan.[237]

The mainly favorable images of Japan and the Japanese lasted until the middle of the 1910's. Even Japanese fighting on China's soil, first against the Boxer Rebellion (1900) and then against Russia (1905), did not affect the positive Chinese attitude substantially.[238] It is not surprising that Mao was very interested in learning about Japan at the beginning of his student career. He was impressed by a "False Foreign Devil," a Japan-returned student, who taught Mao music and English and told him about Japan when Mao was sixteen. Mao recalled a Japanese song learned from the teacher:

> At that time I knew and felt the beauty of Japan and felt something of her pride and might in this song of her victory over Russia. I did not think there was also a barbarous Japan--the Japan we know today.[239]

Before that, Mao was depressed after he read a pamphlet telling of the dismemberment of China. It told of Japan's occupation of Korea and Taiwan, along with China's loss of other territory and tributaries. Mao thought it was the beginning of his political consciousness, which was a typical nationalist beginning, but held no particular hostility against Japan.

Mao's interest in Japan was well evidenced in his "Classroom Notes" taken in October-December, 1913. It was, as we indicated in the first chapter, extracted from what Mao had heard and read as a student, but it reflected what he believed or interested him. In the Notes, Mao recorded something about Japan with admiration. When Mao noted down some important Chinese philosophers' ideas emphasizing practicality rather than idealism, he took Fukuzawa Yukichi, one of the advocates of modern and Western ideas during the Meiji Restoration, as an example to prove Zeng Guofan's teaching. Zeng was a key person on political and philosophical scene in the late Qing Dynasty and Mao greatly admired him then. Mao wrote:

> Do not do overly impractical things: Fukuzawa Yukichi started Keio University and considered education to be his vocation. He was not greedy, but was fair in dealing with money. Mr.Fukuzawa was learned in many different fields, and had the resolve to teach untiringly.[240]

Mao recorded the importance of physical education, "If many are frail, then a nation cannot be strong. This is the case of our nation now, and because of it, she cannot compete with the foreign countries," and he turned to Japan:

> If you visited Japan, you would see a totally different picture....In Japan, schools attach the greatest importance to sports....It is the same with the Western countries....All these are ways to cure bodily frailty, and to encourage young people.[241]

Mao also appreciated the Japanese economic view:

> It is better to manage one's houses and clothes and shoes carefully, rather than spending money and losing the interest. Therefore, the principal is important. The Japanese value the principal so much that they hardly have any extra clothes in their closets, nor extra grain in their barns.[242]

From the "Classroom Notes" one can conclude that Mao respected Japan and the Japanese in late 1913, especially their way to strengthen the nation and people, and their sense of practical life and economics.

Less than two years later, Mao copied an epigraph, printed in *Mingchi Pian* (*Essays on the Sense of Shame*), compiled and published by his school. "The seventh of May,/The Republic suffered extraordinary shame./How to achieve revenge?/Through our students!" The book was an angry reaction to Yuan Shikai's acceptance, on May 7, 1915, of Japan's "Twenty-one Demands." As Mao noted, "Students and others raised fund and printed this booklet." It "succeeds in conveying a general picture of the Sino-Japanese negotiations."[243] Mao's own emotional indignation was expressed in his couplets in memory of his friend and schoolmate who died of illness at that time. He denounced the Japanese as "island savages" because "the barbarians have engaged in trickery....The feelings I hold in my breast are like fire."[244]

In fact, the Twenty-one Demands was part of a fixed policy of Japanese expansionism since the later nineteenth century. It also was a Pyrrhic victory for Japan in every sense, because it made Chinese hate Japan and the Japanese. Tokyo's attempt to forestall republican nationalism in China so as to guarantee its own position ended by advancing that nationalism in China and focusing it against Japan.[245]

Because of this and Japanese ambitions in the Asia-Pacific region, Chinese nationalist passion never changed its target during the most of the twentieth century. For Mao, Japan was no longer the beautiful place; instead, he experienced "a barbarous Japan."

(2) **In practice, there is a dual situation in respect to mutual relations** Dual situations always existed in relations between China and Japan, Chinese and Japanese. The duality is manifested at two levels: official contacts and personal ties. It is also displayed in two aspects: political confrontation and non-political cooperation. The divergence appeared more notable after Japan became the major target of Chinese nationalists and made mutual relations distinctive.

Reading biographies of influential Chinese, one finds that many had very good personal ties with important Japanese politicians, intellectuals, and ordinary people. Warm personal relations could parallel bad official relations at the same time. Moreover, both could occur between the same persons. Normally, personal ties were non-political and culturally oriented. These friendly sentiments reflected historical and geographical as well as cultural intimacy between the two nations and were natural outcomes of individual experiences. Despite the fact that Mao had no personal experience in Japan or associated with individual Japanese, he held this dual feeling and attitude toward Japan and the Japanese.

Although the Twenty-one Demands invited unprecedented wrath against Japanese imperialism, two groups of Japanese still enjoyed the admiration of Chinese. One group was those who helped or were assisting China's political revolution, like Miyazaki Toten who was a Japanese friend and supporter of the Chinese revolutionaries of the generation of Sun Yat-sen and Huang Xing. The other group was those prominent figures who contributed their thinking to Japan's Meiji Restoration, like Fukuzawa Yukichi. This was reflected in Mao's behavior in 1917. In March, Miyazaki arrived at Changsha to bid farewell to Huangxing's grave and coffin. Mao co-signed with one of his close friends a letter to him, in which Mao expressed his greatest admiration:

You, sir, supported Mr. Huang in life with your spirit; in death, you mourn him with your tears....Your lofty friendship reaches as far as the sun and the moon; the sincerity of your mind moves demons and gods. This is something rarely heard of throughout the whole world and never before encountered either in the past and in the present.[246]

Mao had a chance to meet Miyazaki when he paid a visit to Mao's school, the Changsha First Normal. A month later, Mao wrote a long letter to his teacher and friend, Li Jinxi, who used to teach in Mao's school and moved to Beijing University as a professor. In the letter, Mao revealed his comparisons between Chinese and world affairs focused on cultures and thoughts. Mao recalled what he had learned from Yang Huaizhong in class. It was an introduction to leading world class thinkers' ideas, including Fukuzawa Yukichi's denunciation of Oriental thought. Mao said,

> According to Mr. Huaizhong, a certain Japanese gentleman says that Oriental thought entirely fails to correspond to the reality of life. It is well said. But in my opinion, Western thought is not necessarily all correct either, very many parts of it should be transformed at the same time as oriental thought.[247]

Apparently, Mao did not accept Fukuzawa's idea without reservation, but he put his reservation in such an indirect way because of his respect for Fukuzawa.

Mao never limited himself to view Japan and the Japanese with passion. He remained sober-minded and warned:

> But our compatriots still sleep on without noticing and pay little attention to the east. In my view, no more important task confronts our generation; if we wish to consolidate our own situation, in order to preserve our descendants, we must sharpen our resolve to resist Japan. The Japanese know all about our domestic circumstances, while many of us, ourselves, do not know; and their domestic situation is understood by very few of us....I look forward to our encouraging one another in this.[248]

To practice the idea of knowing Japan, Mao wrote a farewell poem for his friend Luo Zhanglong leaving for Japan. It was the first go-abroad action taken by the New People's Study Society. Mao designed some Japan related questions for further study in his Problems Study Society. Mao maintained his study of Japan in his later revolutionary life. His general knowledge and sound analysis about Japan appeared in his writings, especially during the Sino-Japanese war.

Besides numerous criticisms and objective analyses, too many to list here, Mao's admiration of Japan's modernization deserves mention. This existed simultaneously with his hatred for Japan's China policies. As early as 1917, in his famous article, "A Study of Physical Education," published in *New Youth*, Mao used the arts of *bushido* and *jujitsu* as examples to explain the extreme importance of physical practice and education in projecting national strength. To argue the point, Mao recognized fully that Japan was a civilized nation.[249] In 1920, Mao again took Japan as example to illustrate the possibilities of the Hunan self-rule movement. Mao dreamed of his home province becoming a pioneer in all-round reform for the whole country, like Switzerland in the West and Japan in the East. He even compared the conditions and situations in today's Hunan with Japan in the Meiji period. He admitted, "We do not have the knowledge, abilities, and training that the Japanese or the Swiss have."[250] Mao, like many Chinese revolutionaries and intellectuals, separated current politics and non-politics in terms of his perceptions of Japan and Japanese. Even in the Sino-Japanese war of the 1930's, Mao continued to admire the national characteristics of the Japanese while calling loudly for an anti-Japanese war. Thus Mao told the CCP senior leaders in March 1938, they "should have a correct appraisal of Japan. Japan is a powerful and astute imperialism. The Japanese nation is intrepid; their weapons are advanced."[251]

(3) Japan, as political problems for China, complicated China-related international politics Ever since the later nineteenth century, Japan has become an extremely crucial factor for China's foreign relations. Japan's victory over China in the first Sino-Japanese war shocked Chinese as well as the rest of the world. Japan's expansionist policy complicated the political situation in East Asia. First it had to face the challenge of Russia on the Korea issue. Then Japan had to yield to Triple Intervention (France, Germany and Russia) on the Liaodong Peninsula issue. Meanwhile the United States "Open Door" policy contained a potential check on Japan's imperialism. Victory over Russia on Chinese territory satisfied Japan's ambitions in Korea, the Liaodong Peninsula, and southern Manchuria. In the mean time, it made Japan appear too greedy for the world powers in East Asia, particularly in China. Its various treaties and agreements with the major powers on East Asian issues led to future disputes and rivalries. Third, the advantages Japan had taken through

World War I invited strong backlash not only from China but also from other world powers, especially Great Britain and the United States.

The contradictions eased only temporarily in Paris and Washington. Since the late 1920's, Japan's preparation for further expansion in the Asia-Pacific region and the outbreak of the second Sino-Japanese war marked the collapse of the entire Washington system. Thus from a Chinese foreign relations perspective, international relations in East Asia became multi-national situation more often in triangular.

Mao showed awareness of this when in 1916 he predicted an alliance between China and the U.S. against Japan. In 1919 he denounced a previous secret agreement between Tsarist Russia and Japan aimed at China. To avoid isolation in the triangle and to gain an ally against the major enemy, Mao was ready to see the triangles of China-Russia-Japan and China-United States-Japan as means to his goals. This emerged in his Jiangxi and Yanan views. Although he was still far from being the statesman who would have a decisive say in China's foreign policy, Mao would never give up any opportunities to gain the upper hand in the triangular game by using his political skill.

(III) Mao and other powers: Great Britain, France, and Germany

Mao and Great Britain   The British presence in modern Chinese history, particular since the Opium War of 1840-1842, has fluctuated from success to failure from the British perspective, and from extreme animosity to co-operation from the Chinese perspective. One should avoid any generalization evaluating a century of history from the early 1840's to the early 1940's from either perspective. Nevertheless, to understand Mao's view we must know what was the mainstream Chinese view of the British and their relations with China as well as what Mao said about Britain and the British during the period we are discussing.

Great Britain was the first imperialist force to invade China and was the most interested foreign power in China. However Britain's traditional privileged position was shaken after the World War I. Although different opinions exist on the motivations and consequences of foreign powers in China, Mao's version was representative within

China.

The role the British played in China since the 1840's was thoroughly negative and invited Chinese nationalist grievance, even animosity. The negative perception of Britain and the British increased during the Chinese nationalist revolution in the 1920's. In 1923, Mao published an article, "The English and Liang Ruhao," in response to negotiation of the Weihaiwei issue between China and Britain. To prove that "British imperialism's aggression against China has been still worse than that of Japanese imperialism," Mao declared that "the rendition of Weihaiwei is about to turn Weihaiwei into a second Xianggang [Hong Kong]." He also condemned the moves the English had taken in southern China and the Yangtze River area, Britain's traditional sphere of interest.[252] This area was one of the birthplaces of the Chinese nationalist revolution.

It was inevitable that the British would be the major obstacle for Chinese revolutionaries including Mao, and the major target for them as well. The situation did not change in the Jiangxi period. However Great Britain, *via* the League of Nations, did play a major international role responding to Japan's increasing ambitions in China. This partially improved its position in the eyes of nationalist Chinese, but it did not affect Mao's attitude. He continued to reproach Great Britain for its unfair treatment of Japan's aggression in China and extending British influence in China's western area, particularly its intention of building a "Xizhang Guo" (State of Tibet).[253] Mao's conclusion came in December 1939, when he wrote his interpretation, a combination of nationalist mood and communist rhetoric, of modern Chinese history in which the British played an important role. He made three points: (a) foreign capitalism accelerated the disintegration of China's traditional social economy; (b) the purpose of the imperialist powers was to transform China into their own semi-colony or colony; (c) to this end they used military, political, economic and cultural means of oppression in China.[254]

Mao also felt Great Britain was becoming an out dated power. He did not show it much respect, in contrast to the United States, Germany, and Japan. In 1919, young Mao Zedong teased Lloyd George, then British prime minister, by citing his speech of July 3, 1919. Following the politician's words "Let us not waste our strength prematurely in fighting each other," Mao jeered at him, "Such is the great talent of a politician. Such is the great magic of a politician."

Mao thought Lloyd George wanted to stop people attacking the government over their problems and ended his comments:

> I hereby formally announce to politicians such as Lloyd George that we reject all your big speeches as nothing but "lies" and "nonsense." We have already awakened. We are not as we used to be. You can just pack up and go now, and do not ever come back again.[255]

Eighteen years later, Mao returned to the attack. Talking with the British journalist, James Bertram, on October 25, 1937, Mao pointed out that the first imperialist war was against people's interests, necessitating an absolutely centralist government like that of Llyod George.[256] Besides his ideological stance, Mao's critique of Britain included a clear analysis of power politics in the world. When he received American journalist T. A. Bisson on June 22, 1937, Mao asserted:

> It is impossible for Britain to establish the kind of Far Eastern balance of power you have outlined. It is true that Britain long ago adopted the balance of power policy and traditionally followed it. But,...under contemporary world conditions, any such balance can only be temporary.[257]

In view of Britain's disability, Mao noted with derision,

> Of course, the Anglo-Saxon peoples have always prided themselves on their freedom of thought. They can have any kind of thought they like, but ... thinking is not always the same as acting.[258]

Although Mao saw Great Britain as a fading world-class power, the CCP did not realize, in the second half of the 1930's, that Britain was too weak in the Far East to take a strong line toward Japan.[259] Therefore, Britain's role in the region became a major target for the CCP and many Chinese as well.

Britain's China policy was seen as another Munich. Except for the very few words of appreciation of British assistance for China's anti-Japanese course, most of Mao's writings went to expose this Eastern Munich. Most Chinese believed was this was British policy in the area until Chamberlain stepped down in May 1940.[260]

In early 1935 Mao accused Britain's trying to compromise with

Japan in order to save strength to deal with its major opponents--the Soviet Union, United States and Italy.[261] In 1937 Mao attacked the current negotiations between Japan and Britain that were at the cost of China's interests. On the one hand, he recognized there was common ground for these countries in terms of their respective interests in China. On the other hand, Mao was alarmed that he could not count on Britain in the anti-Japanese movement, "We should get a clear understanding of the nature of Britain, then we will not be taken in."[262]

In 1938, Mao continued to criticize Britain's appeasement of Japan. In his important report to the Enlarged Plenum of the Sixth CCP Central Committee, he discussed the policy of Chamberlain after the Munich Agreement. Under the subhead, "Britain's compromise policy will result in a larger size war among the fascist countries," Mao predicted, "'Lift a rock only to drop it on one's own feet,' this will be the natural result of Chamberlain's policy."[263]

At the beginning of 1939, Mao announced that the CCP would approve Roosevelt's policy while opposing Chamberlain. In mid-1939, Mao expressed appreciation of British help in China's struggle but he carefully distinguished the British government from the British people, attributing the help to the latter. Still concerned about the policy of the government, he said, "We ask you [British people] to pay strict attention to your government's attitude,...to put drastic pressure on the government."[264] After the outbreak of the European war, Mao condemned it as an imperialist war, standing on the Soviet side to declare that Britain was the worst of all imperialist countries. Therefore the CCP would oppose both sides in the war, with emphasis on British imperialism.[265]

Obviously, there were ideological reasons for Mao to make such a statement. Nevertheless it was also a consistent attitude toward Britain's China policy. Mao anticipated that the war might cause a more unfavorable British appeasement policy.[266] Mao's anticipation was proven incorrect a few months later, mainly because of the changed political scene in the world and particularly in Great Britain. As a result, Mao muted his grievances against Britain's Far Eastern policy as well as changed the CCP attitude toward the European war after May 1940.

Mao and France The French, together with the Russians, once were the only serious rival of the British in empire-building on the

Asian mainland. However, France had different imperial aspirations and different means of achieving them.[267] For the Chinese there was no substantial difference between the French and the British. This is particularly true when talking about the transition period between the two world wars.

France was one of the major targets for Mao during the Paris Peace Conference, expressing his dislike for these "strutting and prancing men of the present peace conference," specifically Clemenceau and Lloyd George.[268] Several essays criticized their actions in the conference.[269] Mao warned of a gloomy future for France and Britain in their relationship with Germany.[270] While France was his number one villain in 1919, in the 1930's he saw it as only a junior partner of Britain.

The fate of France in the second world war was not unexpected. Twenty years before, on July 21, 1919 Mao predicted, "Clemenceau's great joy is the German's great sorrow. I guarantee that in ten to twenty years, you Frenchmen will yet again have a splitting headache. Mark my word."[271] This prediction illustrates Mao's approach to the international politics as a disinterested observer. In his two essays on relations between France and Germany, four elements support prediction. First, the historical element embodied mutual hostility handed down through generations. Clemenceau's great joy in 1919 was a reaction to the French document of submission to Wilhelm I and Bismarck in 1871. At that time Germany's victory over France was to some extent a reaction to the King of Prussia's submission to Napoleon from 1800 to 1815. That French victory over Germany in turn had some connection with the invasion of France by German and Austrian Holy Alliance armies in 1789. For Mao, history was probably the most important lesson to be taken by politicians and statesmen.[272]

Second in importance is the political element, the superiority of political pragmatism to diplomatic agreement. As already noted, Mao's politics were very practical-oriented; he never believed in the permanency of diplomatic outcomes. In light of this, Mao teased, "Ignorant old man Clemenceau, clutching this gray-yellow thick volume [i.e. the peace treaty] under his arm, thinks that the signatures on it make it as stable and solid as the Alps. How pitiful! "[273]

In third place is the psychological element, including the national mentality, societal sentiment, and people's, particularly leader's, emotions. Mao listed many facts to illustrate that "France fears

Germany as if it were a tiger or a wolf. Even after Germany has suffered such a great defeat, France is still terribly afraid of her." Then Mao asked "Why should she have such fear?" He gave no answer; it seemed to him that the fear was not reasonable based on reality. "I think this phenomenon bodes no good for France!"[274]

Last but not least is the philosophical element, the dialectic chain of cause and effect. Mao thought the alternation and transition between joy and suffering was a theme of philosophy, "The greatest joy, however, also contains within it a certain amount of suffering." "When the joy of one side reaches an extreme, the suffering of the other side will inevitably also reach an extreme." In accord with this philosophical point, Mao cited the history of mutual relations between France and Germany, as given above. He then predicted that when French joy reached an extreme, it would be time for them to experience suffering again.[275]

Personally, Mao felt more positive toward France than Britain. He had absorbed the thoughts of many Western thinkers, including British and French. Since his youth he admired Napoleon, regarding him as a hero. Mao considered the French Revolution a model of political revolution, while the Russian Revolution was treated as a model of social revolution. He respected the French who "are very proud and heroic people."[276] Mao also praised Paris as "a magnificent commercial city," despite never having been there.[277] Although these words were written in his youth, these positive impressions remained his entire life.

Mao and Germany In the first half of the twentieth century, Germany played a very important role in international politics. However, Chinese perceptions of Germany were not identical with those of others who suffered from German aggression. For many Chinese, Germany was famed for her military renown ever since it had defeated France in 1871. Moreover Germany first entered the Far Eastern balance of power by playing a leading role in checking Japan's territorial demands on China in the mid-1890's. Between 1900 and 1914, Germany made a conscious effort to reinforce its precarious footing in China by increasing its intellectual influence. This was after a short period of opposing Chinese during the Boxer Uprising.[278]

Although the relationship between Germany and China was by no means friendly, yet Chinese held a relatively positive attitude toward Germans before the First World War as a result of the generally soft interactions in the previous several decades. Mao shared in and reinforced this image of Germany. A close friend recalled that Mao and he "talked a lot about Germany, since at that time, Chinese felt a special respect for Germany and Japan, though we realized that Japan imitated Germany."[279] At that time, the main topic for Mao and his friends was how to promote physical education and military training in order to strengthen the bodies of Chinese. This was perhaps one of the hottest point to be debated among Chinese young intellectuals. Mao published his first article on the *New Youth* in 1917, which was entitled "A Study of Physical Education." Awareness of the need came from the German victories of 1914-16.[280] Mao also envied the successful reform transition of Germany in modern time. In his study notes on reading a German philosopher, Mao expressed his admiration of such a change. He wrote,

> I used to worry that our China would be destroyed, but now I know that this is not so. Through the establishment of a new political system, and a change in the national character, and a reforming of society, the German states became the German Reich. There is no need to worry.[281]

After Germany's defeat in the First World War, Mao continued to show faith in Germany's changed political system. He said, "I would venture to make a rough judgment on this." What was "this?" Mao predicted that Germany "has already changed from an imperial monarchy into a republic. In the second turnaround, perhaps they will not even want to be a republic." Mao's prediction was based on his view of the current political tendency in the world that was influenced by Russian revolution.[282] History has shown that Mao was partially correct; Germany did not remain a republic. However, he was really wrong because the fact was in opposite to his expectation. Germany took the fascist road.

Mao's faith in Germany was based on his admiration for the riches of its culture and spirit. He felt great sympathy for Germany's fate at the Paris Peace Conference. Mao "focused solely on the pain and suffering inflicted on the spirit of the German people," when his journal, the *Xian River Review*, reported the detailed negotiation of the treaty. He made a further "Editorial Comment" with a stress on German national characteristics, spirit and philosophy:

Germany is made up of the Germanic peoples, who have long been celebrated in history for possessing the characteristic of towering strength. When one dynasty is on the brink of collapse, a new sharp sword appears which the peoples of the whole world can scarcely resist. We do not see the bellicose spirit of Germany as having been unleashed solely by one man, the Kaiser. The Kaiser is the crystallization of the German people. Because there are German people, there is a Kaiser. The German people have in recent years been molded by the philosophical ideas of "striving upward," of "action," of Nietzsche, Fichte, Goethe, and Paulsen. The call to arise when opportunity strikes has been loud and clear. Even today, they still do not admit defeat. "No war guilt." Of all the peoples of the world, the spirit of the German people is richest in "greatness." A spirit of "greatness" alone can overcome all difficulties, it can seek to realize, it brings to fruition this "greatness." Even while detesting the Kaiser's bellicose spirit and indiscriminate use of force, we can also shed tears of warm sympathy, moved by his spirit of "greatness."[283]

It was not strange for Mao to feel great sympathy for defeated Germany. Seeing Germany as an oppressed nation like China was widespread in Chinese intellectual circles during the May Fourth era.

However this bias did not affect Mao's view on Germany's responsibility in launching the world war. In fact, he not only described the war as "barbaric" but also warned of the possible ganging up of Germany and Japan. If that were to happen, Mao anticipated that "the danger will be truly great."[284] As for German philosophy, Mao did not accept it completely without criticism either. For instance, Mao disapproved of Germany's spirit of self-satisfaction and her highly nationalistic environment.

Positive aspects were manifested by German military missions to China, although they caused political problems both domestically and internationally in the 1930's. In the first half of the decade, German military advisors to the KMT darkened Mao's positive view of Germany. Also at that time a German national Comintern agent in Jiangxi enhanced Mao's negative impression of German arrogance. However, the geographic distance between the two countries substantially limited Mao's attention to and interest in German fascist expansion in Europe. Thus in September 1939, as noted before, Mao even perversely anticipated a possible alliance between the Soviet Union and Germany against Britain and France.

Mao's view of the world powers in the period we are discussing was not an important element in international politics or China's diplomatic relations at that time. It was only a matter of Mao's personal or at most, the CCP attitudes toward various foreign countries and foreign peoples. These attitudes were directed by Mao's view of the world as a whole and his vision of the individual powers. Some basic elements made his viewpoints take shape, such as geographical, historical and traditional settings; Chinese experiences of mutual relations in modern history; the influence of current domestic or international events; personal feelings and insights through his learning, knowledge, and career; ideological faith and commitment; nationalistic environment, practical needs and political considerations. No doubt, in the future Mao's attitudes toward the world powers, his perceptions of these powers and all the elements listed here that affected Mao's attitudes and perceptions, would have an important impact on CCP and PRC foreign policies and foreign relations.

PART THREE

MAO'S CONCEPTS OF THE WORLD: PRACTICE, PRINCIPLE AND THEORY

The emergence of Maoism in Yanan period, particularly from 1938-1940,[285] was the systematic synthesis of Mao's thinking and experience--the CCP ideology and policies as made by Mao down to that time. This experience, policy, and theory later became Mao Zedong Thought, which included his long-time world watching, his distinctive perceptions of the world, and the practices, principles, and theories arising therefrom. A conceptual analysis of Mao's practice and theory is a logical continuation of this study.

There are three groups of concepts linked to various degrees with Mao's world view. They were, (1) external affairs specifically, the concept of *Wai Jiao*, (2) abstract principles such as nation-state and sovereignty, and (3) Mao's famous revolutionary strategy and tactics, such as semi-colony, self-reliance, united front, popular mass, and revolutionary war. Combining the three groups provides a comprehensive sketch of Mao's world view at the conceptual level with practical and theoretical dimension of his political thought.

Chapter 7

Mao's World View in Practice And Principle: *"Wai Jiao,"* "Nation-State" And "Sovereignty"

(I) What Did *Wai Jiao* Mean To Mao?

The Chinese word "wai jiao" literally means any kind of outward relations conducted by certain social entities. Here "any kind" originally refers to both international and domestic relations so long as they have an external connection for a particular subject. However it gradually became a political concept identical with "foreign relations" or "diplomacy." To be true, the original Chinese meaning, interconnecting domestic politics and international politics was still alive when Mao used the term "wai jiao."

As indicated in the first chapter Mao, in his youth, studied two major diplomatic officials, Li Hongzhang and Guo Shongtao, who heavily influenced China's *wai jiao* in the second half of the nineteenth century. One noteworthy aspect of Mao's early use of *wai jiao* in its original Chinese sense was his positively reference to Su Qin and Zhang Yi, two leading masters of *wai jiao* in ancient China's Warring State era. Both were famed for their political strategy and eloquence. Mao noted "Su and Zhang created great alliances."[286] Nevertheless, Mao did not experience his own style *wai jiao* until the starting of the Yanan period.[287]

These aspects of *wai jiao* emerged in the Yanan period. First, its meaning expanded from the limits of the Red Border Region to the stage of both domestic and international politics. Mao linked foreign affairs to the associations outside the CCP and its border region as two interrelated tasks encompassed in *wai jiao*. In the spring of 1936, he held a Politburo conference where one of the important issues was *wai jiao*; actually, it was the issue of domestic united front. That June he also talked about *wai jiao* as relations between the CCP controlled area and others. Meanwhile, *wai jiao* also referred to normal foreign affairs. In the Standing Committee of the Politburo in May 1936, Mao connected the international united front and the domestic united front in explaining CCP foreign policy. Two months later, Mao received two American visitors, Ma Hai-teh (Dr. George Hatem) and Edgar Snow at the Foreign Ministry of the Chinese Soviet Central Government that was built in the Jianxi period.[288] On July 16, 1936, Mao started his famous interview with Snow on the issue of CCP foreign policy. Later, the word "wai jiao" still carried these two interrelated meanings but tended to relate more to foreign affairs.

Second, Mao tried to re-organize the decision-making structure and procedure for handling the CCP's foreign affairs, although little was achieved at this time. Mao had no intent to institutionalize the process. Rather he preferred to put foreign affairs under the control of the highest authority in the party. On July 30, 1936, Mao stressed to the Standing Committee of the Politburo that "the work of *wai jiao* should have an independent institution in principle."[289] Interestingly enough, the foreign ministry that was operative from the Jianxi period was abolished not long after Mao's statement. No such an organ existing again until 1949. The best explanation is that Mao wanted to control foreign policy himself. For instance on May 26, 1941, he attended a Politburo conference and made a report regarding the current international situation. Talking about CCP propaganda, Mao declared "In the past, external propaganda was not unified in usual practice. The manifestation of this disunity was the difference in policies on external propaganda among various base areas. From now on, it must be centralized."[290]

Third, some distinct features of CCP external affairs were cultivated through Mao's personal practice. One emphasis was on international propaganda. Although Mao purposely separated diplomacy (international *wai jiao*) and international propaganda as two different tasks to be strengthened,[291] the main endeavor of propaganda was self-promotion rather than ideological export. After the Long March and establishment of his *de facto* leading position in the CCP, one of the immediate needs for Mao and the CCP was to let outside audiences, both at home and abroad, know him and his political force. On August 5, 1936, in his letter to all who had survived the Long March, Mao called for a collection of writings to be compiled in a book *Records of Long March*. Mao told his comrades it was "for international propaganda...extending worldwide influence of Red Army."[292] On January 20, 1939, Mao wrote a preface for the English translation of his famous essay, *On Protracted War*, which were lectures from May 26 to June 3, 1938. In the beginning of the preface he stated, "I am certainly very happy to know that a friend in Shanghai is translating my *On Protracted War* into English."[293]

The most prominent examples of Mao's external propaganda in the early Yanan days[294] were his interviews with many foreigners. Most of them were American journalists to whom he spoke with extraordinary patience, frankness, and enthusiasm. It is well known that Edgar Snow made a breakthrough contribution in this regard, his *Red Star Over China* becoming a classic that brought the Chinese Communists and Mao to world-wide attention. Not only was Snow's personal competence made him to be the first one in the world to have done this, Also he was helped by "combination of factors," in John K. Fairbank's term. Namely, in mid-1936 and 1937, the Chinese communists "were ready to tell their story to the outside world. Snow had the capacity to report it."[295]

Following Snow, two American women arrived Yanan in 1937. Agnes Smedley entered in January and had a formal interview with Mao on March 1, 1937. Nym Wales (Helen Foster Snow), the then wife of Snow, arrived in April 1937 to continue Snow's work. Her book, *Inside Red China*, won a similar reputation. From 1937 to 1939 Yanan and the Chinese Communists had great attraction for foreigners, especially American journalists, while the opportunity to cross the border between the CCP and the KMT areas was changing month by month. Generally speaking, 1937 was the time of blockade for entering Yanan but 1938 was an open-door period. Then in 1939 the KMT re-imposed the news blockade, effectively isolating the CCP from contact with the West for nearly four years. Again, it was Edgar Snow who became the last foreigner received by Mao in September 1939, ending this first wave of Western contact with the Chinese Communists.

During these three years, there were over a dozen formal interviews conducted between Mao and these Westerners. In many cases, the interviews covered extensive topics and extended time. Those records are invaluable in terms of Mao studies, including study of his world view. However it must be pointed out that this first wave of the contact between the CCP and the outside world had no diplomatic significance. None of those foreigners who visited Yanan had any official color except for Evans Carlson, who had two lengthy talks with Mao in 1938. Because of Carlson's political and military career, especially his personal relation with Roosevelt, his visit was considered as the first American with an official capacity to enter the CCP area. Moreover, his agreement with Roosevelt to confidentially report his experiences in China to the president made his trip even more distinctive.[296]

Aside from propaganda, a second point of emphasis was the pursuit of political and military goals. When Mao called for an independent system for CCP foreign affairs, he focused on political and military aspects.[297] Besides welcoming friends from outside Yanan, Mao tried to establish official channels to the world after he became CCP leader. Logically, Mao first and foremost need was to establish means of reaching Moscow to legitimate his position in the party.[298] He also hoped for possible material support from Soviet Russia.[299]

Other than seeking a reliable route to the Soviet Union, Mao's efforts in contacting the outside world in his early Yanan time were limited but noteworthy. For example, on the second day of the Xian Incident, December 13, 1936, Mao ordered an official response to the event at a Politburo meeting. The package of policies and approaches that the CCP was supposed to implement included inviting British and American approval through actively associating with these two very influential world powers. Again in the mid-1941, making contact with the officials of Britain and the United State was proposed again. On the day of the Pearl Harbor attack, Mao ordered a high CCP official,

Liao Chenzhi, to "liaise boldly with British government in Hong Kong." A few days later, Mao telegraphed to Zhou Enlai, "The British Ambassador and somebody else want us to send representatives to Singapore; it is good for us using this opportunity to have persons there."[300]

A third point was to hold a principled criterion of attitude toward external relationship, as quoted in chapter three, "Befriend all those helping us; be hostile to all those assisting our enemy." Of course the precondition of this criterion is to have a target for attack. In the 1930's, Japan was definitely the main enemy. However, other domestic or international forces might serve as a temporary target, such as the KMT or Great Britain. Yet identifying a major enemy was not Mao's main concern in setting up this criterion of attitude. In the sense of *wai jiao*, the main objective, in Mao's words, is not searching out an enemy, but rather strengthening different types of external unity. In the second half of the 1930's, Mao called several times for an anti-Japanese front. When he presented this idea, Mao always put the term *wai jiao* before the idea of the united front. This implied that *wai jiao* was less of an ideological domain for Mao and the CCP; it was more strategic and tactical than propagandistic. In other words, practicing *wai jiao* was implementing "real policy." In line with this, Mao set up another important principle for external activity. As he said on March 4, 1941, "We must distinguish propaganda and real policy."[301] Apparently the term propaganda here was an ideologically oriented word. It even differed qualitatively from previously mentioned "international propaganda."

A fourth consideration for Mao was how to address the issues of foreign policy and diplomacy as a legitimate regime in international society. Although Mao's power in Yanan was still limited, he wanted to address the CCP future, including its foreign policy. Two main issues were first, mutually beneficial relations with foreign countries, particularly those with interests in China, and second, relations with China's major neighbors. These concerns in turn linked China's domestic and foreign affairs.

On several occasions in Yanan, Mao defined future mutually beneficial relations. In 1936, Mao told Snow:

> When China really wins her independence, then legitimate foreign trading interests will enjoy more opportunities than ever before. The

power of production and consumption of 450,000,000 people is not a matter that can remain the exclusive interest of the Chinese, but one that must engage many nations. Our millions of people, once really emancipated, with their great latent productive possibilities freed for creative activity in every field, can help improve the economy as well as raise the cultural level of the whole world.[302]

In 1938, Mao answered Evans Carlson's question about the CCP plan for the post-war period. As for international relations, Mao stressed equality, "We feel that cordial relations should be established and maintained between China and other nations which are willing to meet us on a basis of equality."[303] Mao had described China's future under two circumstances: an independent China and a coalition government. But what if China took the socialist road? In 1939, he received another American journalist, Robert Martin. Assuming a "socialist country," Mao spoke as he had to Snow and Carlson, but went further:

> When China enters socialism, if Great Britain, the United States, and France are still capitalist countries at that time; and if those countries do not militarily offend China, the Chinese government will guarantee (with preparation of paying the cost) the foreign investments and foreigners' properties in China.[304]

In sum, independence, equality, and mutual benefit were to be general principles of foreign policy.

As for China's neighbors, besides Soviet Russia and Japan, Mao was most concerned about relations with India, Korea, and Southeast Asia or Nan Yang, as it was called in Chinese then. Given the size of India's territory and population, and rich cultural traditions that had been the precious heritage of both India and China, Mao kept his eyes on what was going on in this neighbor. Both Snow and Smedley recorded his knowledge and interest in India. Two factors prompted him to praise India. First was personal contact between Mao and Jawaharlal Nehru, through telegrams and the India Medical Mission sent to China by Nehru as chairman of the Indian National Congress. Second and more important was the common stand on the anti-Japanese war and on the European war in 1939, when Nehru objected to Britain's intention of bringing India into the war. As Mao put it:

India is a great nation with three hundred and twenty million populations. This time Great Britain enforced India entering the war, the Indian National Congress, standing for the people of the whole nation, issued a declaration to oppose joining the war, oppose the imperialist war. The leader of the Indian National Congress is Mr.Nehru, who has been to Chongqing not long ago. Mr.Nehru sent the Indian Medical Mission to assist China. China and India, the two great nations, unite to down Japanese imperialism.[305]

Nevertheless, Mao did not approve all the ideas of famous Indian leaders such as Gandhi and Nehru. He "had definite opinions on that country. Chief among these was that Indian independence would never be realized without an agrarian revolution."[306]

Because of its historical tributary relationship with China, Korea arouses more concern among the Chinese people in the twentieth century than any other neighbor. In his youth, Mao sympathized with the Koreans under Japanese colonialist rule. The historical heritage and the currently similar fate of Chinese and Koreans directed Mao's ideas about China and Korea in the future. Snow asked for Mao's ideas about China's lost territories and the influence of Chinese communism in other Asiatic or colonial and semi-colonial nations. Mao did not include Korea in China's goal of regaining territory lost to the Japanese, although he incorrectly thought Korea once was China's colony, rather than only a suzerainty. However, Mao believed that China's revolution was a "key" factor in the world situation. "When the Chinese revolution comes into full power the masses of many colonial countries will follow the example of China and win a similar victory of their own."[307] Korea was certainly among these countries. Differing from other Asiatic nations, Korea was still treated specially by Mao as he said the same thing on Taiwan and Inner Mongolia. Mao told Snow, "When we have re-established the independence of the lost territories of China, and if the Koreans wish to break away from the chains of Japanese imperialism, we will extend them our enthusiastic help in their struggle for independence."[308] History shows that Mao lived up to his promise fifteen years later, however, under different circumstance with different results.[309]

Southeast Asia was special for Chinese, not only because of the very tight connections in history but also due to the very active overseas Chinese and their monetary contributions to contemporary China. Mao, like his predecessors in the revolutionary movement, put his hope in this region, particularly on the Chinese there. In his 1920 promotion of the overseas student movement, Mao turned his attention from France, the ideal of most Chinese youth who wanted to go abroad at that time, to Southeast Asia. During the Sino-Japanese war, Mao directed his followers several times to enhance the work among the overseas Chinese, particularly, in Nan Yang (Southeast Asia).

(II) How Did Mao Exercise "Nation-State" And "Sovereignty"?

There were many types of states that developed at various times in the course of history and on the soil of different civilizations. Among the states were two groups: the Western and the Eastern ones, both prominent, but incompatible with each other. Thanks to the power of modern science, the industrial revolution and a new cosmopolitan vision, the Western type nation-state gained its momentum from a world-wide international system through European expansion to incorporate all the other nations, particularly, Eastern nations represented by China.

For China, from the middle of nineteenth century, the process was painful but inevitable. From the 1910's onward, Chinese intellectuals, both in and out of government, made attempts to get China to participate in the international system as an equal member. Here, the basic principles of a Western type nation-state such as national sovereignty and equality became the instrument for China's national revival, national reverence, and national re-unification. However the traditional Sino-centrism, although a fading standard, was still embodied within the nationalist mentality.

This was the context Mao had when he encountered the concepts of the nation-state and sovereignty during the 1910's. In his *Classroom Notes* of 1913, Mao recorded three points that he learned from his teacher, Yang Changji. First, the Chinese "people lack the concepts of state and politics" because the relationship between the government and the people has been simple and loose since ancient times. Second, because of the peculiar relationship between the state and the people in traditional China, the Chinese situation was more favorable than the Western one.[310] Third, compared to what the French did in Vietnam and the Japanese in Korea, "China was very generous toward its vassal nations; apart from their obligation to pay tribute and betrothal gifts, they were allowed to enjoy autonomy."[311] The question of the impact of Yang's three points on young Mao remains open.[312]

In a modern political sense, the May Fourth era witnessed the birth of a Chinese nation with a growing consciousness of her outward looking profile and position.[313] However, it was just a start. The process of remolding China as a modern nation-state lasted several decades. In such a process, Mao's words and actions occupied a crucial position. From the May Fourth era to the Yanan era, Mao presented his ideas and practices on building a "state" in a modern political sense in Hunan, in Jiangxi, and in Yanan respectively.

Mao's first striving for a new state was at the Hunan Autonomy Movement in September and October 1920, just before he committed himself being a Marxist. The Movement was, on the one hand, an exhibition of their self-confidence and self-respect, because of the outstanding performance of the Hunanese in China's modernization from the middle of the nineteenth century. On the other hand, the Hunan Autonomy Movement was in practical opposition to Chinese efforts to build a "Great Republic of China." Mao concluded, "The only method is for us to pursue self-determination and self-government, and create a `Republic of Hunan' in the territory of Hunan," to save Hunan and save China as well.[314] In nearly two months, Mao published sixteen articles promoting this goal. Although he said he had a lengthy theory on the question of the "country of Hunan," he never had a chance to write it down. His sixteen articles presented his argument about the rule of causation between states and the federation, his advocacy of a citizens' movement, his draft of a constitutional proposal for Hunan people, and so on. These writings showed Mao's earliest thought on constructing a state.[315]

Mao accepted the political science concept of "country." He wrote, "A `country' has the essential elements of land, people, and sovereignty, of which the most essential is sovereignty." Therefore, the first step was to achieve "complete self-rule" for Hunan as well as other provinces all over China. Only after building up "many Chinas," that is many states, could one begin talking about a federation. On this issue, Mao cited the example of Germany and the United States, "Both Germany and the United States had states before they joined together in federations. Once states are created, federation will be simply the natural result."[316] There is no doubt that Mao was not merely talking about regional autonomy; he was enhancing Hunan as a state in the full sense of the word. Mao appealed to a citizens' movement. As usual, he used Western history and politics as a model, "The political and social reforms of the Western countries all started with movements of the citizens....The power of the citizens is truly great! The citizens are truly the proudest people under Heaven!"[317] The movement of citizens should not be separate from cultivating the individual citizens, "If the individual citizens are not healthy and sound, one cannot expect the citizenry as a whole to be healthy and sound."[318] In line with, Mao made it clear the preference should be for social organization over political organization and small localities over the big country. At this point, Mao rejected Lenin's path of the Russian Revolution, although he admired it greatly.[319]

To be sure, the "Hunan Republic" would be democratic. Mao carefully chose the term "constitutional convention" as the most appropriate to modify the vehicle that would give birth to the constitution. Once again, he used the American state constitutions or the German state constitutions as examples.[320] It was not difficult to discover the Western democratic nature in the law he adopted for the new state, including "direct election" and "universal suffrage" as drafted by Mao.

The Hunan Autonomy Movement was obviously a utopian scheme and quickly aborted. However it could have been an experiment for Mao in the concept of the modern state, Western in general, America or Germany in particular. Thus a Western brand may be put on Mao's first experience of building a state in the modern political sense. However this changed once he accepted the communist idea.[321]

A formal state, the Chinese Soviet Republic, was created by the CCP during the Jiangxi period. While this period marked a temporary decline of Mao's power, first from the Party, next from the Red Army, and finally from the government, Mao held the chairman's post throughout the entire period of the soviet-type state. His influence was particularly prominent at the First National Soviet Congress in 1931. The Chinese Soviet Republic was Mao's second chance to form a state. The differences from the previous one were obvious. Unlike the proposals only presented in newspapers in his Hunan time, this was an authentic state run by the CCP and Mao who had been effectively controlling certain territory, peoples, and armies. This state was a formal political entity in every sense of the word. It provided tremendous propaganda value to the communists to support their claim of being an "alternative road" for the Chinese people to that offered by the KMT.[322]

Another important aspect of the Chinese Soviet Republic in Jiangxi was that it differed qualitatively from the Hunan Autonomy Movement in its political and ideological base. In Hunan, Mao took the Western states as model. Now in Jiangxi, he followed Soviet Russia's pattern (even borrowing the name "soviet"). It reflected the positive side of the relationship between Mao and Moscow.[323] The internal workings of the Chinese Soviet government were identical to Soviet ideology. A constitutional outline of the Chinese Soviet Republic asserted that the state was to be a workers' and peasants' democratic dictatorship; a transitional form *en route* to a proletarian dictatorship. This form was identical with the one Lenin employed in 1905. It was even more radical than Lenin's by reason of the one party dictatorship claimed by the Chinese Soviet Republic. Freedom of speech, assembly, and the press belonged only to the workers and the peasant laboring masses. No democracy was available for landlords and bourgeoisie. The priests, monks, and other clergy were deprived of the right to vote, although the republic declared there was true religious freedom. As for foreign policies, the soviet regime showed its willingness for revolutionary alignment with the world proletariat and oppressed nationalities, while proclaiming its loyalty to Moscow. This was the line espoused by the Comintern's policy after the Manchurian Incident.[324] As for the policy toward world powers, Mao drafted an economic policy for the Soviet Republic:

> Article 1 In order to secure an entirely independent Soviet government, it will nationalize all the fatal economic (properties and enterprises) that were in imperialists' hands (concessions, banks, railways, navigation, mining, factories, etc.,...). For the present, it will allow some of foreign enterprises to re-negotiate leases, so as to continue production. But (they) must obey all the rules and laws of the Soviet.[325]

From Jiangxi to Yanan, Mao experimented to construct and operate the power of the communist trinity (party, army and government). He inherited the Jiangxi tradition, but he had to draw a new blueprint for the future extended power of the CCP. In the autumn of 1936, Mao admitted, "we are a state, but today we are not yet a full-fledged one, for we are still in the first period of the civil war, and the state is far from a perfect one."[326] Apparently Mao was referring to the situation from the Jiangxi period at this point, but the change had been already planned. As Mao indicated, "Why did we change the `workers' and peasants' republic into a `people's republic?" Mao's answered theoretically: "Our government represents not only the workers and peasants but the whole nation"; practically "the Japanese invasion had altered class relations in China".[327] The worker-peasant revolution, with its aim of establishing a dictatorship of the working classes, was no longer appropriate to China's situation. Instead, accompanied by the birth of the united front of all national classes in 1937, Mao's communist state gained its class-coalition base. This also became the keynote for his comment on the principles of the future state of the whole nation during Yanan time.[328]

In his article "On the New Stage" (1938), Mao specified his idea of a state, "What kind of state are we going to build? The answer: Establish a republic with the Three People's Principles." Mao used Sun Yat-sen's famous ideas and ideals to express the CCP's proposition of establishing the state of the whole nation. The central principle of the state was equality, international equality, political equality, and economic equality within and without China.[329]

Although Mao's conception of the nation-state contained Leninist and Sun Yat-sen's nationalistic origins, Mao tried to distinguish himself by identifying his ideas with a concept of "new democracy." Mao's argument contained the following points. First, the numerous types of state systems in the world can be reduced to three basic kinds according to the class character of their political power. Republics under a bourgeois dictatorship Mao called "the old European-American form of the capitalist republic, ...which is the old democratic form and already out of date." Republics under the dictatorship of the proletariat, or a socialist republic such as the Soviet Union, Mao praised for a dominant state and governmental structure and pointed out it could only be happened in the industrially advanced countries. Republics under the joint dictatorship of several revolutionary classes Mao believed would be adopted in the revolutions of all colonial and semi-colonial countries. He named this the "new-democratic republic." For China it would be labeled "The Chinese democratic republic", a republic of the genuinely revolutionary new Three People's Principles with their Three Great Policies.[330]

Second, the question of the "state system" (*Guo Ti*), being tossed about in China for several decades, was simply a question of the status of the various social classes within the state. The kind of state needed today was a dictatorship headed by the Chinese proletariat consisting of all the revolutionary classes maintaining power over the counter-revolutionaries and traitors. Third, the question of "the system of government" (*Zheng Ti*) was a matter of how political power being organized or the form a social class choosed for arranging its apparatus of political power to oppose its enemies and protect itself. China needed a system of universal and equal suffrage, irrespective of sex, creed, property or education. Such a system is democratic centralism.[331]

A vertical display of Mao's conception of nation-state from Hunan, from Jiangxi, and from Yanan, offers a conceptual interpretation of the subject discussed here. Due to the minor political position Mao held in the entire nation, the concept of the nation-state he developed was assumptive and tentative by and large. However his views of the nation-state, particularly as formulated while in Yanan, were a blueprint and theory for a new China later.

In Mao's writings, from youth to maturity, national sovereignty was a major concept in developing a nation-state or any dealings of China related to international issues. As early as the Hunan Autonomy movement, Mao was aware that sovereignty was "the most essential" element among the three basic elements of a nation-state. His great concern for national sovereignty was a natural outgrowth of his personal background as a politician and statesman combined with nationalism and Marxism-Leninism.

Complete independence and territorial integrity are two frequent issues in modern China that called for national sovereignty. Not being a formal colony, a commonwealth country, or an allied state, but rather being semi-colonial and politically "independent" only in form, China's international status since the 1840's was more inferior than an ordinary colony. That is why Sun Yat-sen used the term "quasi-colony" instead of "semi-colony". For this reason Chinese efforts were directed toward complete independence from all unequal treaties and foreign privileges.

Mao's first mention of national sovereignty appeared to be in December 1919. He had been deeply engaged in the campaign of expelling Hunan's governor Zhang Jingyao, a notorious non-Hunanese warlord. On December 27 Mao sent a dispatch to the People's News Agency calling for the ouster of Zhang, in which Mao exposed

Zhang's secret agreement to sell the Hunan mines to foreign businessmen under unequal contracts. Mao called for new regulations that would safeguard national sovereignty whereby "mining regulations stipulate that in all joint-capital mining ventures between Chinese and foreigners, both parties must remain equal in terms of capital, so as to protect the nation's sovereign rights."[332]

Mao's voice for sovereign rights became more audible within the nationalist and communist movements in the first half of the 1920's. Since the focus of the Chinese revolution in that period was anti-imperialism and anti-warlordism with a nationalist mentality, it was the time to attack unequal treaties, extraterritorial rights, the trade tariffs, and foreign concessions. Mao's writings in the period were full of specific charges of foreign economic aggression.[333] With the lapse of time, these attacks on concrete targets of the nationalist revolution yielded to the more refined synthesis of national independence demands. In Yanan, Mao concluded how China was deprived of her independence by military, political, economic, and cultural factors in modern history. The crucial cause was the imperialists' aggression against China. They "imposed their ruthless rule on China, reducing an independent country to a semi-colonial and colonial country."[334] Mao assumed that negotiations with world powers to abolish the unequal treaties might be adopted by China's future government after the victory of Sino-Japanese war. The basic need was to avoid "any measure that may place China at a disadvantage in her struggle against Japanese imperialism."[335] Mao interpreted his version of the so-called "independent state":

> It does not allow any external interference and will not interfere in any foreign countries. That is to say, it will change China's original semi-colonial position. It stands up independently. Meanwhile, it will absolutely not reduce itself to imperialism, no matter how strong it will be. Based on the equal spirit, it will have peaceful contacts with all the friendly nations who respect China's independence, co-exist with them and share benefits mutually.[336]

Territorial integrity was another important issue that was closely related to modern nationalism. In fact, it was a product of the nation-state system. All Chinese politicians with nationalistic mood, no matter how different ideologies they held, are irredentists to some degree. Generally, main concerns of territorial issues should include, but not be limited to, strategic security, economic interests, national dignity, and politicians' or statesmen's personal reputations. In this period, given his minor position in the nation, Mao's focal point was on the last two aspects: national dignity and personal reputation, not strategic security and economic interests. Thus, Mao's irredentism claim was characterized with more nationalist passion but less operational significance.

As previously cited, the young Mao realized land was one of the three essential components of a state, and one of the two undestroyable factors. In the 1920's nationalist revolution, Mao engaged in China's territorial issues, such as the issue of Weihaiwei in 1923, the issue of foreign concessions in Shanghai (1925), Tianjin (1926), and Hankou (1926). In the early 1930's, while at Jiangxi inland, Mao listed all of China's remote areas that he thought might the KMT sell out to the western powers. These territorial-related problems plus Japan's threats in North China justified Mao's revolution under the nationalist banner. He lost no opportunity to call for the "Chinese nation's independence, liberalization and territorial integration."

In Yanan, Mao's interview with Snow covered more specific territorial problems. After declaring "It is the immediate task of China to regain all our lost territories, not merely to defend our sovereignty below the Great Wall," Mao specified several important places that were under Japanese occupation. Manchuria, Mao asserted "must be regained." Inner Mongolia "is populated by both Chinese and Mongolians. We will struggle to drive Japan from there and help Inner Mongolia establish an autonomous state." Korea was formerly under Chinese suzerainty but he did not include it within the scope of his irredentist claim. Curiously, Mao treated Taiwan the same as he did Korea, with only one remark after his addressing Korea, "The same applies for Formosa."[337] Mao repeated the statements about Taiwan he had made to Snow in July 1936. For instance, in August 1937, he proposed an anti-Japanese foreign policy to "unite with the worker and peasant masses of Korea, Taiwan and Japan against Japanese imperialism." (In later officially published writings, "Taiwan" has been removed from the text for an obvious reason.)[338] Two months later, in his essay, "On the New Stage", Mao paid equal attention to the Koreans and Taiwanese again. This time he went farther because he considered Taiwan an independent nation the same as Korea and Japan. These nations were all outside China; therefore, people in all three nations were the objects for China to build a united front.[339] (This essay has been excluded from the official edition of Mao's writings.)

Samuel Kim believed that Mao's irredentist claims appear to be less sweeping compared to that of Sun Yat-sen and Chiang Kai-shek.[340] The Taiwan case and vague words on China's territorial losses may prove Kim was right. But Mao's proposal to establish a Chinese federation addressed his territorial concern from another direction. On July 23, 1936, a week after his allusions to Inner Mongolia autonomy and Taiwan and Korean independence, Mao told Snow,

> When the People's Revolution has been victorious in China, the Outer Mongolian republic will automatically become a part of the Chinese federation, at its own will. The Mohammedan and Tibetan people, likewise, will form an autonomous republic attached to the Chines federation.[341]

The concept of federalism did not have a place in traditional Chinese world order thinking and had no substantial influence on China's nation unity in modern history. Federalism is a western idea. It was introduced into China for building national unity by force from below, rather than from above. The most prominent person to advocate this idea was Hu Shi, during the heyday of "worldism" in the 1920's.[342] Hu Shi greatly influenced Mao with western ideas in the May Fourth era. Mao's conception of the nation-state and national sovereignty, including the idea of territorial integrity, reflected the influence of the Westphalian model in modern China's political culture. This model is the normative basis for a state-centric international order. It stresses national sovereign rights with territorial states at the center and it obeys the logic of the competitive balance-of-power system. As such it has remained dominant in the Chinese image of a world order since Mao.[343]

Chapter 8

Mao's Famous Revolutionary Concepts and His World View

Three interlocked reasons justify separating discussion of Mao's famous revolutionary concepts that basically reflect domestic politics, from the dimension of Mao's world view. First, the history of modern China features the impact of external forces, events, and ideas on internal politics. Second, one of the salient characteristics of Chinese traditional political culture is that Chinese did not substantially differentiate internal affairs from external ones; for them, the principle would be the same. Thirdly, Mao had a subtle mind that linked international and domestic affairs, and then developed his own feasible and efficient strategies and tactics. These were conceptualized as important parts of Maoism and have received careful scholarly study, particularly from China's domestic angle. In discussing Mao's conception of the world, one cannot pass over these revolutionary concepts. However, a new perspective is a necessary one that contains international basis for these ideas, external application of these strategies and tactics, and world wide influences of these concepts.

The concept of semi-colony. This fundamental theme conceptualized the basic nature of China's political, economical, cultural and societal condition. The concept of semi-colony linked closely with Mao's world view as argued previously, such as his view of world imperialism and colonialism, his understanding of the dominant influence of external forces upon China's internal situation, and his point about the confrontation and conflict between Chinese nationalism and imperialist powers and between different groups of capitalism. In turn, Mao's theory of semi-colony substantiated his world view, because it illustrated the features of his worldview, such as: emphases on the interlock between international and domestic politics, the skillful use of contradictions, and always being optimistic on the general course of world history.

The theme of Mao's idea of semi-colony is very distinctive compared with other contemporary views of Sun Yat-sen, Lenin, and Stalin.[344] Although Mao and his opinion were in the minority at the time of Jiangxi, whether within the CCP or the whole communist world, Mao and his views were eventually proved applicable with far-reaching significance that inspired later CCP and PRC foreign policy.[345]

After arriving in Yanan, Mao broadened his concept of semi-colony. On the one hand, Mao used it to describe China's society in detail. In doing so he added "colony" to Stalin's concept "semi-colony and semi-feudalism," in view of Japan's invasion of China. By listing ten aspects of the changes caused by imperialist aggression since 1840, Mao drew a "blood-stained picture of feudal China being reduced to semi-feudal, semi-colonial and colonial China."[346] Mao then analyzed six characteristics of Chinese society. The characteristics brought various contradictions. Among which two, the contradiction between imperialism and the Chinese nation, and the contradiction between feudalism and great masses of the people, were basic in modern Chinese society. Of the two, the contradiction between imperialism and the Chinese nation was the principal one.[347] This description suited the need of Chinese nationalistic motion during the Sino-Japanese war.

On the other hand, Mao did not want to lead people into a general anti-imperialist and even anti-foreigner path. This would be at odds with his strategy, tactics, and policies. The strategy, tactics and policies were identical with Mao's major theoretical contribution to the Chinese revolution in the later 1930's known as "New Democracy." This general introduction to Chinese politics, economics, culture, and society was also a base line for the CCP revolution in contemporary China. In interpreting his theory of New Democracy, Mao utilized the concept of semi-colony, together with semi-feudalism and colony, to analyze the Chinese bourgeoisie's dual character--possible participation in the revolution on the one hand and proneness to conciliation with the enemies of the revolution on the other--with respect to their attitude toward revolution. Such a dual character of Chinese bourgeois was not unique compared with the bourgeoisie elsewhere in the world, but it was much better cultivated in the colonial and semi-colonial soil. As Mao indicated, "Being a bourgeois class in a colonial and semi-colonial country and so being extremely flabby economically and politically," the trait of dual character "is more pronounced in the Chinese bourgeoisie."[348] With this analysis in mind, Mao developed two main themes in his theory of new democracy: leadership of the proletariat via the CCP in the new democratic revolution, which was still a bourgeois revolution by nature, and associating different classes including the bourgeoisie under the united front, resulting in new democracy in China.

For our purpose Mao's approach toward grasping complicated world politics requires further exploration with his utilizing the concept of semi-colony as example. First of all, Mao never limited himself to the descriptive level when he talked about world affairs or China's situation. Certainly, the term "semi-colonialism" was not his invention. However, only Mao, through the concept of semi-colonialism, structured a whole set of revolutionary theory. This included the explanation for the existing communist political power ("divided rule"), the major force of the revolution ("peasant struggle"), strategy of the revolution ("encircling the cities"), strategy and tactics of the revolution ("the wavering bourgeoisie"), and the independence and importance of China's revolution ("China's uniqueness").[349] Second, Mao purposely used the external elements as an instrument for his revolution. According to his concept of semi-colonialism, "collusion yet contention" was the most prominent feature of relations among the world powers. Citing the facts of "collusion," Mao could call for either socialist revolution against world capitalism or nationalist struggle against imperialist powers. Using the contradiction of "contention," not only did Mao build up his semi-colonialism theory but he also left room for a new united front. In the long run, Mao was famous for skillfully playing the game by taking advantage of contradictions between the powers. Third, Mao was good at highlighting the distinctiveness or uniqueness of the problems he encountered by comparing China to others. Through the concept of semi-colony, Mao made himself the only authoritative source of interpretation of Chinese modern history, China's politics, economy, culture and society. Thus Mao built up his revolutionary theory to differ from his Chinese predecessors and Soviet orthodoxy.

The concept of self-reliance. If the concept of semi-colony reflected external elements functioning upon Chinese society, the idea of self-reliance responded to external elements as received by the CCP. Mao had held strong "self" consciousness views since his youth, as he organized the Self-Study University, the Self-Strengthening Society, and promoted local self-government. However his concept of self-reliance was not crystallized until the end of 1935, the start of the Yanan period. Thereafter it became one of the major ideas in Maoism. The question arises, why was it in the Yanan time but not the Jiangxi era, when Mao stressed self-reliance? Further, what is the implication behind the concept with reference to Mao's world view? A clue lies in Mao's words in late 1935 and early 1936.

At the December 27, 1935, conference of party activists held at Wayaobao, northern Shaanxi province, Mao gave a report titled "On Tactics Against Japanese Imperialism." He put the idea of self-reliance in the discussion about the relation between the Chinese and the world revolution. Mao declared publicly, "We Chinese have the spirit to fight the enemy to the last drop of our blood, the determination to recover our lost territory by our own efforts, and the ability to stand on our own feet in the family of nations."[350] A few months later, in much narrower context but higher level CCP conference, Mao lectured his comrades while debating association with the Soviet Union,

> Chinese things should be handled by ourselves. Believe in ourselves. In the past, we created a soviet because we had confidence. Why should we loss our confidence today? However, having a friend is better. In conclusion, in the first place, hold faith with ourselves; in the second, it would be wrong to deny friends.[351]

Mao's words suggested that two factors might facilitate the crystallization of self-reliance. The first was the urgent need of help from outside the CCP and outside China, with this possibility emerging in the new environment. In view of this, the Jiangxi era, despite being truly a self-reliance time without any remarkable external aid, offered no reason to promote self-reliance. The concept accompanied Mao's declaration that "We can no longer be isolated" so as to welcome "international support," the sub-title of the final section of Mao's report at the Wayaobao Conference.

The second factor was the great sense of self-dignity stimulated by the unfavorable external situation in terms of the *wai yuan*-- assistance from outside the CCP, particularly, from Moscow at that time. This was shown by Mao's calling for confidence in front of his high ranked comrades in March 1936. Comparing Mao's faith about Soviet support a few months before,[352] his self-confidence call provided an emotional and psychological basis for the idea of self-reliance.

These two factors, one objective, the other subjective, remained in Mao's concept of self-reliance permanently. From 1936 to 1941, whenever Mao talked about self-reliance, it would be either when seeking outside aid or responding to external pressure. An official formula took shape later on, expressed as "primarily relying on our own efforts, while not ignoring any possibility of securing help from abroad."[353] His concept of self-reliance throws another light on Mao's conception of the world: an interdependent world versus a non-dependent self with its extension, being the party, the nation, and the country.

The concept of united front. Mao's united front doctrine is often seen from strategic and tactical perspectives. This is generally correct, as Mao himself, on many occasions, spelled out the concept of united front in this way.[354] However, with respect to Mao's world view, his united front doctrine was creative compared with that of Lenin. It was also essential considering that united front was part of Mao's revolutionary career for nearly a life-time. And finally it was intrinsic with the concept of Mao's world view at both the practical and principled levels.

The idea of united front is rooted in both Chinese tradition[355] and Leninist ideology. However, the actual term "united front" was not used until the 1920's, when it was employed by the Comintern with reference to communist collaboration with Social Democratic parties in Europe and the "national bourgeoisie" in the colonies and semi-colonies.[356] Mao's concept of united front undoubtedly had very much to do with those Chinese and foreign sources. Also, it can be regarded as creative because Lenin saw it as a "transitional" policy, a temporary expedient to be employed only during periods of Communist weakness, while for Mao it was the first three basic components for winning the revolution's goals.[357] In application Lenin's work was only embryonic, primarily because he was less interested in "winning over" the middle forces than in having them reveal their inadequacies. Mao's idea was more comprehensive and systematic, especially his stress on the importance of pulling the middle forces over to the CCP side, for which Mao made a sophisticated analysis of the middle-force question.[358] In theory, neither Lenin nor the Comintern interpreted the concept of "struggle" so essentially and intellectually as Mao did. For him, "struggle" had to be seen as good in itself because of its "consciousness-raising" side effect and as a necessary part of a protracted revolutionary process. In light of this, united front, which contains "unity and struggle" for Mao, meant not just a short-term alliance with specific friends opposing particular enemies, but a "grand strategy" during the continual, step-by-step revolutionary progression.[359]

Also the concept of united front was essential practice and theory in Mao's revolutionary life. Mao's gift of persuading and rallying others to work with him was shown in his work of mass education and of uniting a number of small associations and groups when he was a young patriot. Han Suyin concludes that "the mass education movement was an attempt at forming a broad united front, a grand alliance of the masses."[360] Han further argues that "Mao Tse-tung had already indicated his option for a united front in 1922" with the description of a "united front of workers, peasants, and petty bourgeois," shortly after his conversion to communism. This came before the Russian pressure on the CCP, over the opposition of the CCP delegation in Moscow to a united front.[361] From that time on, Mao was to play an important role in "united front work" that referred particularly to the cooperation of the CCP and the KMT. In the article entitled "External Forces, the Warlords, and the Revolution," published in April 1923, he announced there were only three factions (*Pai*) in China: the revolutionary democratic faction, the non-revolutionary democratic faction, and the reactionary faction. Both the CCP and the KMT fell into the first category.

The main body of the first united front was the two major political parties in the revolutionary camp. It was changed later, yet "the division of the totality of social forces into three was, and would remain, highly characteristic of Mao's approach to politics and to revolution," as correctly pointed out by Schram.[362] The Jiangxi period was not significant in terms of Mao's concept of united front. However, Mao's victory over all CCP factions in the Zunyi Conference exhibited his political skill in CCP politics, utilizing the same strategy, tactics and underlying principle united front. Specifically it was "to make use of contradiction, win over the many, oppose the few and crush our enemies one by one."[363] The Second United Front, marked by the Xian Incident during the second Sino-Japanese war, showed Mao's concept to be theoretically and empirically mature. The practical and theoretical differences from Lenin and Stalin on the issue of united front were fully manifest in this period.

Mao even extended this concept to the international scene through his sophisticated exposition in Yanan caves. Mao's important article "On Policy" explained this:

> The Communist Party opposes all imperialism, but we make a distinction between Japanese imperialism which is now committing aggression against China and the imperialist powers which are not doing so now, between German and Italian imperialism which are allies of Japan and have recognized "Manchukuo" and British and U.S. imperialism which are opposed to Japan, and between the Britain and the United States of yesterday that followed a Munich policy in the Far East and undermined China's resistance to Japan, and the Britain and the United States of today that have abandoned this policy and are now in favor of China's resistance.[364]

In the above argumentation, a methodological point intrinsic to Mao's world view needs to be highlighted: policy was based on distinctions. Mao always took seriously the making and implementing of policy. He frequently said, "The policy we adopt is of decisive importance."[365] Regarding policy making, particularly CCP foreign policy, Mao argued, "On our part we must draw certain distinctions, ...we build our policy on these distinctions."[366] Hence, united front was a decisive and distinctive policy for the CCP, namely a subject to the distinction of various factors, such as friends and foes, elite and masses, alliance and struggle, external help and self-reliance, and so forth. In a sense, one may say that the united front is a principal means for attaining the ends and also is one of the central concepts of Mao's world view on practical level.

The Concept of popular mass. This concept was another distinctive point of Maoist ideology and practice when he was conducting the Chinese revolution and dealing with foreign affairs. However the importance and uniqueness of this concept for Mao and of Mao were very realistic and empirical, especially in domestic politics.[367] By comparison, Mao's concept of popular mass on the international stage was less practical and more ideological--although it was by no means irrelevant to his world view, given the mixture of his strong background of *Pin Min Zhu Yi* (an *ism* for average people) in youth, and sinicized Marxism-Leninism later.

There were two traditions of patriotism in China, higher one and lower one responding to the growing pressure caused by foreign powers after the late nineteenth century. The gap between the two was increasingly pronounced owing to the behavior of different social forces. The higher one was elite patriotism led by reformists such as Kang Youwei, while the lower was mass nativism that had two shapes. One was the Boxer type, famous for its xenophobia; and the other was the nationalist revolutionary type led by Sun Yet-sen who promised access to the global network of Chinese secret societies.[368] Mao's *Pin Min Zhu Yi* in his youth tried to bridge the gap. Especially in his masterpiece, "Great Union of the Popular Masses" in July 1919, he first of all recognized popular mass as a historical rule and the current tendency using the strength of the people through creating the great union that he had learned from the world. Mao then expressed his nationalist commitment to China's greatness through her struggle against imperialism.[369]

Mao argued eloquently in the May Fourth era for the basic point of his concept of popular mass. The concept was modified by some Marxist-Leninist ideas such as class analysis and class struggle, internationalism, and patriotism. In essence, the method of class analysis offered a more meticulous way to mobilize the popular masses. The idea of class struggle agitated for a deeper social movement accompanied by national revolution. The doctrine of internationalism invited a more favorable environment for the Chinese people. The slogan of patriotism promoted the scope of united front as broad as possible. In any case, Mao's conception of popular masses occupied a crucial position in view of the strength of people. If there was any contradiction between orthodox Marxism-Leninism and Mao's concept, Mao would remove or refine the former in order to fit the latter. For example in the early 1920's, Mao once put the Chinese merchant class in the central position of China's nationalist revolution. This was not a mistake in his approach to class analysis. Rather it was a logical outcome of Mao's political and social analysis and did no harm to his concept of popular masses since the merchant class was the critical element in the Chinese population at that time.[370] In this sense, Mao's famous doctrine of the Chinese peasantry should be viewed similarly.

In international politics, the concept of popular masses served differently. On the one hand, Mao appealed to the world-wide communist parties, ordinary people, and overseas Chinese for their international help in China's patriotic course. On the other hand, he told popular masses in China that the emphasis should be put on patriotism, namely nationalism, rather than on internationalism. As Mao told Agnes Smedley:

> The Chinese Communists are internationalists; they are in favor of the world Communist movement. But at the same time they are patriots who defend their native land...This patriotism and internationalism are by no means in conflict, for only China's independence and liberation will make it possible to participate in the world Communist movement.[371]

Returning to the concept of popular masses on an international scale, Mao knew that he had very little to do with ordinary people outside China in any practical way. Appeals for foreign aid would be successful only from those in office. However, the popular masses or the common people would be a source of political and social pressure that could be put on a certain government. As a result, this might be able to affect its China policy. This was why Mao placed hope on the British people in the late 1930's.

On ideological aspects, the function of Mao's concept of popular masses in the international scene was much more apparent. His contact with foreign communist parties, particularly the Communist Party of the United States, showed Mao's strong commitment to the international communist path. His urgent command to develop the CCP influence in *Nan Yang* in 1941 gave further proof of his communist revolutionary ambitions. On the same ideological line, Mao repeatedly taught his comrades, "We must draw certain distinctions...between the people of Britain and the United States and their imperialist governments."[372]

The concept of revolutionary war. One of the key points of Mao turning from a non-Marxist-Leninist into a Marxist-Leninist was his acceptance of the idea of class struggle favoring a bloodshed revolution or revolutionary violence.[373] The communist doctrine was identical with his pronounced admiration for the martial spirit, courage, and violence continued from his youth. Later on, in Mao's style of revolution, war became a key concept that gave specific content to the revolution, a crucial means of the revolution, and in some sense, war was even the revolutionary course itself.[374]

It was quite natural for a politician in the 1920's and 1930's to talk about war on daily base. There were real wars now and then, here and there in China's territory. There also were real and potential wars on the wider international screen that exploded worldwide not long after this period. However Mao neither passively accepted war as a revolutionary context nor merely restricted his thinking within narrow military limits. Instead on the one hand, he actively shaped and changed the context by directing the Chinese revolutionary war; on the other hand, he synthesized long famous war-related views. This included, for instance, the concept that war is politics and war itself is a special political action to sweep away obstacles in the way of politics. Also political power grows out of the barrel of a gun. With the gun at one's disposal one can really build up the party organization. The essence of guerrilla tactics and the military principles have been one of the distinctive heritage of the CCP since the Jinggang Mountain period. In the sense of the distinctive heritage of the CCP, war, or to be precise the Chinese revolutionary war itself became a course for Mao devoting himself to it. For only through the Chinese revolutionary war was Mao able to present himself as a unique political leader in China and the world, especially in the communist world.

To connect Mao's conception of revolutionary war with his world view, one may adopt Schram's approach,[375] namely, generalizing the meaning of what Mao said about the subject, with recognition of war as a central and daily issue in Mao's revolutionary career, particularly before 1949. The imprint of Mao's conception of revolutionary war on his world view was many-faceted. However at least two aspects deserve detailed attention.

First, Mao's theme on the interrelation of revolution and war was, to a great degree, a reflection of his commitment to Leninism and Stalinism.[376] The linkage between World War I and the Soviet Revolution provided an empirical demonstration of Lenin's admonition of "turning the imperialist war into the proletarian revolution." Even in his youth before converting to Marxism-Leninism, Mao forecast that a future war would be a class war. The winner would be the Marxist-Leninist ideology and these socialists.[377]

However, the interrelation between revolution and war had not crystallized for Mao until his Jiangxi period. In March 1932, after an analysis of the international situation with a purely communist ideological tone, Mao wrote, "This is a time of an historical new era, a time of revolution and war."[378] In December 1935, Mao continued to use the theme of revolution and war to identify the current international situation. This time Mao indicated prudently that it was "the eve of revolution and war in the world." Obviously with the causal relationship of World War I and the Soviet Revolution in mind, Mao conceived that revolution and war was some kind of historical cycle and anticipated that "the new cycle of world-wide revolution and war was pending." His further forecast was that "a great war and great revolution will bury all the anti-revolutionaries in the world." For Mao, it was very good for the Chinese revolution, because it had gotten rid of isolation in the past and would contribute greatly to the world revolution.[379]

Second, Mao's stress on the uniqueness of the Chinese revolutionary war expressed the nationalistic and independent facet of his world vision. For instance, the famous proposition--"Encircling the cities from the countryside" is part of the core strategic thinking for his type of revolutionary war. It became extremely important and very influential.[380] At that time it was exclusively Chinese. In 1938, Mao clearly explained the uniqueness of this idea. He concluded, "It is impossible to conceive of a protracted guerrilla war carried on by the peasants in the countryside against the cities in a country such as England, America, France, Germany, Japan, etc. Such a thing is also impossible in a small semi-colonial country..."[381] While the uniqueness of Chinese revolutionary war could confirm China's difference from the rest of the world, the independence of the Chinese revolutionary war could assert the superiority of Mao's line to other communists. In "Strategic Problems of China's Revolutionary War," considered as one of the three major theses on revolutionary war that Mao wrote in the 1930's,[382] he declared that "The laws of China's revolutionary war must be studied and understood by anyone directing China's revolutionary war." He continued,

Although we must value Soviet experience, and even value it somewhat more than experience in other countries throughout history, because it is the most recent experience of revolutionary war, we must value even more the experience of China's revolutionary war, because there are a great number of conditions special to the Chinese revolution and the Chinese Red Army.[383]

Schram points out the significance of this text as the affirmation of Mao's theme of China's grandeur and uniqueness, and also her independence from even superiority over the Soviet experience.[384]

Chapter 9

Mao's World View in Theory: Understanding the World and Changing the World

In 1941, while studying *A Course in Dialectical Materialism,* a Soviet Marxist philosophical book authored by Sirokov and Aizenberg, Mao expressed his emotional regret by saying: "the Chinese struggle is so great and plentiful, and yet has not produced a theoretician,"[385] To some extent, Mao's sigh was a rhetorical question or even a complaint to the CCP Center. There had been a remarkable problem of designating an authoritative theoretician within the CCP up to 1941.[386] However, the problem was soon solved without setbacks because of Mao's victories over his opponents in the party's political, military, and organizational affairs after the Zhunyi conference. Consequently, Mao emerged as the sole and exclusive theoretical authority in the CCP by the end of 1941. In view of this fact, this chapter tries to pinpoint the philosophical base for Mao's world view that was discussed from a political dimension throughout this thesis.[387]

The Chinese translation of the term of world view--*shi jie guan*-- is usually in accord with the English words, either world view or world outlook. The latter often appears in the official Chinese translation in a philosophical sense. Language always carries cultural significance. The meaning of the Chinese term *shi jie guan* can be two-sided in a political and philosophical sense. It identifies philosophy with a political orientation, but it also in accord with the traditional Chinese world view, which broadly emphasized politics with a philosophical base. Such a cultural perspective takes into account the philosophical aspect of Mao's world view, not only for its importance, but for its objective existence in Mao's "stormy career", borrowing Schwartz's words.

In fact, most of Mao's writings attributed and contributed to his new title as the CCP theoretical authority in Yanan were completed before the party's Rectification Campaign (1942-1944). Among them, Mao's lecture on dialectical materialism in the early Yanan period produced two very important chapters in terms of Mao's philosophy. They are:"On Practice" and "On Contradiction".[388] To understand Mao's mature philosophy produced at Yanan time, it is necessary to examine his philosophical world view that converged with the insight gained in his youth. These two periods appear to be the major sources for fulfilling this task.[389]

Mao offered a philosophical proposition on the relationship between "necessity and freedom" that reflects his philosophical belief of the world and its connection to human beings. In late 1941, Mao wrote,

> From the realm of necessity to the realm of freedom, man has to pass two procedures--understanding the world and changing the world. Europe's old philosophers had discovered the truth of "freedom is understanding the world." Marx's contribution is not to reject this truth, rather to admit it then to replenish its insufficiency by adding the truth of changing the world based on understanding of the world.[390]

Then Mao proposed his version, "Freedom is understanding the necessity and changing the world."

It is Marxism. It is Maoism too, because the philosophical point is identical with Mao's political ambitions: changing China and the world, a political direction for the New People's Society reordered by Mao and his radical friends by the end of 1920 and retained in his whole life.[391] Furthermore,one can trace Mao's conception of freedom back to when he was twenty-four and twenty-five, writing notes on a western philosophical book. At that time, Mao had faith in the principles of realism and individualism, and believed that "Only what is in accord with these two ideas can be called true freedom, can be called true self-perfection."[392] By connecting Mao's philosophical point, political ambitions, and thinking in his youth and in Yanan, we detect two strands of Mao's world view converging at the abstract level: his understanding of the world, and his viewpoint on changing the world. Mao's world outlook could not be separated from his philosophical outlook on human life since he considered freedom the reward for man's endeavor of understanding and changing the world.

Philosophically, Mao's theoretical world view is his understanding and ideas about the phenomena of the world and the nature of reality. The distinction between "the present world" and "the essential world" with emphasis on the former was conceived by Mao in his youth.[393] Mao, like most Chinese philosophers, showed no great interest in the issues of ontology. He appeared dualistic in his thinking on the question of the noumenon of the world. In his youth, he did not raise the issue of the origin of the universe, while he treated the issues of the material and the spirit equally.[394] Although Mao accepted the idea of materialistic monism in line with his Marxist-Leninist faith, when he spoke of philosophy in the mid-1930's his major concern was on "the present world".

What is the nature of the present world? Three notions combined to form Mao's conceptual world view drawn consistently from his youth to Yanan time. First, Mao held the notion of dialectical unity of the objective world and human beings. Early in 1917-1918, Mao regarded the world as a two-sided coin. On one side, it was objective in that "our minds are limited to concepts, and concepts are limited to phenomena, and phenomena are limited to reality."[395] On the other side, it was man's subjective initiative. "Knowledge, belief, and action are the three stages of our [men's] spiritual activity".[396] Man's spiritual activity will create "the present world" and makes it eventful and colorful. Mao concluded:

> Although we are defined by Nature, we are also part of Nature. Thus Nature has the power to define us, and we have the power to define Nature. Although our power is very small, it cannot be said to have no effect. Nature without us would be incomplete.[397]

Mao's dialectical unity of the subjective and the objective became more sophisticated in Yanan, when he subscribed to the concept of practice as the core of Marxist epistemology interpreted by himself.[398] For Mao, human practice can only be social practice, defined by him in a broad generic way. "As a social being, man participates in all spheres of practical life of society." Theory cannot be formed without practice. The process of acquiring knowledge and establishing theory would be incremental (step by step) and progressive (lower-to-higher), containing the three-step (perceptual, rational, and verification stages) epistemological model. This means that human practice would be historical error without theory. Mao called it the error of "empiricism." Then he gave historical evidence of the indiscriminate anti-foreign struggle of the Taiping and Boxer Rebellions as representing the first and superficial stage of a Chinese cognition of world imperialism.[399]

Secondly, Mao affirmed the notion of contradiction in the world. In his "Classroom Notes" (1913), Mao realized that "In the universe, so many interconnections have arisen among myriad phenomena" that the key to understanding the world was understanding the interrelationship of things.[400] In his notes on a German philosopher's book (1917-1918), he saw the world in a dialectical way. He wrote, "In essence, the many are one, and change is permanence."[401] Mao never concealed his favorite distinctions, comparisons and differentiation. He said,

> Our various forms of human mental activity are composed of these distinctions and comparisons, and without these distinctions and comparisons historical life would not be possible. Evolution is the succession of differentiation. Only after there are distinctions can there be language and thought, without distinctions they would not be possible.[402]

It seems the sense of distinctions, comparison and differentiation were most likely a subjective truth for young Mao because he identified with these subjective concepts, saying, "Reality itself does not make distinctions; distinctions are only conceptual, in order to facilitate language and memory."[403]

This conceptual understanding of the world was permeated by dialectical reasoning Mao learned from ancient Chinese thought and Western philosophy. Later in the 1930's, it was known as his famous thought on the law of contradiction, which is commonly accepted as the central theme of Mao's philosophy. The major content of the law of contradiction included the universality of contradiction versus the particularity of contradiction, the principal contradiction and the principal aspect of a contradiction, the identity and struggle of the aspects of a contradiction, and the place of antagonism in contradiction.

To be in accord with his Marxist-Leninist belief, Mao linked his concept of contradiction with the theory of dialectical materialism. Therefore, every contradiction represents an objective reality in Mao's world outlook, rather than merely a subjective need.[404] However, Mao's emphasis was consistently on the subjective side. In Mao's world outlook, all objectively existing contradictions can be understood, analyzed and resolved properly by the people who had grasped dialectical cognition and approach, which was the dynamic kaleidoscope of Mao's world outlook. The identicalness of objective contradictions and subjective dialectical epistemology, as well as dialectical methodology, makes the law of contradiction very practical and operational for Mao's revolutionary course, especially in international affairs. Just as Mao indicated, "This dialectical world outlook teaches us primarily how to observe and analyze the movement of opposites in different things and, on the basis of such analysis, to indicate the method for resolving contradiction."[405] Scholars discovered the theoretical base of the previously discussed Mao's world view in his explanation of the law of contradiction.[406]

Thirdly, Mao asserted the notion of development of the world. In addition to stressing man's subjective activity in the subject-object relations to manipulate contradictions of things in the present world, Mao, in principle, welcomed all changes and developments. This was another crucial point Mao established since his youth for understanding the world.[407] Once established, Mao had never reversed the idea in his entire "stormy career".

In 1917-1918, Mao wrote the following words which were a vivid reflection of his taste of history, human life, philosophical world outlook:

When we read history, we always praise the era of the Warring States, the time of rivalry between Liu [Bang] and Xiang [Yu], the time of the struggle between Han Wudi and the Xiongnu, the era of the struggle among the Three Kingdoms. It is the times when things are constantly changing and numerous men of talent are emerging that the people like to read it about. When they come to periods of peace, they are bored and put the book aside. It is not that we like chaos but simply that the reign of peace cannot last long, it is unendurable to human beings, and that human nature is delighted by sudden change.[408]

In Yanan, Mao's desire for change and development became a confirmed philosophical principle mingled with dialectical materialism. This meant that change and movement (development) were not merely Mao's personal philosophical taste. The point of movement (or development), together with the point of materiality, were elevated as one of two basic principles of dialectical materialism.[409]

In his lecture on dialectical materialism, Mao copied Soviet Russian and Chinese Marxist philosophers' introduction to dialectical materialism to explain the point of movement (or development). His own interpretation of this point was also remarkable nevertheless. Summarizing Mao's writings and speeches from his youth to his Yanan time, three patterns of Mao's own view of the movement or development of the world may be drawn. (1) The movement, or development, takes wave-like form. In his youth, Mao talked with optimism of the waves of peace and disorder, and life and death. Later, he described the wave-like development of revolution as the law of revolutionary logic. By using wave-like patterns of movement, or development, Mao made his world view optimistic in strategy and practicable in technique. The wave-like form should be treated as a component of Mao's philosophy.[410] (2) Unevenness is the normality of a thing's movement, or development. Mao generated this idea from a peculiar but sound reasoning on China's political, economic, and societal situation in his Jiangxi period. It had philosophical roots in his thinking of the disharmony of the world however. Since the unevenness of China's national condition brought great benefit to Mao and his revolution, as his theory of semi-colony evidenced, Mao reaffirmed his faith in the normality of unevenness in his early Yanan days. Later he never gave up this faith and even made efforts to break the evenness in domestic as well as international affairs. (3) There exists a basic or common law of historical development, regardless of the differences of time and space. From his teachers in Hunan, at twenty, Mao noted, "Though the system has changed over time, the reasoning has not changed. For instance, the military,...systems have changed, but the justification for maintaining an army is to devise strategies,...Has the reasoning become any different?"[411] The belief of a basic law in historical development makes great sense for understanding Mao's prestigious character that was permeated with the teachings and lessons of human history--first Chinese history, then world history. Also, it provides a convincing explanation of Mao's desire to spread his ideas and philosophy to the whole world. Mao saw this as a more important step in his world outlook--to change the world to his understanding of it.

Mao's viewpoints on changing the world, the second cluster of his theoretical world view, were virtually his methodology of approaching and handling international-related matters. His methodology was closely linked to the epistemology or his philosophical way of understanding the world. The latter offers theoretical guideline to the former, while the former is a crystallization of the latter.

Several renowned features constitute Mao's methodology of resolving "the most important problem", which "does not lie in understanding the law of the objective world and thus being able to explain it, but in applying the knowledge of these laws actively to change the world."[412] First of all, struggle is universal and absolute in Mao's methodology. The point is well explained in his concept of contradiction. Mao argued,

> The combination of conditional, relative identity and unconditional, absolute struggle constitutes the movement of opposites in all things....Yet struggle is inherent in identity and without struggle there can be no identity.[413]

There is no doubt such a philosophical argument reflects Mao's basic faith. In his youth, Mao proclaimed the boundless joy in struggles against heaven, earth, and human beings; in his later years, Mao even identified the Communist Party's philosophy with struggle. A protracted and tireless struggle was Mao's life commitment to his philosophy and the CCP conversion to the ideology of Marxist-Leninist philosophy. Yet Mao was by no means a blind fighter. He warned of the dangers of indiscriminate analysis and application of the contradiction. According to Mao's theory, all things are supposed to be characterized by their nature of contradictions, to typologize their categories, and to prescribe proper methods for resolving the contradictions. Mao either defined the concept of struggle at the abstract level, or alternated the method of struggle with non-struggle means, such as building a united front.

Secondly, value is placed on guiding and judging in Mao's methodology. The question of value is a question of the justification and orientation of practice. Man's practice will follow perceived values, and the value accepted by man will be valuable only after it is put into practice. With the influence of leading Chinese intellectuals in modern China, Mao made value analyses of traditional Chinese thought and compared it with western concepts he learned in his youth. As a result, his value system contained various elements of western philosophy, modern Chinese thinking, and older Chinese traditions, particularly non-mainstream traditions.

What Mao valued was the sacrifice of historical life, the belief in the present, personal achievement, nationalist consciousness, and after his conversion to Marxism-Leninism, "revolutionary causes or values."(As defined by Samuel Kim)[414] These concepts were significant for changing the world.

For interpreting historical life, Mao denied ethical humanism; instead, he valued historical life with a reference to historical judgment or historical will, which pays little attention to human's joy or morality. As a youth, Mao accepted the statement, "A nation does not reckon the cost of its ideal. It strives for freedom, or power, or glory, without calculation of how much happiness is gained or lost."[415] At the same time, he questioned the argument, "The evil person of their age, though they may attain the highest position and honors, will be unknown after they die." Mao did not accept the criterion of historical reputation, such as goodness or evil, to value a person's historical contribution.[416]

This attitude was connected tightly with another of Mao's values maintained from his youth--belief in the present. Liang Qichao labeled such a belief as a new ism--*Xian Zai Zu Yi*, was often repeated by modern Chinese intellectuals, including Mao. Mao's justification for stressing the present was, "If we want to grasp something real, we can do so only in the immediate present; if we have the present, we have a whole lifetime."[417] His belief in the present gave Mao freedom to cite historical instances, lessons, and teachings, both from Chinese and foreign histories, for serving today's purpose, but not for reproducing history;[418] His belief in the present allowed Mao to devote himself to today's course, no matter what kind of historical reputation he may obtain.[419]

Apparently, his belief in *Xian Zai Zu Yi* echoed Mao's philosophy of human life, just as Mao learned from his teachers when he was twenty years old: "Stressing the present has two important meanings. One is valuing oneself. (Seek within oneself.) (Do not depend on others.) The other is to understand the present age thoroughly."[420] It reveals Mao's concern about his personal life, the development of his own self and the fulfillment of his life in the age he was living. Mao had proven himself, insisting that the values learned earlier in life led to his later practice of changing the world, albeit he did no longer disclose his philosophy of life so frankly, nor did he identify himself as an "egoist", or an "individualist" any longer. Despite the fact that Mao used to love these terms, Mao was never an egoist or individualist in the full sense of the words, because Mao exposed himself as an enthusiastic nationalist and revolutionary from the time of his youth. There were impressive evidences of Mao's regard for national consciousness and revolutionary causes and values presented in this thesis.

Thirdly, flexibility was very important to political or ideological principles in Mao's methodology. In other words, one of Mao's methods for dealing with the world affairs was a combination of the two, or conversely the alternative utilizing of the two. Mao's definition of flexibility from a military perspective as of May 1938, can be extended to a general philosophical theme. The definition states: "What is flexibility? It is the concrete realization of the initiative in military operations;...The ancients said: `Ingenuity in varying tactics depends on mother wit.' This `ingenuity,' which is what we mean by flexibility, is the contribution of the intelligent commander."[421] Clearly, flexibility is the theme of man's subjective initiative, which was stressed most by Mao when he talked about the subject-object relation.

In a sense of practice and operation, flexibility can be regarded as a principle that people "ought" to learn and be able to carry out. Still, it is a tactic for obtaining strategic goals and the ultimate aim. For instance: Many times Mao's two-division and three, or multi-division methods for describing world order have been mentioned. The two-division picture of world order Mao drew was often linked with his ideological commitment, strategic need of Moscow's help, and more important, his emphasis on struggle. However, it somehow reflected Mao's social ideal. The three, or multi-divisional view of world order Mao took was usually the outcome of his strategic thinking about the world under a much larger context based on the interests of the Chinese nation and a method of non-struggle. The alternative or simultaneous use of these two approaches was a manifestation of Mao's flexibility. The ever-existing and never-discarded two methods in the CCP theoretical storage room were evidences of Mao's persistence of these principles.

A controversial question arises when making an assessment of Mao's achievement on the relation between "necessity and freedom" on the issue of his world view, either at a practical level or at a philosophical level. It seemed to Mao that he came close to the realm of freedom, although he recognized that man's cognitive process from the realm of necessity to the realm of freedom had no limits. By the end of 1941, his goal of becoming a leading theoretician had been achieved. One does not have to admit Mao's greatness on his world view, but one should acknowledge his outstanding consciousness, and somehow, uniqueness.

CONCLUSION

Having presented a historical and thematic description, and moved from micro to macro analysis of Mao Zedong's world view during his early life (up to 1941), conclusions can now be drawn.

The two hypotheses introduced in the beginning of this work have gained factual and logical validation. Mao was a three-faceted world watcher: (1) **A lively observer.** Samuel Kim pointed out that "even in his Yanan cave Mao seldom lost sight of the larger realities of the international situation."[422] Kim's point was well taken. However, studies of Mao frequently convey a false image of him as a narrow-minded or shortsighted person in terms of the international sense. The conclusion drawn here goes beyond Kim, namely, that Mao's broad vision of the world had been developing since a very young age, and that he never faltered. On this point the differences in Mao's life stages were not qualitative even in his guerrilla life at Jingang Mountain.

(2) **An enthusiastic commentator.** John Gittings, correctly recognized that Mao's revolutionary contemplation after the Jiangxi period was "the inspirational source" of CCP foreign policy and its working out in practice.[423] But his belief that "Mao has shown no great inclination to speculate, except in vague global terms, about the prospects for revolution elsewhere" was incorrect.[424] In his youth, especially in the May Fourth era, Mao was *the* editor as well as the only columnist for the international news and commentary *Xian River Review*. In Yanan Mao showed great interest and sound knowledge in presenting his opinions about other countries, such as the United States and India. However Gittings correctly noted that "when he [Mao] discusses the international situation it is with the purpose of

ascertaining the prospects which it allows for China's own revolution."[425]

(3) **A bold predictor.** No matter whether in his youth or in Yanan time, Mao appeared as a predictor of international affairs. Many were China related; some were not. His predictions were direct, specific, and bold. Some were subtle and amazingly valid; some were sloppy and embarrassingly groundless. Generally, Mao's historical knowledge and political sense played a positive role in his predictions. He anticipated another German-French war, ten or twenty years later after the end of the First World War, and he foresaw the inevitable political and military clash between the United States and Japan in Asia-Pacific area. This showed Mao's predictions to be historically and politically grounded while possessing a philosophical base. In addition, Mao's thorough comprehension of Chinese conditions offered him a perfect vision for forecasting the course of the Sino-Japanese war. In contrast to these predictions, Mao's ideological commitments might have embarrassed him because his revolutionary prophecies often failed to match reality. The most salient instance was his ignorance or defense of Moscow's selfish policies dealing with Germany and Japan in the later 1930's and early 1940's. As a bold political predictor, Mao did not care too much for the accuracy of his words. One reason may have been the typical way the CCP handled these personal statements. The CCP could officially hide every document it saw as unfavorable or unsuitable for the publication.[426] Moreover, Mao did not formally present himself as being in the forefront of the Party's foreign affairs. This position allowed him to make comments without stigmatizing himself if he was in error on a situation. This device of secondary place became a formula for the CCP top leaders in later times.

Through observing, commenting, and predicating, Mao had shaped his world view based on four aspects. First, he began practicing *Wai Jiao*--the CCP's informal foreign relations, and foreign affairs in the Yanan caves. To say this, one must put the CCP long-time relations with Moscow aside.[427] Because the relations with the Soviet Union and the Comintern were special, sometimes the bilateral contact could be regarded as internal issues within the communist world on an ideological basis.

Second, Mao made commentaries and criticisms on current world affairs from the end of the World War I to the beginning of the Pacific

War. With his mixture of communist and nationalist complex, he had adopted a two-division method and a three or multi-division method alternatively as needed, to interpret the world as a whole and to identify China's position in the world.

Third, Mao set up precedents and patterns in his attitude toward those major powers, particularly the Soviet Union, the United States, Japan, Great Britain, France, and Germany. He also offered opinions on important neighbors such as Korea, Mongolia, and India. To a large extent, Mao's attitude represented the Chinese mentality and feelings that developed during modern history. Conversely, Mao's view of these individual countries became stereotyped by CCP attitudes and policies.

Fourth, Mao's theoretical world outlook was the foundation of his world view in the preceding three aspects. Dialectical materialism was the epistemological and methodological match between Mao's own philosophical belief and his Marxist-Leninist faith. More importantly, Mao sinicized it by stressing a subjective initiative in subject-object relation, by illuminating the concept of contradiction in all things, by endorsing the law of movement or development in human history, and by emphasizing, and practicing the task of changing the world.

Mao's relationship with Moscow was the most practical issue in the chosen period. Many factors made the relationship complex and even confusing. This work has attempted to reveal the differentiation and disagreements between Mao and Moscow. The ideological element that significantly brought the two together was noticeable nevertheless. Besides ideological common ground with Moscow, Mao occasionally held similar views with Moscow about Chinese revolutionary strategy after the tragic event of 1927, although the ideas of Moscow were fragmentary or contradictory while Mao's theory was consistent and systematic.[428] Understandably Mao used the red umbrella to protect himself and legitimatize his policy.[429]

Compared with Mao's admiration of Moscow, his grievance against Moscow was a major point after the middle of the 1920's.[430] The sources of Mao's unhappiness were various. There had been no personal communication between the leaders in Moscow and Mao. Although he had a dream of studying in Soviet Russia since early 1920, he never realized it. Compared to many Chinese communists who had the experience of studying or living there, Mao was an alien element to any factions in the Comintern or Soviet Communist Party.

Certainly he was known in Moscow before the Jiangxi period because he was a member of the first group of Chinese communists. Also he wrote *Report On An Investigation Of The Peasant Movement In Hunan* that was reprinted by the Comintern. Nevertheless, Mao, as a Chinese revolutionary and communist leader, never won Moscow's official endorsement until the late 1930's.[431]

Mao developed divergent views on almost every crucial issue from the representatives of the Comintern to the Russian returned students. He had encountered conflict with the Comintern representatives and the Comintern discipline. The conflict kept Mao in a precarious position in the CCP throughout the Jiangxi period. In fact, he was removed from the top post several times. Therefore this period remained a most frustrating time for Mao's revolutionary career. It widened the gap between Mao and Moscow and had never been truly purged.

As noted before, Mao rebelled against external pressure and mental despotism since he was a young student. He could not tolerate the Moscow-backed delegates arrogance and discrimination against him. Li De "pounded his fists on the table. He told Mao and others that they knew nothing about military matters; they should heed him;"[432] Mao responded with anger. Even harder for Mao was his belief that Wang Ming and his followers saw him as no more than an "agrarian revolutionary," a "Marxist in the mountain valley". Given the unfavorable situation he encountered at that time, Mao adopted a "wait-and-see" tactic. Meanwhile, he used his political skill to survive and appease his comrades. However, his anger was building. Naturally, whenever he gained chance to fight with the *benben zhuyi*, (literally, "bookism," a term he created to label those dogmatists), he would do so after he took over and solidified his power in the party and in the nation. His personal characteristics explained Mao's first words spoken to Stalin in their initial meeting, as cited in the Note 9 of this Conclusion.

The sources of Mao's world view were diversified. They fall into two categories, Chinese tradition and foreign influence, that can each be divided into two major parts. There are two interrelated and qualitatively distinct Chinese traditions; (a) an older, ancient one and (b) a newly established tradition in modern China. Under the category of foreign influence are (c) at first Western thought and later, (d) Marxism-Leninism. Both played a crucial role in shaping Mao's world view in the modern sense.[433]

Among the parts, (b) and (c) have not received enough attention and research in Mao studies. They often were lumped together with (a) and (d), respectively, although they are extremely important to the study of Mao's world view. It does not suffice to identify Mao's thoughts and ideas with only a single source. The challenge is to produce a dynamic analysis of each part of the source, to discover the logical intercross of each part, and to re-construct an intellectual base of Mao's world view in view of the synthetic and eclectic features of writings, speeches, and thinking with regard to his intellectual and cultural sources.

Each of the four parts functioned to influence Mao's world view in one way or another. However, the influences overlapped to a certain extent. (a) The older Chinese tradition, both mainstream and non-mainstream, had two levels of impact on Mao: a traditional Chinese cultural complex of self-esteem for being the great center of the world, and the self-given responsibility to the other part of the world. The first is a rational source for the "new type of sino-centrism" in Mao's world view. The second is cultural behavior at the operational level. Mao had used identical concepts and approaches in both foreign and domestic politics, investing his time and energy in personalized foreign relations.

(b) The newly established tradition in modern China provided a political environment for Mao's international perspective. It also offered an unprecedented opportunity for his actions on the stage of Chinese politics that were closely linked to the world at large. Ideas have to be defined in context. Mao's every perception and conception, practice and theory, was inseparable from the modern Chinese context and his personal background within this environment. More importantly, Mao continued to hold the nationalist banner that was the most prominent new phenomenon in modern China's politics and international relations. The nationalist mentality directed Mao's way of thinking and behavior. No longer was his world view under the illusion of Chinese civilization being complete and destined to rule "all under Heaven." Neither could Mao tolerate China's weakness in international society, especially in politics.

(c) Western thought, which Mao learned mostly in his youth, oriented his approach to political themes in the modern sense.[434] For example, the commonly recognized theme in modern Chinese politics is to seek national identity from many aspects, including China's position in a world of other nations. Since the turn of the century when China entered the family of nations, the growing self-consciousness of nationalism in international affairs centered on national independence, egalitarianism, and sovereignty. This self-identity of China as a nation-state framed Mao's nationalistic attitude toward the issues and events relevant to China. This framework of international politics is a product of the Westphalian model developed in Europe centuries ago. It provided the main normative basis for a state-centric international order and has remained dominant in the Chinese image of world order thus far.

(d) Marxism-Leninism was the source of legitimacy and authority for Mao in the communist world. He had to label himself as a Marxist-Leninist to solidify his position in the party. It provided the social ideal and ideological faith for Mao among the various *isms* of the modern world. He would not totally abandon it when he observed the world. However on many occasions he might set it aside. Marxism-Leninism promoted Mao's dialectical thinking and behavior, although it was not the only intellectual resource for his philosophy. In spite of these positive factors, the function of Marxism-Leninism in shaping Mao's world view cannot be explained too simplistically nor must it be exaggerated. Mao's effort to build his own authority for revolutionary theory in the CCP illustrated its limited influence. Therefore, the notion and the fulfillment of sinicized Marxism-Leninism provide a proper tension for balancing Mao's need for Marxism-Leninism and finding freedom from its outward ideology.

The significance of Mao's world view down to 1941 for Mao and the later CCP years is too complicated to be summarized here, particularly if one links the question of continuity versus change in the study of Chinese foreign affairs.[435] However a basic approach to reveal the possible answer is suggested here.

The main text of this work should be classified into two large categories: Category A contains all the tangible contents of Mao's world view--his viewpoint on concrete political figures and events, his vision of the world system, major powers and their connection with China, and his strategic and tactical thinking and behavior under domestic and international circumstances. The degree of significance of Mao's world view under this category needs further exploration. Contrasted with Category A, Category B refers to the hidden meanings that may be found in Mao's world view from an abstract perspective. Those meanings implicitly accompanying Mao's tangible world view offer a more endurable impact on the CCP and the PRC foreign affairs than Category A. Mao's epistemology and methodology, his philosophy of history and human nature, his personal characteristics and the political culture Mao inherited and created are the components of the intangible contents of Mao's world view under Category B. The question of the historical and logical connection between Mao's world view in earlier and later periods, divided by 1941, remains open.

ENDNOTES

Introduction

[1] While people may attribute historical preeminence to such great figures as Sun Yan-sen or Deng Xiaoping, I am firmly convinced that, in terms of the breadth and depth of his influence, the life of Mao Zedong (viewed either as a positive or negative element) was unquestionably the most influential person shaping the history of twentieth century China.

[2] When reviewing scholarly literature (in both Chinese and English) on Mao, one is impressed by the sheer number of biographies, treatises, and reminiscences. Considering these, and the number of important studies on China's foreign policy, it is surprising that little research has been done on the development of Mao's perceptions of the world prior to 1941. However, some research is relevant, such as: Stuart R. Schram's long-time Mao studies, Samuel S. Kim's chapter-length discussion of the "Maoist Image of World Order" (*China, the United Nations, and World Order*), John Gittings, *The World and China, 1922-1972*, and James Reardon-Anderson, *Yenan and the Great Powers, the Origins of Chinese Foreign Policy, 1944-1946*, as well as others.

[3] Yaacov Y.I. Vertzberger finds that the reflection of the living world in people's minds, particularly in decision-makers' minds, is a matter of information processing. It involves many subjective and objective elements in the process. He distinguishes two different levels of knowing: direct knowing (a perception-based knowing), and indirect knowing (a cognition-based knowing). See Yaacov Y.I. Vertzberger, *The World in Their Minds, Information Processing, Cognition, and Perception in Foreign Policy Decision-making* (Stanford, Stanford University Press, 1990) p. 9.

[4] To my knowledge and experience, people tend to stress the peculiarity of Mao's lack of experience abroad compared with many other politicians and statesmen of the same level. This fact has invited either high appreciation of his consciousness on Chinese matters from one extreme, or, from the other extreme, a simple ridicule of his capability to handle international affairs. Both have accepted a pre-assumption that Mao was generally "a man of the interior" since his youth. For

instance James Reardon-Anderson argues: "In an age when most of the radical intellectual youth of China flocked to the treaty ports or sought their fortunes abroad, Mao remained a man of the interior." "Unlike many of his contemporaries, Mao never left China or traveled abroad. He spoke no foreign language." See *Yenan and the Great Powers*, p. 8.

[5] Vertzberger, op. cit., pp. 9-10.

[6] Shi Zhe, a long time Soviet Russian expert in the CCP, recalled the history of relations between CCP and Comintern during the 1930's and the early 1940's. In his book are three possible reasons for the declining relationship between the Yanan and Moscow after the second half of 1941: (1) the German attack on the Soviet Union; (2) Mao's soft but insistent rejection of Moscow's request for military cooperation by the CCP in the eastern area of Soviet Union. (3) Moscow's disagreement with or misunderstanding of Mao's Zheng Feng Campaign (Rectification Campaign), which was launched at the end of 1941. See Shi Zhe, *Zai Lishi Juren Shengbian* (Chinese) (Beside the Historical Giants, Shi Zhe Memoirs), (Central Party's Literature Press, 1991) pp. 150, 201, 204-205,   213-215.

[7] The challenges included: externally, the "second anti-Communist onslaught" and the most intensified blockade of the CCP's Border Region by the Nationalist Party, i.e. Kuomintang (KMT), and the philosophical attack on Mao's sinicized Marxism-Leninism by Yei Qing, a former leader of the CCP and Mao's old foe. Internal dissension were tough, too, such as: the "ultra-left viewpoint" on the issues of military strategy, the united front, the cadre education movement in mid-1940, the disputes on cultural problems, and more seriously, the disapproval, or hesitant acceptance of Mao's authority as a Marxist-Leninist theorist among some high ranking persons. Refer to Raymond F. Wylie, *The Emergence of Maoism, Mao Tse-tung, Ch'en Po-ta, and the Search For Chinese Theory 1935-1945* (Stanford University Press, 1980) pp. 130-161.

[8] Immanuel C. Y. Hsu made an excellent description and analysis of ancient China's tributary relations. See Hsu: "The Meeting of the Western and Eastern Families of Nations," from his books *China's Entrance into Family of Nations: the Diplomatic Phase, 1858-1880* (Harvard University Press, 1966), and *Reading in Modern Chinese History* (Oxford University Press, 1971).

[9] There are many scholarly studies in English on traditional Chinese conceptions of the world: John K. Fairbank (ed.), *The Chinese World Order, Traditional China's Foreign Relations* (Cambridge, Mass.: Harvard University Press, 1968), C. P. Fitzgerald, *The Chinese View of Their Place in the World* (Oxford University Press, 1966), Mark Mancall, *China At the Center, 300 Years of Foreign Policy* (London: Collier Macmillan Publishers, 1984), Samuel S. Kim, *China, the United Nations, and World Order* (New Jersey: Princeton University Press, 1979).

Nevertheless, it needs to be pointed out that some scholars, especially Chinese scholars, have developed positive arguments on Chinese traditions in responding to the economic achievement in East Asia during recent two decades. As for Chinese traditional world view and relevant institution, some people found it was factually incorrect to generalize Sino-centrism and tributary system in the whole Chinese history.

[10] Benjamin I. Schwartz, "The Chinese Perception of World Order, Past and Present," See John K. Fairbank, *The Chinese World Order, Traditional China's Foreign Relations* (Cambridge: Harvard University Press, 1968) pp. 278-279.

[11] Ibid. pp. 284-285.

[12] In a modern political sense, the May Fourth era witnessed the birth of a Chinese nation with reference to the growing consciousness of her outward looking profile and position. As Dr. John Dewey, then in Beijing, wrote: "To say that life in China is exciting is to put it mildly. We are witnessing the birth of a nation, and birth always comes hard." See Robert Payne, *Mao Tse-tung, Ruler of Red China* (London: Secker and Warburg, 1951) p. 69.

[13] Levenson indicates that Chinese nationalism began as a paradox, a doctrine with increasingly obvious internal tensions between nationalism and traditionalism, performed as culturalism. "The nationalist protected tradition so that he might *be* a nationalist and be able to attack it. And a tradition requiring protection instead of compelling belief became increasingly open to attack." See Joseph R. Levenson, *Confucian China and Its Modern Fate, The Problem of Intellectual Continuity* (University of California Press, 1958) p. 108.

[14] Stuart R. Schram, "The Marxist," See Dick Wilson ed., *Mao Tse-tung In the Scales of History* (Cambridge University Press, 1977) p. 35.

[15] Richard Herrmann, "The Empirical Challenge of the Cognitive Revolution: A Strategy for Drawing Inferences about Perceptions" *International Studies Quarterly* Vol. 32, No. 2, June 1988, pp. 175-203.

[16] According to Richard Herrmann, the theory of cognitive balance is a theory of image and perhaps of propaganda, which stresses a subject's emotional sentiments that will direct cognitive attention; self-serving imagery that a subject will use to define the situation; perceptions of some basic notions like threat, opportunity, capability, relationships and cultural differences, which can determine the imagery. Refer to "The Empirical Challenge of the Cognitive Revolution: A Strategy for Drawing Inference about Perceptions," *International Studies Quarterly* Vol. 32 No. 2, June 1988, pp. 182-183.

[17] People have very divergent points on this issue but the tendency is to find the relations, no matter what type of academic linkage, between Mao's earlier thinking and the Mao Zedong Thought that matured in Yanan. Schram has an interesting thesis on the continuity of these two periods, the only two in Mao's revolutionary career before 1949 when Mao invested so much time and energy in philosophical work. He wrote, "Intriguingly, in Mao's early encounters with Western thought, the problem of epistemology, to which he later attached his name with the essay 'On

Practice,' looms large." See Stuart R. Schram: "Introduction, The Writings of Mao Zedong, 1912-1920," Stuart R. Schram, ed., *Mao's Road to Power, revolutionary Writings, 1912-1949*, Volume I The Pre-Marxist Period, 1912-1920 (M.E. Sharpe, 1992) p. xxvi.

Chapter One

[18] Li Rui, James C. Hsiung trans., *The Early Revolutionary Activities of Comrade Mao Tse-tung* (New York: M.E. Sharpe, Inc., 1977) p. 3.

[19] Edgar Snow, *Red Star Over China* (New York: Grove Press, Inc., 1968) pp. 133-134.

[20] Ibid. p. 138.

[21] Mao had a famous saying in Yanan: "It is a weakness for a person not to read the newspaper for one day. It is a mistake for a person not to read the newspaper for three days." See Gong Yuzhi, etc., *Mao Zedong de Dushu Shenhuo* (*Mao Zedong's Reading Life*), (Beijing: Three Joint Publishing House, 1987) p. 238.

[22] Mao, "Essay on How Shang Yang Established Confidence by the Moving of the Pole" (June 1912). See Stuart R. Schram ed., *Mao's Road to Power, Revolutionary Writings, 1912-1949*, Vol. 1, (The Pre-Marxist Period, 1912-1920), (New York: M.E. Sharpe, Publishers, 1992) (Hereafter: *Mao's Road*) pp. 5-6.

[23] The point Mao cited was Li's failure in his later career, particularly, Li's involvement in diplomacy as a matter of personal capability. The situation would be like "a mass of water" that is not bulky enough to carry a big boat. (See Mao, "Classroom Notes" (October-December 1913), Ibid. Vol.1, pp. 48-49) Here, the key was laid to specific persons and their personality. This point needs to be kept in mind when discussing Mao's domestic or international politics.

[24] Mao, "Classroom Notes," Ibid. Vol.1, pp. 31-32.

[25] It sounds an evangelical Chinese "Darwinism" tendency in dealing with states. However, Social Darwinism used to permeate among Chinese intellectuals during the first decade of twentieth century, thanks to Yan Fu's translation. Mao's early thinking certainly bore the imprint of such an intellectual context. However Mao, as usual, likes to cite similar ideas from Chinese source.

[26] *Mao's Road.* p. 15.

[27] Ibid. pp. 16-17.

[28] Li Rui's book records many evidences of young Mao's activities for purposely acquiring various experiences of the world. However, he was unable to go abroad then and even later he went to the Soviet Union only twice. This may have affected Mao's world view in some ways; it did not result in a lack of awareness of world affairs.

[29] Mao, "At Changsha" (1925), See *Reverberations, A New Translation of Complete Poems of Mao Tse-tung*, with Notes and Translated by Nancy T. Lin (Hongkong: Joint Publishing Co., 1980), p. 7.

[30] Mao, "Letter to Xiao Zisheng" (July 25, 1916), See *Mao's Road*, Vol. 1, p. 104.

[31] Details will be given in Chapter 6.

[32] Although the "third power" was not named in the treaties, some scholars believed that the United States might be one of the targets of the Russo-Japanese alliance that was doomed because of the revolution in Russia a few months later. See David J. Dallin, *The Rise of Russia in Asia*, (New Haven: Yale University Press, 1949), p. 122.

[33] Mao, "Letter to Xiao Zhisheng," See *Mao's Road*, Vol. 1, p. 103.

[34] Interesting enough, a Sino-Japanese War became true roughly 20 years later. China survived the war and came out from the Japanese shadow. Mao's ideology and his political force benefited from the war.

[35] Gao Jucheng, etc., *The Young Mao Zedong*, (Beijing: Party Historical Material Press, 1990), p. 60.

[36] Mao: "Letter to Xiao Zisheng," See *Mao's Road*, Vol. 1, p. 103.

[37] Ibid. p. 103.

[38] Ibid. p. 104.

[39] Ibid. p. 104.

[40] Schram, "General Introduction: Mao Zedong and Chinese Revolution, 1912-1949, " Ibid. p. xxix.

[41] Mao, " Marginal Notes to: Friedrich Paulsen, *A System of Ethics*," Ibid. Vol. 1, pp. 274-275.

[42] Ibid. p. 253.

[43] Mao, "Manifesto on the Founding of the *Xiang River Review*" (July, 14, 1919), Ibid. Vol. 1, p. 318.

[44] Mao, "Declaration of the Xiangtan Society for the Promotion of Education" (July, 31, 1920), Ibid. Vol. 1, p. 536.

[45] Mao, "Declaration on the Occasion of the Founding of the Association for Promotion Reform in Hunan" (April 1, 1920), Ibid. Vol. 1, p. 511.

[46] Mao, "The Founding and Progress of the `Strengthen Learning Society'" (July 21, 1919), Ibid. Vol. 1, p. 372.

[47] Mao, "The Great Union of the Popular Masses" (July 21, 1919), Ibid. Vol. 1, p. 389.

[48] Mao, "Declaration of the Xiangtan Society for the Promotion of Education," Ibid. Vol. 1, p. 536

[49] According to Han Suyin, Mao refuted both Russell and Dewey in December 1919, but she had only cited Mao's words criticizing Russell, and admitted that "John Dewey's influence persisted in some circles, promoted by Hu Shi and other

intellectuals." See Han Suyin, *The Morning Deluge: Mao Tse-tung and the Chinese Revolution, 1893-1954*, (Boston: Little, Brown and Company, 1972) p. 77.

[50] Not until the 1950's did the fierce criticism of pragmatism occur in Mao's political domain, because Mao needed to eliminate Hu Shi's influence among Chinese intellectuals after he grasped power and was angry about Hu Shi's political stand.

[51] Mao, "Statutes of the Problem Study Society" (September 1, 1919), See *Mao's Road* Vol. 1, pp. 407-413.

[52] Mao, "The Founding and Progress of the `Strengthen Learning Society,'" Ibid. Vol. 1, p. 376

[53] Mao, "Letter to Li Jinxi" (June 7, 1920), Ibid. Vol. 1, p. 518.

[54] Mao, "The Fundamental Issue in the Problem of Hunanese Reconstruction the Republic of Hunan" (September 3, 1920), Ibid. Vol. 1, p. 543.

[55] Mao, "Clearing up the Doubt" (September 27, 1920), Ibid. Vol. 1, p. 558.

[56] Mao, "Oppose Unification" (October 10, 1920), Ibid. Vol. 1, p. 579.

[57] Mao, "The Great Union of the Popular Masses" (Part I) (July 21, 1919), Ibid. Vol. 1, p. 378.

[58] Mao, "Manifesto on the Founding of the Xiang River Review," Ibid. Vol. 1, p. 318.

[59] Mao's idea of popular masses became one of his famous revolutionary concepts. A detailed discussion is given in Chapter 8.

[60] Gao Jucheng, etc., *The Young Mao Zedong*, p. 102.

[61] The terms "Alliance" and "Entente" Mao used were current of the time. Later, "Allies" replaced the "Entente" commonly, referring to " Allies "(including the U.S.) and the "Central Powers." See *Mao's Road*, p. 319 & p. 319n2.

[62] Mao, "For the Germans, the Painful Signing of the Treaty" (July 21, 1919), Ibid. Vol. 1, p. 366.

[63] Mao, "So Much for National Self-determination" (July 14, 1919), Ibid. Vol. 1, p. 337.

[64] Mao, "For the Germans, the Painful Signing of the Treaty", Ibid. Vol. 1, p. 366.

[65] The term mainstream faction is an English translation of the Chinese term *Guangyi Pai*, which was used by Mao and his generation referring to the "genuine socialists" represented by Russian Revolutionaries. See Mao, "The Waves of Strikes in Various Countries" (July 14, 1919), Ibid. Vol. 1, p. 321.

[66] Some Mao cultists believed that Mao's concentration on domestic affairs made him find a unique road to power.

[67] Some Mao critics insisted that Mao's lack of foreign experience caused him to fall into a narrow line of the Chinese revolution.

[68] Mao, "Letter to Li Jinxi" (September 5, 1919), See *Mao's Road*, Vol. 1, p. 415.

[69] Mao came into trouble from his writings and behavior with Zhang Jingyao, a Hunan governor and warlord. He challenged Zhang's authority and led a movement to expel Zhang. To this end, he went to Beijing and Shanghai again.

[70] Cai was another core member in the New People's Study Society, who won the compliment among the comrades as a "theorist" in contrast to a "practitioner" that was praise to Mao.

[71] Mao, "Letter to Tao Yi" (February 19, 1920), See *Mao's Road*, Vol. 1, p. 491.

[72] Mao, "Letter to Zhou Shizhao" (March 14, 1920), Ibid. Vol. 1, pp. 505-506.

[73] Mao, "Letter to Zhou Shizhao" Ibid. Vol. 1, p. 505.

[74] Mao, "Letter to Li Jinxi" (August 23, 1917), Ibid. Vol. 1, p. 132.

[75] Mao, "Letter to Cai Hesheng" (December 1, 1920), See *Mao Zedong Shuxin Xuanji* (*Selected Letters of Mao*), (Beijing: People's Publishing House, 1983) p. 2 (Hereafter: *Mao's Letters*).

Chapter Two

[76] Mao, "Letter to Cai Hesheng" See *Mao's Letters* p. 15.

[77] The word "national" in the bracket was a missing word in English translation.

[78] Mao, "Analysis of Classes in Chinese Society" (February 1, 1926), See M. Henri Day ed., *Mao Zedong, 1917-1927, Documents* (Stockholm, 1975), p. 293. (Hereafter: *Mao's Documents*).

The reason for removing words later by the CCP was unclear. Possibly it was because the early 1950's was the time for the CCP to stress the particularity of Mao's style of revolution. Mao did not give up his idea of universality of revolution in his later life. However, the direction of revolutionary current should flow from the Chinese model to others, not vice versa.

[79] A KMT operated journal started in the end of 1925 when Mao was an acting head of the KMT's Propaganda Department.

[80] Mao, "Reasons For Publication of the Political Weekly" (December 5, 1925), See *Mao's Documents*, p. 205.

[81] Mao, "The National Revolution and the Peasant Movement" (September 1, 1926) Ibid. p. 303.

[82] Mao, "Report on an Investigation of the Peasant Movement in Hunan" (March 28, 1927), Ibid. p. 342-343.

The words appear in Mao's "Report on an Investigation of the Peasant Movement in Hunan "published on March 28, 1927, and became a famous quotation from Mao Zedong forty years later in China's Cultural Revolution.

[83] Mao, "Analysis of the Classes in Chinese Society" (March, 1926), See *Selected Works of Mao Tse-Tung*, Vol. 1 (Beijing: foreign Language Press, 1975), p. 13 (Hereafter: *Mao Xuan*).

[84] As noted before, this article was rewritten to a considerable degree after Mao's revolutionary victory. An important change was made for omission of a sentence, in which Mao tried to give prominence to the issue of revolutionary strategy. He wrote that the problem of old revolution "is not because its aims have been wrong, but rather, only and entirely because its strategy has been wrong." (See *Mao's Documents*, p. 292.) What is the explanation of the change? To synthesize Mao's revolution-related world view then and later, it must be recognized that Mao's stress on revolutionary strategy was as important as the question of distinguishing "friend or enemy?" In view of this, one must conclude that the omission of the sentence that emphasized on the revolutionary strategy, was a distortion of Mao's original idea.

[85] A more conspicuous example to illustrate Mao's pragmatic utility of the term "imperialism" was in "General Principles for the Propaganda of the Chinese Guomindang (the KMT) in the War Against the Fengtian Clique" (November 27, 1925). The war began in October 1925 when a Zhili Clique warlord Sun Chuanfang in Zhejiang province attacked Fengtian Clique troops in Jiangsu province. It quickly developed into a general anti-Fengtian war, with the Zhili Clique, the force of Feng Yuxiang—another warlord with no clique affiliation, and the KMT all more or less allied in the attempt to defeat Fengtian Clique. Interestingly, Mao showed positive attitude toward the Feng Yuxiang faction by saying "Feng had no connexion with imperialism and supports the National Revolution [*Guomin Geming*] ..." (See *Mao's Documents*, p. 199) The attitude was proved by the CCP, too. This was not exactly true because Feng was not entirely innocent of client-like relations with the foreign powers although he personally seemed to have been heartily disliked by the powers. This fact was well-known at the time. Mao, and the leaders of the KMT and the CCP, could hardly have been unaware of this. The best explanation was to employ what Mao called "a tactical necessity."

[86] Mao, "Declaration of the First Congress of Peasant Representatives of Hunan Province" (December, 1926), See *Mao's Documents*, p. 333.

[87] Mao, "External Forces, Warlords and Revolution" (April 10, 1923), See Takeuchi Minoru ed., *Mao Zedong Ji Bujuan* (Supplements to Collected Writings of Mao Tse-Tung), Vol. 2 (Tokyo: Sososha, 1986) p. 110 (Hereafter: *Mao Bu*).

[88] Ibid. p. 111.

[89] Mao, "The Beijing *Coup d'Etat* and the Merchants" (July 11, 1923), See *Mao's Documents*, p. 160.

[90] Mao, "External Forces, Warlords and Revolution," See *Mao Bu*, Vol. 2, p. 160.

[91] Mao, "Analysis of Classes in Chinese Society," See *Mao's Documents*, p. 292.

[92] For the same reason, the official edition of 1951 had no such three-division expression. But no one thought Mao had abandoned this point or his approach for organizing his political forces. For example, Mao told people in the 1960's that "As

long as human beings exists, there are three categories among them: left, middle and right." Mao had even extended his three-division approach and popular mass concept to the world political stage.

It is noticed that some scholars indicated the significance for such a revision was that it showed an important correction in the developing process of Mao's thought. The point is not accepted here.

[93] Mao, "General Principles for the Propaganda of the Chinese Guomindang in the War against the Fengtian Clique," See *Mao's Documents*, p. 197.

[94] Chang Kuo-t'ao, *The Rise of the Chinese Communist Party, 1921-1927*, Vol. 1 (Lawrence: The University Press of Kansas, 1971), p. 510.

[95] Edgar Snow, *Red Star Over China*, p. 163.

[96] Ibid. p. 165.

[97] The CCP authorities collected "ten short pieces occupying only 152 pages in the English version, all of which were retitled, cut, rearranged, or otherwise extensively modified before the author pronounced them worthy of inclusion." The reason why the CCP Center and Mao himself took a good deal of trouble in selecting and revising Mao's writings in this period is a question beyond the mission of this research. Nevertheless, it has very much to do with the relationship between the CCP and Stalinist Russian. Referring to Kenneth E. Shewmaker, *Americans and Chinese Communists, 1927-1945: A Persuading Encounter* (Conell University Press, 1971) p. 33.

[98] Mao, "Letter to the Center Committee of the Chinese communist Party" (November 28, 1929), See *Mao's Letters*, p. 27.

[99] Gong Yuzhi, etc., *Mao Zedong de Dushu Shenghuo (Mao Zedong's Reading Life)* (Beijing: Three Joint Publishing House, 1986), p. 239.

[100] For some reasons this relevant chapter of the Resolution Mao wrote was entirely deleted by the CCP when this article was formally published in the early 1950's under the title of "Why is it that red political power can exist in China?"

[101] Mao, "The Current Political Situation and the Tasks of the First Front Red Army and the Party in Jiangxi" (October 26, 1930), See *Mao Bu*, Vol. 3, p. 160.

[102] Mao, "The Directive of Provisional Center Government to the First Soviet Conference of the Workers, Peasants and Soldiers in Fujian Province" (March, 1932), See Takeuchi Minoru ed., *Mao Zedong Ji (Collected Writings of Mao Zedong)* (Tokyo: Hokubosha, 1970), Vol. 3, p. 108 (Hereafter: *Mao Ji*)

[103] Mao, "The Proletariat and Oppressed Nations of All Over the World, Unite!" (August 30, 1933), Ibid. Vol. 3, p. 361.

[104] Mao, "The Report of the Central Executive Committee and the People's Committee of Chinese Soviet Republic on the Second National Soviet Representative conference" (January 24-25, 1934), Ibid. Vol. 4, p. 220.

[105] Mao, "The Declaration of the Central Government of Chinese Soviet Republic on the Selling out of Northern China by the Guomingdang" (June 19, 1934) See *Mao Bu*, Vol. 4, p. 216.

[106] Mao, "On Tactics Against Japanese Imperialism" (December 27, 1935), See *Mao Xuan*, Vol. 1, p. 170.

[107] A detailed discussion of Mao's semi-colonial theory is given on Chapter 8.

[108] Mao, "The Report of the Central Executive Committee and the People's Committee of Chinese Soviet Republic on the Second National Soviet Representative Conference" (January 24-25, 1934), See *Mao Ji*, Vol. 4, p. 221.

[109] Mao, "On Tactics Against Japanese Imperialism "See *Mao Xuan* Vol. 1, p. 159.

Chapter Three

[110] *Reverberation, A New Translation of Complete Poems of Mao Tse-tung*, with Notes by Nancy T. Lin (Hong Kong: Joint Publishing Co., 1980), p. 37.

[111] Ibid. p. 41.

[112] Zhang Ruxing, a young party theoretician who had come to Yanan from Shanghai writing in the journal *Communists*, March 20, 1941, began the notion "comrade Mao Zedong's thought." Two years later, Wang Jiaxiang, an important leader in the CCP, used the term "Mao Zedong thought" in his article in the Yanan newspaper *Liberation*, which was regarded as the first use of the term. See Xin Jianfei, "Ma Keshi Zhuyi Zhexueshi Dashi Nianbiao, Zhongguo Bufeng" [The Chronology of Marxist Philosophical History (China: 1893-1988)], *Zhexue Dachidian, Ma Keshi Zhuyi Zhexue Juan (Philosophical Encyclopedia, The Volume of Marxist Philosophy)*, (Shanghai Lexicography Press, 1990), pp. 1068-1069.

[113] Documental Study Division of the Central Committee, *Mao Zedong Nianpu (1893-1949) (A Chronicle of Mao Zedong's Life)*, (Beijing: People's Publishing House, 1993), (Hereafter: *Mao Nianpu*), Vol. 1, p. 541.

[114] Edgar Snow, *Red Star over China*, pp. 102-105.

[115] *Mao Nianpu* Vol.1, p. 561.

[116] Mao, "A Talk about the Problem of China and Japan, and Xian Incident" (March 1, 1937), See *Mao Ji*, Vol. 5,   pp. 175-188.

[117] Mao, "Policies, Measures and Perspective for Resisting the Japanese Invasion" (July 23, 1937), See *Mao Xuan* Vol. 2, p. 17.

[118] Evans Fordyce Carlson, *Twin Stars of China: A Behind-the-Scenes Story of China's Valiant Struggle for Existence by a U.S. Marine Who Lived & Moved with the People* (New York: Dodd, Mead & Company, 1941), p. 168.

[119] Mao, "Problems of Strategy in Guerrilla War against Japan" (March, 1938) See *Mao Xuan*, Vol. 2, p. 102.

[120] Mao, "On New Stage" (October 12-14, 1938), See *Mao Ji*, Vol. 6, p. 184.

[121] Mao, "On New Stage," Ibid. Vol. 6, pp. 234-236.

[122] Ibid. p. 237.

[123] Mao, "On New Stage," Ibid. Vol. 6, pp. 238-239.

[124] Ibid. p. 238.

[125] Mao, "On the Connections between Anti-Japanese War and Foreign Assistance–Preface *On Protracted War* (English Version)" (January 20, 1939) See *Mao Bu*, Vol. 6, p. 20.

[126] Mao, "An Outline of Counter-capitulationism" (June 10, 1939), Ibid. Vol. 6, pp. 56-57.

[127] *Mao Nianpu*, Vol. 1, p. 129.

[128] It was especially true when the matters had no direct impact or negative affect on the CCP's course. Besides, Mao was still hoping for more China aid from Moscow. Therefore, it was not unusual for Mao to echo Comintern propaganda that explained Soviet Union's "socialist peace policy."

[129] Mao, "Identity of Interests between the soviet Union and All Mankind" (September 28, 1939), See *Mao Xuan*, Vol. 2, pp. 279-283.

The formula of the CCP's propaganda regarding this story has maintained until the 1980's.

[130] The term refers to the Treaty of BrestLitovsk signed by Soviet Russia and Germany on March 3, 1918, which was treated as a model of flexibility of Leninism in the communist world.

[131] Mao, "Identity of Interests between the Soviet Union and All Mankind," See *Mao Xuan*, Vol. 2, p. 281.

[132] Mao, "Conversations with Snow in 1939" (September 25 & 26, 1939), See *Mao Bu*, Vol. 6, p. 123.

[133] Mao, "The Chinese Communist Leader Mao Zedong on Current International Situation and China's Anti-Japanese War" (September 1, 1939), See *Mao Ji*, Vol. 7, p. 15.

[134] The words "incontestable principle "were omitted from the official version of *Selected Works of Mao Zedong.*

[135] Micheal Schaller, *The United States and China in the Twentieth Century* (Oxford University Press, 1979), pp. 56-57.

[136] The two-division approach was an oft-used way for Mao to describe the international situation, particularly in later 1939 and early 1940. For instance, on December 21,1939, Mao declared that, "Today, the world is divided into two struggle fronts: one is imperialism, a front suppressing people; another one is socialism, a counter-suppressing front." Mao, "A Speech at the Ceremony of Stalin's Sixtieth Birthday in Yanan" (December 21, 1939), See *Mao Bu*, Vol.7, p.141.

[137] Mao, "The Resolution of the Center of Chinese Communist Party About the Current Situation and the Party's Policy" (July 7, 1940), See *Mao Bu*, Vol. 6, pp. 155-156.

[138] Ibid. p. 156.

[139] *Mao Nianpu*, Vol. 2, p. 221.

[140] Mao, "Telegram to Zhou Enlai, An Assessment on the International Relations and the Relations between the KMT and the CCP" (March 17, 1941), See *Mao Bu*, Vol. 7, p. 45.

[141] This was an official statement issued by the CCP on April 21, 1941. See Charles B. Mclane, *Soviet Policy and the Chinese Communists, 1931-1946* (New York: Columbia University Press, 1958) p. 136.

[142] Mao, "A Circular to Zhou Enlai: On the Development of Current Affair" (January 30, 1941), See *Mao Bu*, Vol. 6, p. 303.

[143] This is the official CCP statement on the Soviet-Japanese Pact, John Gittings, *The World and China, 1922-1972*, p. 82.

[144] *Mao Nianpu*, Vol. 2, p. 279.

[145] Mao, "The Critic in Yanan States: the 'Fireside Chat' Has Dual Character–Forcing Germany to Compromise and Preparing to Enter the War, The Far Eastern Munich Needs Great Attention" (May 30, 1941), See *Mao Ji*, Vol. 7, pp. 325-326.

[146] *Mao Nianpu*, Vol. 2, p. 312.

[147] Mao, "A Statement of the Center of the Chinese Communist Party on Current International Events" (August 19, 1941), See *Mao Ji*, Vol. 8, pp. 21-22.

[148] *Mao Nianpu*, Vol. 2, p. 334.

[149] Mao, "Comrade Mao Zedong Appealing to Enforce Unite on the East Anti-Fascism Conference" (October 30, 1941), See *Mao Ji*, Vol. 8, p. 31.

[150] *Mao Nianpu*, Vol. 2, p. 343.

Chapter Four

[151] It has been pointed out that "China was accepted in 1918-1920 into the international society." See Zhang Yongjin, *China in the International System, 1918-20: The Middle Kingdom at the Periphery* (Macmillan Academic and Professional Ltd., 1991), p. 5.

[152] Mao, "Letter to Xiao Zisheng" (September 6, 1915), See *Mao's Road*, Vol. 1, p. 79.

[153] Mao, "The Current Political Situation and the Tasks of the First Front Red Army and the Party in Jiangxi" (October 26, 1930), See *Mao Bu*, Vol. 3, p. 160.

[154] Mao, "The Chinese Revolution and the Chinese Communist Party" (December, 1939), See *Mao Xuan*, Vol. 2, p. 309.

[155] Mao, "Letter to Zhou Shizhao" (March 14, 1920), See *Mao's Road*, Vol. 1, p. 505.

[156] In Chapter 1, we have introduced Mao's analysis of "the tide of change" in the world during May Fourth era. This was a factual base of Mao's new type of Sino-centricism.

[157] George Modelski, "The Long Cycle of Global Politics and the Nation-State," *Comparative Studies in Society and History*, (April 20, 1978) p. 224, See Samuel S. Kim, *China In and Out of the Changing World Order*, (Center of International Studies World Order Studies Program, Occasional paper, November 21, Princeton University, 1991) p. 4.

[158] Some regulations, like debts' collection, rules of war, and rights and obligations of neutrals, and the machinery of voluntary arbitration, like a permanent court of arbitration, were provided for.

[159] Mao, "Statutes of the Problem Study Society" (September 1, 1919), See *Mao's Road*, Vol. 1, p. 409.

[160] Mao, "For the Germany, the Painful Signing of the Treaty" (July 21, 1919), Ibid. Vol. 1, p. 366.

[161] Mao, "Contents of the Treaty" (July 28, 1919), Ibid. Vol. 1, p. 391.

[162] In 1919, Mao noticed that France, England, and the United States had replaced Germany to be the greatest powers in the world. The new powers "will be social and economic." See Chapter 1.

[163] Mao, "Manifesto on the Founding of the *Xiang River Review*" (July 14, 1919), Ibid., Vol. 1, p. 318.

[164] Li Yongshou, *Mao Zedong Yu Da Geming* (Mao Zedong and Great Revolution), (Shichuan People's Publishing House, 1991), p. 97.

[165] Mao, "External Forces, Warlords and Revolution" See *Mao Bu*, Vol. 2, p. 110.

[166] Mao, "The English and Liang Ruhao" (August 29, 1923), See *Mao Documents*, p. 167.

[167] Mao, "On Tactics Against Japanese Imperialism" See *Mao Xuan*, Vol. 1, pp. 153-154.

[168] Mao, "A Talk about the China's Problem and Xian Incident" (March 1, 1937), See *Mao Ji*, Vol. 5, pp. 182-183.

[169] See Chapter 3 for detail.

[170] In Chapter 2, we have discussed Mao's concept of imperialism in the first half of the 20's.

[171] The Leninist theory of imperialism contains the following points: (a) imperialism is the highest stage of capitalism, capital export is the major economic feature; (b) monopoly is the deepest economic foundation of imperialism, it appears both domestically and internationally; (c) therefore, imperialism links the world together for competition, it is the source of the modern war; (d) as a result, it is also

the last stage of capitalism. Along with and after the imperialist war, socialist revolution will take in action and win the world. Refer to *Zhexue Dachidian, Ma Keshi Zhuyi Zhexue Juan* (Chinese) (*Great Dictionary of Philosophy--the Volume of Marxist Philosophy*), (Shanghai Lexicographical Publishing House, 1990), pp. 739-740.

[172] See Chapter 8 for detail.

[173] Mao, "The Election of This Year" (September 6, 1933), See *Mao Ji*, Vol. 4, pp. 13-14.

[174] The CCP had to give up the concept of "the second imperialist war" for identifying the European war in late 1939. This article does not show up in Mao's official works.

[175] Edgar Snow, *Red Star Over China*, p. 142.

[176] The other three evils of demons are the churches, monarchy, and the state. Mao, "Marginal Notes to: Friedrich Paulsen. *A System of Ethics*" (1917-1918), See *Mao's Road*, Vol. 1, p. 208.

[177] Mao, "The Founding and Progress of the `Strengthen Learning Society'" (July 21, 1919), Ibid. Vol. 1, p. 373.

[178] "Mr. Mao Zedong's Lecture," *Guangzhou Minguo Rebao* (*Guangzhou Republic Daily*), (October 28, 1925), See Li Yongshou, *Mao Zedong and Great Revolution*, p. 219.

[179] Mao, "Analysis of the Class in Chinese Society," See *Mao Xuan*, Vol. 1, p. 15.

[180] Mao, "Declaration of the First Congress of Peasant Representative of Hunan Province" (December, 1926), See *Mao Documents*, pp. 336-333. ¹

[181] Mao, "Letter of the Fourth Section of Chinese Red Army to the Soldiers of Guomingdang Army "(January, 1930), See *Mao Bu*, Vol.3, p.62

[182] Mao, "The Working Report of the First Anniversary of Provisional Central Government to All Voters" (November 7, 1932), Ibid. Vol. 4, p. 91.

[183] Mao, "The Report of the Central Executive Committee and the People's Committee of Chinese Soviet Republic on the Second National Soviet Representative conference" (January 24-25, 1934), See *Mao Ji*, Vol. 4, p. 220.

[184] Mao, "On New Democracy" (January, 1940), See *Mao Xuan*, Vol. 2, pp. 343-345, 355, 360.

[185] The Treaty of Nerchinsk (1869) was the first treaty between Russians and Chinese. It resulted from conflict between Tsar Peter I and the Kang Xi Emperor. Before the treaty, Russians had penetrated into the Amur region for commercial purpose through military pressure. After the treaty, Russians were obliged to withdraw from the occupied territory and to abandon military means. Later, Russians established a trading agent and an Eastern Orthodox church in Beijing. The treaty marked the beginning of a period of 170 years of peace on the Siberian-Manchurian border.

[186] Even the Russian Revolution in 1917 was one of a negative element that paralleled the unhappy history between the two nations, as Mao pointed out, "Soviet Union differs from us: (1) Tsar Russia was an imperialist; (2) later, there was the October Revolution. Therefore, many Russians are very arrogant and cocky." See *Mao Xuan*, Vol. 5, p. 287.

[187] Allen S. Whiting, *Soviet Policies in China, 1917-1924*, (New York: Columbia University Press, 1954), p. 248.

[188] Mao, "In Memory of a Friend—Yi Yongxi" (May, 1915), See *Mao's Road*, Vol. 1, p. 61.

[189] Mao, "Letter to Xiangsheng" (June 25, 1915), See *Mao's Road*, Vol. 1, p. 64.

[190] Mao, "Letter to Xiao Zisheng" (July 25, 1916), See *Mao's Road*, Vol. 1, p. 102.

[191] Mao, "The Secret Treaty Between Japan and Germany" (July 28, 1919), See *Mao's Road*, Vol. 1, p. 392.

[192] Russia's posture was carried on a famous, but controversial document, known as Karakhan Manifesto in July 1919. The later development of Sino-Soviet diplomacy evidenced that the Russia's posture was no more than lip service, particularly on the issue of Chinese Eastern Railway, "The Soviet Union was able to benefit from the Chinese people's goodwill while giving up nothing in exchange" by subtly changing the crucial promise that was to return the Chinese Eastern Railway to China without any compensation. See Bruce A. Elleman, "The Soviet Union's Secret Diplomacy Concerning the Chinese Eastern Railway, 1924-1925," *The Journal of Asian Studies*, Vol. 53, No. 2, May, 1994, p. 459.

[193] Mao, "Study the Extremist Party" (July 14, 1919), See *Mao's Road*, Vol. 1, p. 332.

[194] Mao, "Break Down the Foundationless Big China And Build up Many Chinas Starting with Hunan" (September 5, 1920), Ibid. Vol. 1, p. 546.

[195] Ibid. p. 547.

[196] Mao, "Letter of the Fourth Section of Chinese Red Army to the Soldiers of Guomingdang Army" (January, 1930), See *Mao Bu*, Vol. 3, pp. 62-63.

[197] Otto Brawn, *A Comintern Agent in China, 1932-1939* (Stanford University Press, 1982), Dick Wilson's "Introduction," p. xii.

[198] Kenneth E. Shewmaker, *Americans and Chinese Communists, 1927-1945: A Persuading Encounter*, p. 29.

[199] There are several of Mao's writings dealing with the Party's history during the Jiangxi period, especially, from 1931-1934. The most important document is "Resolution on Some Historical Problems," adopted by the Seventh Enlarged Plenary Session of the CCP's Sixth Central committee, on April 20, 1945. "All the major divergence of policy between the Mao group and Russian returned students can be found in this statement," but it did not directly attribute the faults to Moscow. However, the impact of Pavel Mif, Stalin's disciple, on the Jiangxi soviet

was liquidated in the Yanan period. Refer to Tso-liang Hsiao, *Power relations within the Chinese communist Movement, 1930-1934, A Study of Documents* (Seattle: University of Washington Press, 1961)

[200] This is called "a policy of double dealing: give aid to Chinese revolutionary forces through the Comintern, while promoting friendly relations with the domestic enemies of those same forces (like the Beijing Government and the warlords) through the Soviet Government." Refer to Shinkichi Eto, "China's International Relations 1911-1931", John K. Fairbank & Allert Feuerwerker, *The Cambridge History of China, Republican China 1912-1949*, Part 2, Vol. 13 (Cambridge University Press, 1986) p. 109.

[201] Edgar Snow, *Red Star Over China*, p. 444.

[202] Harry Schwartz, *Tsars Mandarins and Commissars, A History of Chinese-Russian Relations* (Anchor Books, 1973),   p. 119.

[203] Mao spoke in a meeting of the Politburo shortly after arriving in Yanan, "We must link the revolution with the nation..." See *Mao Nianpu*, Vol. 1, p. 525.

[204] Edgar Snow, *Red Star Over China*, p. 444.

[205] Ibid.

[206] It is commonly recognized that Soviet aid in the first several years of the Sino-Japanese war was major foreign assistance for China. However, little was sent to Yanan directly except for the period before the Sino-Soviet Pact had been signed. According to Li De (Otto Braun), a disgraced Comintern agent in Yanan, "Bitter sarcasm was voiced in Yanan, such as `weapons to the bourgeoisie, books to the proletariat' (books referred to communist political literature)." He believes the voice bears the mark of Mao's sayings. Otto Braun, *A Comintern Agent in China, 1932-1939* p. 209.

[207] Allen S. Whiting and General Sheng Shih-tsai, *Sinkiang: Pawn or Pivot?* (Michigan State University Press, 1958) See the book for details.

[208] The story is that Stalin refused to let Sheng join the CCP and ordered him to join the Russian Party instead. Obviously, the purpose of Stalin to do so was his unwillingness to see Xinjiang's future being fallen into Chinese nationalists, including the CCP. Ibid.

[209] Benjamin I. Schwartz, *Chinese Communist and the Rise of Mao* (Cambridge: Harvard University Press, 1951), p.136

[210] Shu Yang ed, *Zhongguo Chu Le Ge Mao Zedong, Zhongwai Mingren de PingShou* (*China Had a Mao Zedong, the Commentaries of Famous Persons within and without China*), (People's Liberal Army's Publishing House, 1991), p. 383.

[211] See *Mao Nianpu*, Vol. 1, p. 502.

[212] Ibid. Vol. 2, p. 90.

[213] Mao, "On New Democracy" (January, 1940), See *Mao Xuan*, Vol.2, p. 364.

[214] See *Mao Nianpu*, Vol. 2, p. 267.

[215] Ibid. p. 312.

[216] Ibid. p. 313.

[217] Moscow criticized that the CCP was busy purging the Comintern influence in his Rectification Campaign, when it was the most dire time of the Soviet-German war. See Fan Xianchao, *Mao Zedong Shixiang Fazhan de Lishi Guiji* (Chinese) (*The Historical Orbit of the Development of Mao Zedong Thought*), (Hunan People's Publishing House, 1993), p. 1029.

Chapter Six

[218] Michael Hunt, *The Making of a Special Relationship: the United States and China to 1914* (New York: Columbia University Press, 1983)

[219] Akira Iriye, *Across the Pacific, An Inner History of American-East Asia Relations* (New York: Harcourt, Brace & World, Inc.,1967), pp. 34-35.

[220] This is based on mainstream Chinese images of the U.S. No doubt there always existed various opinions on the same issue.

[221] As Mao recalled, he was impressed by a quotation: "After eight years of difficult war, Washington won victory and built up his nation." See Edgar Snow, *Red Star Over China*, p. 138.

[222] Mao, "Letter to Xiao Zisheng" (July 25, 1916), See *Mao's Road*, Vol. 1, p. 104.

[223] Mao, "Reply to Zeng Yi from the Association for Promoting Reform in Hunan" (June 23, 1920), Ibid. Vol. 1, p. 526.

[224] Mao, "Letter to Li Jinxi" (March 12, 1920), Ibid. Vol. 1, p. 501.

[225] Ibid. p. xxx. Stuart Schram, "General Introduction. Mao Zedong and the Chinese Revolution, 1912-1949"

[226] Akira Iriye, *Across the Pacific, An Inner History of American-East Asia Relations*, p. 124, pp. 128-129.

[227] See Chapter 1 for detail.

[228] Mao, "On Democracy in Anti-Japanese war and the Northern Youths" (1937), See *Mao Ji*, Vol. 5, p. 229.

[229] T.A. Bisson, *Yenan in June 1937: Talks with the Communist Leaders* (The Regents of the University of California, 1973), pp. 59-60.

[230] Mao, "Savage Bomb Attacks" (July 14, 1919), See *Mao's Road*, Vol. 1, p. 339.

[231] Mao, "Poor Wilson" (July 14, 1919), Ibid. Vol. 1, p. 338.

[232] Mao, "The Despotism of Industry Is Unacceptable" (July 14, 1919), Ibid. Vol. 1, p. 340.

[233] Mao, "The Beijing *Coup d'Etat* and the Merchants" (July 11, 1923), See *Mao Documents*, p. 217.

[234] Mao, "The Declaration of the Central Government of Chinese Soviet Republic on the Selling out Northern China by the Guomingdang" (June 19, 1934) See *Mao Bu*, Vol. 4, p. 217.

[235] Mao, "Outline of the Lecture On the Second Imperialist War" (September 14, 1939), See *Mao Ji*, Vol. 7, p. 44.

[236] Mao, "What Does the KMT Shorten?" (June 17, 1941), Ibid. Vol. 7, p. 329.

[237] For instance: Li Hongzhang, a crucial person in late nineteenth century China, particularly in foreign affairs, was alarmed as early as the 1870's, "While our own weakness remains chronic, our strong neighbor [i.e. Japan] daily becomes a threat to us;" Liang Qichao, one of the most influential intellectuals in modern China, had very bad personal experience in Japan where he was under constant police observation for fourteen years. This had something to do with his anti-Japanese attitude.

[238] Akira Iriye, *Across the Pacific, An Inner History of American-East Asia Relations*, p. 83, 91.

[239] Edgar Snow, *Red Star Over China*, pp. 137-138.

[240] Mao, "Classroom Notes" See *Mao's Road* Vol. 1, p. 10.

[241] Ibid. p. 15.

[242] Ibid. p. 34.

[243] Mao, "Letter to Xiangsheng" (June 25, 1915), Ibid. Vol. 1, p. 65.

[244] Mao, "In Memory of a Friend, Yi Yongxi" (May, 1915), "Epigraphies to *Mingchi Pian*" (*Essays on the Sense of Shame*) (Summer, 1915), "Letter to Xiangsheng"(June 25,1915), Ibid. Vol. p. 61, 66, 64.

[245] John K. Fairbank & Albert Feuerwerker ed., *The Cambridge History of China: Republic China, 1912-1949*, Part 2, Vol. 13 (Cambridge University Press, 1986) pp. 97-100.

[246] Mao, "Letter to Miyazaki Toten" (March, 1917), See *Mao's Road*, Vol. 1, p. 111.

[247] Mao, "Letter to Li Jinxi" (August 23, 1917), Ibid. Vol. 1, p. 132.

[248] Mao, "Letter to Xiao Zisheng" (July 25, 1916), Ibid. Vol. 1, p. 103.

[249] Mao, "A Study of Physical Education" (April 1, 1917), Ibid. Vol. 1, p. 114.

[250] Mao, "Reply to Zeng Yi from the Association for Promoting Reform in Hunan" (June 23, 1920), Ibid. Vol. 1, p. 529.

[251] *Mao Nianpu*, Vol. 2, p. 57.

[252] Mao, "The English and Liang Ruhao" (August 29, 1923), See *Mao Documents*, pp. 166-168.

[253] Mao, "The Open Telegram on Opposition to the Report of International Fact-finding Mission" (October 6, 1932), See *Mao Ji*, Vol. 3, p. 139.

Mao, "The Declaration of the Central Government of Chinese Soviet Republic on the Selling out Northern China by the Guomingdang" (June 19, 1934) See *Mao Bu*, Vol. 4, p. 216.

[254] Mao, "Chinese Revolution and Chinese Communist Party" (December, 1939), See *Mao Ji*, Vol. 2, pp. 309-310.

[255] Mao, "Politicians" (July 28, 1919), See *Mao's Road*, Vol. 1, p. 393.

[256] Mao, "Interview with the British Journalist James Bertram" (October 25, 1937) See *Mao Xuan*, Vol. 2, pp. 57-58.

[257] T.A.Bisson, *Yenan in June 1937: Talks with the Communist Leaders* (University of California, Berkeley, 1973), pp. 54-55.

[258] Ibid. p. 54.

[259] When a British Journalist, Gunther Stein, later raised the question to Bo Gu, a senior leader of the CCP, and an important man in Yanan's world affairs. Bo Gu answered: "I admit that we did not know then that Britain was so weak, Her weakness surprised us later. But the main point is that all the weakness of Britain arose from her wrong imperialist policies in general." Gunther Stein, *The Challenge of Red China*, New York: McGraw-Hill Book Company, Inc., 1945), p. 445.

[260] Bo Gu gave a typical CCP version Britain's policy toward China from 1937 to 1941, "The policies of the British and French governments were still fundamentally determined by imperialistic considerations." Ibid. pp. 444-445.

[261] Mao, "Resolution of Current Political Situation and the Party's Task" (December 25, 1935), See *Mao Ji*, Vol. 5, p. 20.

[262] Mao, "On Democracy in Anti-Japanese War and the Northern Youths" (1937), Ibid. Vol. 5, pp. 228-229.

[263] Mao, "On New Stage" (October 12-14, 1938), Ibid. Vol. 6, pp. 236-237.

[264] Mao, "The Chinese and the British Peoples Are Standing on the Same Line" (June 1, 1939) Ibid. Vol. 6, pp. 339-340.

[265] Mao, "The Outline of Lecture on the Second Imperialist War" (September 4, 1939) Ibid. Vol. 7, p. 46, 43.

[266] According to Stein's notes, Bo Gu denied that the CCP attitude toward the European war followed Moscow's instruction. It was entirely an independent judgment, "Our general estimate of British and French policies influenced our attitude toward the European war, "said Bo Gu. However, he did not reject Stein's thought that the CCP attitude toward the war was wrong because it was more like ideological propaganda than practical politics. Gunther Stein, *The Challenge of Red China*, pp. 445-446.

[267] Robert Lee, *France and The Exploitation of China, A Study in Economic Imperialism, 1885-1901* (Oxford University Press, 1989), p. vii.

[268] Mao, "For the Germans, The Painful Signing of the Treaty" (July 21, 1919), See *Mao's Road*, Vol. 1, p. 366.

[269] For instance: on the issue of German's membership of the League of Nations, Mao said, "Wilson was surrounded by thieves like Clemenceau, Lloyd George,..." Mao, "Poor Wilson" (July 14, 1919), Ibid. Vol. 1, p. 338.

[270] Mao told people that "their [i.e. the politicians of France and Britain] days of famine will come soon! Their days of headaches will arrive!" Mao, "For the Germans, The Painful Signing of the Treaty" See *Mao's Road*, Vol. 1, p. 366.

[271] Mao, "Joy and Suffering" (July 21, 1919), Ibid. Vol. 1, p. 367.

[272] Mao, "Joy and Suffering," Ibid. Vol. 1,   p. 367.

[273] Mao, "For the Germans, The Painful Signing of the Treaty," Ibid. Vol. 1, p. 366.

[274] Mao, "France Fears Germany As If It Were A Tiger" (July 28, 1919), Ibid. Vol. 1, p. 390.

[275] Mao, "Joy and Suffering," Ibid. Vol. 1,   p. 367.

[276] Mao, "France Fears Germany As If It Were A Tiger," Ibid. Vol. 1, p. 390.

[277] Mao, "The Works of The Students" (December 1, 1919), Ibid. Vol. 1, p. 454.

[278] Hsi-Huey Liang, *The Sino-German Connection, Alexander Van Falkenhausen Between China and Germany, 1900-1941* (Van Gorcum & Comp. The Netherlands, 1977), pp. 1-11.

[279] Xiao-Yu, *Mao Tse-tung And I Were Beggars* (Syracuse University Press, 1959), p. 69.

[280] Schram indicated: "The lesson of the nineteenth century, followed by the German victories of 1914-16, had given new prestige to military force, and also to physical strength, as keys to national survival." Stuart R. Schram, "Introduction," See Li Rui, *The Early Revolutionary Activities of Comrade Mao Tse-tung* (New York: M.E. Sharpe, Inc., 1977), p. xxiv.

[281] Mao, "Marginal Notes to: Friedrich Paulsen, *A System of Ethics*," See *Mao's Road*, Vol. 1, p. 258.

[282] Mao, "For the Germans, the Painful Signing of the Treaty" (July 21, 1919), Ibid. Vol. 1, p. 365.

[283] Mao, "For the Germans, the Painful Signing of the Treaty," Ibid. Vol. 1, p. 365.

[284] Mao, "The Secret Treaty Between Japan and Germany" (July 28, 1919), Ibid. Vol. 1, p. 392.

Chapter Seven

[285] Raymond F. Wylie concludes that the 1938 was the year of "the sinification of Marxism," then, Mao emerged as the Prophet in the next two years. See Raymond F. Wylie, *The Emergence of Maoism, Mao Tse-tung, Ch'en Po-ta, and the Search For Chinese theory, 1935-1945* (Stanford University Press, 1980)

[286] Mao, "Letter to a Friend" (July, 1915), See *Mao's Road* Vol. 1, p. 68.

[287] There are three reasons to support this point. First, Mao did not occupy the decisive position in the CCP until Zunyi conference(January 1935). Second, the relationship between the CCP and Moscow, although started much earlier, had to

be treated specially with reference to the common ground of ideology and communist movement. Third, the CCP declared officially the beginning of its diplomatic work in 1944, when U.S. President Franklin D. Roosevelt approved official contacts with Yanan. This became known as the "Dixie Mission," the first American observers who entered Communist territory that July. The CCP considered this event the beginning of its diplomacy; apparently they treated the CCP-Moscow relations as something different. For instance, by directing a warm welcome toward Americans, Yanan seriously announced: "This is the start of our diplomatic work."* However, an operational structure for dealing with foreigners and foreign affairs had been taking in shape before the end of 1941, given the strong sense of international politics Mao had developed since his youth.

* The Central Committee of the Party, "Directive of diplomatic work" (1944) See Jincheng *Yanan Jiaojichu Huiyilu* (*Memoirs of Yanan Association Department*), (Chinese Youth Publishing House, 1986), p. 192.

[288] In the Chinese Soviet Republic, formally inaugurated by the First Congress in 1931 and continued by the Second Congress in 1934, the Foreign Affairs Department was one of the central administrative organs established in the Jianxi Border Area. It was headed by Wang Jiaxiang, who became a leading envoy of the CCP to the Comintern in the second half of 1937 and the first half of 1938.

[289] *Mao Nianpu*, Vol. 1, p. 565.

[290] Ibid. Vol. 2, p. 301.

[291] Mao, "On Protracted War" (May 26, 1938), See *Mao Xuan* Vol. 2, p. 116.

[292] Ibid. p. 566.

[293] Mao, "On the Connections between Anti-Japanese War and Foreign Assistance–Preface of *On Protracted War* (English Version)"(January 20, 1939) See *Mao Bu*, Vol. 6, p. 19.

[294] Including the Baoan period, a small town nearby Yanan where the CCP center rested before it moved to Yanan in January 1937.

[295] Edgar Snow, *Red Star over China*, J. K. Fairbank, "Introduction," p. 11.

[296] Kenneth E. Shewmaker, *Americans and Chinese Communists, 1927-1945: A Persuading Encounter*, p. 102.

[297] See *Mao Bu*, Vol. 1, p. 565.

[298] There were two groups of opponents led by Zhang Guotao and Wang Ming respectively.

[299] This aspect has been discussed in Chapter 5.

[300] *Mao Nianpu*, Vol. 2, p. 343, 345.

[301] Ibid. p. 279.

[302] Edgar Snow, *Red Star Over China*, p. 104.

[303] Evens Fordyce Carlson, *Twin Stars of China*, p. 169.

[304] *Mao Nianpu*, Vol. 2, p. 110.

[305] Mao, "The Speech on a Welcome Party" (September, 1939), See *Mao Bu*, Vol. 6, p. 126.

[306] Edgar Snow, *Red Star Over China*, p. 94.

[307] Ibid. pp. 444-445.

[308] Ibid. p. 110.

[309] Ironically, the Koreans with the leadership of Kim II Sung did not follow Mao's example in foreign relations; rather, Kim played a skillful game between his two Communist big brothers and gained benefits.

[310] Mao noted, "Just because of the lack of relationship, people lack the concepts of state and politics. China has freedom but the Western countries have despotism. China's politics and laws are simple and taxes are light, but the Western countries are just the opposite." See Mao, "Classroom Notes," *Mao's Road*, Vol. 1, p. 22.

[311] Mao, "Classroom Notes" Ibid. Vol. 1, p. 22.

[312] Schram argued: "This articular teaching Yang's does not appear to have had much influence on Mao." See Schram, "Introduction, The Writing of Mao Zedong, 1912-1920," Ibid. Vol. 1, p. xxvii.

[313] As Dr. John Dewey, then in Beijing, wrote: "To say that life in China is exciting is to put it mildly. We are witnessing the birth of a nation, and birth always comes hard." See Robert Payne, *Mao Tse-tung, Ruler of Red China* (London, Secker and Warburg, 1951), p. 69.

[314] Mao, "The Fundamental Issue in the Problem of Hunanese Reconstruction: The Republic of Hunan" (September 3, 1920), See *Mao's Road*, Vol. 1, pp. 543-545.

[315] Schram put an important footnote for the English translation of Mao's terms from Chinese. Mao used several terms for state, including the single characters *guo* and *bang*, and the compound *guojia*. Schram points out that "All of them evoke in some degree both the states as a political entity, and the country more loosely defined." Ibid. Vol. 1, p. 543n2.

[316] Mao, "'Complete Self-rule' and `Semi-Self-Rule'" (October 3, 1919), Ibid. Vol. 1, p. 563.

[317] Mao, "Appeal to the 300,000 Citizens of Changsha in Favor of Self-Rule for Hunan" (October 7, 1920), Ibid. Vol. 1, p. 572.

[318] Mao, "Break Down the Foundationless big China and Build Up Many China Starting with Hunan" (September 5, 1920), Ibid. Vol. 1, p. 546.

[319] See Chapter 5.

[320] Mao, "Proposal That the `Hunan Revolutionary Government' Convene a `Hunan People's Constitutional Convention' to enact a `Hunan Constitution' in Order to Build a `New Hunan'" (October 5-6, 1920), See *Mao's Road*, Vol. 1, pp. 568-569.

[321] A month later, Mao wrote a letter to his comrades of the New People's Society. He said: The movement was the "only expedient measure in response to

the current situation and definitely does not represent our basic views. Our proposals go way beyond these movements," nevertheless, the movement was "also means to achieve a fundamental transformation, means that are most economical and most effective in dealing with our `present circumstances'." Mao, "Comments in Response to the Letter from Yi Lirong to Mao Zedong and Peng Huang" (November, 1920), See *Mao's Road*, Vol. 1, pp. 611-612.

[322] Refer to Derek J. Waller, *The Kiangsi Soviet Republic: Mao and the National Congresses of 1931 and 1934* (Center for Chinese Studies, University of California, Berkeley, 1973), p. 112.

[323] China's politics then gave a reasonable context for such a positive aspect of the relations. The coup by Chiang Kai-shek and the KMT in mid-1927 caused a reaction from the CCP and Soviet Russia; the triple coalition between Moscow, the KMT and the CCP was replaced by a two-party alliance between Moscow and the CCP. The alliance was tighter and more solidly organized, having a political and ideological basis. At least, this was the way it appeared to outsiders.

[324] Derek J.Waller, *The Kiangsi Soviet Republic: Mao and the National Congresses of 1931 and 1934*, p. 32.

[325] Mao, "The Economic Policy of the Chinese Soviet Republic" (December 1, 1931), See *Mao Ji*, Vol. 3, p. 53.

[326] Mao, "Problems of Strategy in China's Revolutionary War" (December, 1936), Ibid. Vol. 5, p. 157.

[327] Mao, "On Tactics against Japanese Imperialism" (December 27, 1935), See *Mao Xuan*, Vol. 1, p. 167.

[328] The multi-class base of the state power was maintained over the next several decades, at least in official rhetoric, except for the period of Mao's Cultural Revolution.

[329] Mao, "On the New Stage" (October 12-14, 1938), See *Mao Ji*, Vol. 6. pp. 232-233.

[330] The Three Great Policies were: alliance with Russia, co-operation with the Communist Party and assistance to the peasants and workers. They were raised by Sun Yat-sen to obtain the help of Russia and to strengthen his political forces in his late revolutionary career. Mao attached these policies tightly to the Three People's Principles and treated this combination of Sun's ideas as the product of the new international and domestic conditions. In doing so he legitimated his concept of the new democratic republic on both nationalist or communist dimensions.

[331] All three points of Mao's conception of state cited here can be found in Mao's "On New Democracy" (January, 1940), See *Mao Xuan*, Vol. 2, pp. 350-352.

[332] Mao, "Petition Opposing Zhang Jingyao's Secret Agreement to Sell the Mines" (December 27, 1919), See *Mao's Road*, Vol. 1, p. 461.

[333] For instance, see his denunciation of Sino-British negotiations for the rendition of Weihaiwei and his condemnation of foreign manipulation of the

cigarette tax. The former was considered as giving away China's territory and state sovereignty; the latter was ridiculed as the Beijing government smelling the foreigners' farts. See *Mao's Documents*, p. 166 & p. 169.

[334] Mao, "Chinese Revolution and Chinese Communist Party" (December, 1939), See *Mao Xuan*, Vol. 2, p. 312.

[335] Edgar Snow, *Red Star over China*, p. 136.

[336] Mao, "On New Stage" (October 12-14, 1938), See *Mao Ji*, Vol. 6, p. 233.

[337] Snow, *Red Star Over China*, p. 110.

[338] Mao, "For Mobilization of all the Nation's Forces for Victory in the War of Resistance" (August 25, 1937), See *Mao Ji*, Vol. 5, p. 254.

[339] Mao, "On the New Stage," Ibid. Vol. 6, p. 218.

[340] Samuel S. Kim, *China, the United Nations, and World Order* (Princeton: Princeton University Press, 1979), pp. 41-44n63.

[341] Snow, *Red Star Over China*, p. 444.

[342] Samuel S. Kim, *China In and Out of the Changing World Order*, (Princeton, N.J.: Princeton University Press, 1991) p. 44.

[343] Ibid. p. 15.

Chapter Eight

[344] Sun Yat-sen preferred to call China's miserable situation as "hypo-colony," and he emphasized the impact of imperialist economic penetration on China's industrial development. This was an essentially urban view of the prospects for national revolution, according to Gittings. Lenin used the term "semi-colony" more frequently in communist literature; however it was descriptive and general. Lenin did not go further to evaluate the effect of the contradiction within imperialism upon semi-colonial countries such as China. Stalin's identification of China as "semi-colonial and semi-feudal" was an oft-used reference for the CCP as well as Mao, but the detailed argument was given out by Mao. More importantly Stalin failed to see that the semi-colonial situation would assist, not retard, the development of China's revolution because of the divisive pressures, not just the preponderant weight, created by different imperialists on China. See John Gittings, *The World and China*, pp. 43-45.

[345] John Gittings, *The World and China, 1922-1972* (New York: Happer & Row, Publishers, 1974) pp. 35-46.

[346] Mao, "Chinese Revolution and Chinese Communist Party" (December, 1939), See *Mao Xuan*, Vol. 2, p. 312.

[347] Ibid. p. 313.

[348] Mao, "On New Democracy," Ibid. Vol. 2, pp. 348-349.

[349] The summaries in brackets are borrowed from Gittings' book, *The World and China, 1922-1972.*

[350] Mao, "On Tactics Against Japanese Imperialism" (December 27, 1935), See *Mao Xuan*, Vol. 1, p. 170.

[351] See *Mao Nianpu*, Vol. 1, p. 525.

[352] Speaking to the CCP activists, Mao referred to "The support of the people of the Soviet Union, which they will certainly give us because they and we are bound together in a common cause." Mao, "On Tactics Against Japanese Imperialism," See *Mao Xuan*, Vol. 1, p. 171.

[353] Mao and the CCP developed the idea of self-reliance further in the later Yanan period and in the PRC. One can find many similar ideas or slogans in those two periods, such as self-sufficient, self-dependence, self-determination, etc. Some were used particularly in China's foreign policy and diplomatic activity.

[354] For instance, in his youth, Mao regarded a certain sort of union as a decisive "technique" for both sides fighting each other. (Mao, "The Great Union of the Popular Masses," See *Mao's Road*, Vol. 1, p. 378.) In December 1935, Mao addressed "the national united front" in his report to CCP activists, in which he defined the Party's basic tactical task as "United Front." (Mao, "On tactics Against Japanese Imperialism," See *Mao Xuan*, Vol. 1, p. 162.)

[355] In Chinese literature, such as *The Art of War* and *the Romance of the Three Kingdoms*, there were many good (and bad) advises and examples about alliance and the tactics to be employed in dealing with powerful adversaries.

[356] See J. D. Amstrong, *Revolutionary Diplomacy, Chinese Foreign Policy And The United Front Doctrine* (University of California Press, 1977), p. 14, 15, 22.

[357] The other two were "armed struggle" and "criticism and self-criticism."

[358] Mao wrote an outline, "Current Problems of Tactics in The Anti-Japanese United Front" on March 11, 1940, for the report he made at a meeting of the Party's senior cadres in Yanan. The report is considered as the first time Mao distinguished the different attitudes toward the anti-Japanese policy among different groups of Chinese bourgeoisie. Mao's emphasis on the middle forces in his detailed analysis was bluntly expressed. As he said, "to develop the progressive forces, win over the middle forces and combat the die-hard forces; these are three inseparable links, ..." "The winning over of the middle forces is an extremely important task for us in the period of the anti-Japanese united front,... the middle forces carry considerable weight in China and may often be the decisive factor in our struggle against the die-hards; we must therefore be prudent in dealing with them." See *Mao Xuan*, Vol. 2, p. 422, 424-425.

[359] The differences between Lenin and Mao on the idea of united front as explained here are, to a considerable extent, spelled out in J. D. Armstrong, *Revolutionary Diplomacy,*   p. 44.

[360] Han Suyin, *The Morning Deluge, Mao Tse-tung and The Chinese Revolution, 1893-1954*, (Little, Brown and Company, 1972), p. 89.

[361] Ibid. p. 108.

[362] John K. Fairbank & Albert Feuerwerker ed., *The Cambridge History of China*, Vol. 13, Republican China 1912-1949, Part 2, p. 808.

[363] Mao, "On Policy" (December 25, 1940), See *Mao Xuan*, Vol. 2, p. 444.

[364] Ibid. Vol. 2, pp. 443-444.

[365] Ibid. Vol. 2, p. 441.

[366] Ibid. Vol. 2, p. 444.

[367] Schram summarizes what Mao explained in later years as one of the reasons for differences between the patterns of the Chinese and Soviet revolutions. It flowed from the exercise by Mao and the CCP of effective political control over varying but often considerable areas and populations, long before the actual conquest of power. Because of this the Chinese Communist movement stood in a threefold relationship to the people: that of a revolutionary army; that of the "vanguard party," and that of government, or state within a state. Attuning to such a reality, Mao developed his concept of popular mass, which differs from Lenin and Stalin along various dimensions. The over-arching idea was that of the "mass line." See John K.Fairbank & Albert Feuerwerker, *The Cambridge History of China*, Vol. 13, Part 2, p. 821.

[368] Dick Wilson, *Mao Tse-tung In The Scales of History* (Cambridge University Press, 1977), pp. 230-232.

[369] A detailed description of young Mao's idea of populism is in Chapter 1.

[370] The case has been discussed in Chapter 2.

[371] See Stuart Schram, *Mao Tse-tung*, (Penguin Books, 1967), p. 201.

[372] Mao, "On Policy," See *Mao Xuan*, Vol. 2, p. 444.

[373] Mao, "Letter to Cai Hesheng," See *Mao's Letters*, p. 15.

[374] By linking the concept of national power, Kim synthesizes the rich repertoire of traditions and experiences about war that Chinese, including Mao, have had. That contains: (1) The classical Sun Zi tradition--to win a war without firing a single shot, instead exploiting the enemy's weakness and internal contradictions. Therefore, war is considered the continuation of statecraft by another name. This tradition profoundly influenced Mao's writing of "On Protracted War" in the 1930's. (2) The Confucian normative tradition--a tradition based on proper behavior, not power. The moral virtue of Confucian China collapsed under the pressure of Western power. Thus Mao never inherited this legacy. (3) The lesson of the Opium War--a national humiliation and a "never again" mentality. An axiom, that China could not stand up to outsiders without military power, let alone win their respect, had convinced most Chinese, regarding of their different ideological stripes. Mao appeared to be a loyal believer in the axiom. (4) Yanan tradition represented by Mao's writings in the 1930's--a way of thinking about the concept of revolutionary war that was a synthesis of the preceding three traditions. In my opinion, perhaps more important, the Yanan tradition was *a conclusion of the CCP's bloodshed experiences and a sinification of Marxist-Leninist doctrine*. Unfortunately, Kim

takes these two critical factors as of no account. (Samuel S. Kim, *China In and Out of the Changing World Order*, Center of International Studies, Princeton University, 1991, pp. 56-58.)

[375] As for the significance of Mao's concept of revolutionary war, Schram made several inspirational points. Besides reaching the political goals, Mao's military principles were also organizational means necessary for the communist revolutionaries' attainment. This was extremely important for a Leninist party. (Stuart R.Schram, *The Political Thought of Mao Tse-tung*, p. 265) Furthermore, Mao's stress on the role of armed force in the Chinese revolution had a spiritual output that pervaded his outlook. To be specific, Schram reveals that it strengthened the emphasis on courage, firmness of heart, and the martial spirit that is visible in his first published article and never left him until the end of his life. (John K. Fairbank & Albert Feuerwerker, *The Cambridge History of China*, Vol. 13, Part 2, p. 820.)

[376] Another well-known ideology-oriented theme was Mao's typology of all wars throughout history into just and unjust wars. This theme contained some pragmatic content. In practice it could be ideologically free because the distinction of just and unjust based on predator and prey was quite ambiguous and too subjective. For example Mao condemned the European war as an unjust imperialist war for both sides in September 1939, and then discontinued this charge against the British and French sides in late 1940. After less than a year, the war turned into a fascist and anti-fascist war, doubtless, the latter side was just at this time.

[377] Mao, "For the Germans, the Painful Signing of the Treaty," See *Mao's Road*, Vol. 1, p. 366.

[378] Mao, "The Directive of Provisional Center Government to the First Soviet conference of the Workers, Peasants and Soldiers in Fujian Province" (March, 1932), See *Mao Ji*,   Vol. 3, p. 109.

Here the theme echoed Stalin's similar view but Mao's major concern was the Chinese communist revolution.

[379] Mao, "The Resolution of Current Situation and the Party's Task" (December 25, 1935), See *Mao Ji*, Vol. 5, pp. 19-23.

[380] In the 1960's, Lin Biao made it even more famous by applying this Chinese revolutionary formula to world-wide revolution. Apparently, Mao approved this interpretation, therefore, enabled this idea to be a revolutionary world view directly.

[381] Mao, "On the New Stage" (October 12-14, 1938), See *Mao Ji*, Vol. 6, pp. 193-195.

[382] The other two are "Problems of Strategy in Guerrilla War Against Japan" (May, 1938) and "On Protracted War" (May, 1938).

[383] Mao, "Strategic Problems of China's Revolutionary War" (December, 1936), See *Mao Ji*, Vol. 5, p. 86.

[384] Mao's these statements were replaced in the official edition of the *Selected Works* (i.e., *Mao Xuan*) by passages saying the exact opposite. Referring to Stuart R.Schram, *The Political Thought of Mao Tse-tung*. p. 266, 276.

Chapter Nine

[385] *Mao Nianpu*, Vol. 2, p. 349.

[386] There seemed to be a strange dualism in the Party's attitude toward Mao's stature as a theoretician even in mid-1941. Some high ranking members, not only the Returned Students, but also those within Mao's faction including Zhu De and Liu Shaoqi, "had shown some misgivings at the first signs of a Maoist cult" that was initiated by some of the Party's theorists such as Chen Boda and Zhang Ruxin. Zhu and Liu switched their allegiance to Mao as the party's leading theorist later. Refer to Raymond F. Wylie, *The Emergence of Maoism*, pp. 157-160.

[387] It is a controversial point for the academic circle of Mao studies to regard Mao as a qualified theoretician, especially a philosopher. Here, we would like to take Benjamin Schwartz's position and approach. When Schwartz was asked to make some reflections on Mao the philosopher, he responded: "I shall interpret the word 'philosophy' in the broadest possible sense to refer to some of the central and dominant themes and ideas which may have shaped his mental world over the course of his stormy career." Benjamin I. Schwartz, "The Philosopher," See Dick Wilson, ed., *Mao Tse-tung in the Scales of History*, p. 9.

[388] People have questioned the original of this philosophical lecture by comparing Mao's writing with some Marxist philosophical works published in Soviet Union. For the purpose of the thesis, we do not pay attention on the question. There is no question that Mao accepted and believed the philosophy dressed by himself. Regarding the question of origination of the text, the most recent and exhaustive discussion was made by Werner Meissner. See Werner Meissner, *Philosophy and Politics in China, The Controversy Over Dialectical Materialism in the 1930's*, (Richard Mann, trans.) (Stanford University Press, 1990), pp. 149-160.

[389] Here, we have touched another quite controversial issue, namely, the question of how to evaluate Mao's writings in his early life, and what was its significance and impact on Mao's later thinking? To our knowledge, the trend of Mao studies on this question is to give a generally positive response and to make some specific analytical links between the early and later periods. For instance, Stuart Schram once pointed out two very important connections of this kind. He believed that Mao's attitude toward the immortality of personal life remained unchanged in his lifetime once he obtained it in his youth. Schram also thinks that one of the philosophical sources of Mao's famous philosophical work "On Practice" should be Western thought on the problem of epistemology, which appeared in Mao's

encounters with Western philosophers in his student life. See Stuart R. Schram: "Introduction, The Writings of Mao Zedong, 1912-1920," Stuart R. Schram, ed., *Mao's Road*, Vol. 1, p. xxvi.

[390] Mao, "The Freedom Is the Understanding of the Necessity And the Changing of the World," See *Mao Bu*, Vol. 7, p. 65, and *Mao Nianpu*, Vol. 2, p. 350.

[391] A redefinition about the aim of the Society indicated a settlement and announcement of Mao's ultimate political concern. The initial goal of the New People's Society, when it was born, was to improve members' self-cultivation toward their leanings, personalities, and behavior. The discussions were held in Shanghai, Paris and Changsha in late 1920 and early 1921 respectively.

[392] Mao, "Marginal Notes to: Friedreich Paulsen, *A System of Ethics*," See *Mao's Road*, Vol. 1, pp. 252-253.

[393] Mao wrote, "Aesthetic education is the bridge between the present world and the essential world (see Mr. Cai's 1912 guideline on the orientation of education), ..." See Mao, "Letter to Xiao Zisheng" (September 6, 1915), See *Mao's Road* Vol. 1, p. 77.

[394] The point of co-existence and the importance of material and spirit in the world was expressed clearly in Mao's "A Study of Physical Education" and "Marginal Notes to: Friedrich Paulsen, *A system of Ethics*," that were two major works of Mao's philosophical thinking in his youth.

[395] Mao, "Marginal Notes to: Friedrich Paulsen, *A System of Ethics*," See *Mao's Road*, Vol. 1, p. 262.

[396] Ibid. p. 271.

[397] Ibid. p. 308.

[398] Actually, Mao's philosophical arguments of practice not only benefited from Marxism, but also stemmed from Western philosophies and Chinese traditional thinking. However, *On Practice* is Mao's most self-fulfilling philosophical work. It reflects his own philosophy—to bridge the subjective and objective through practice.

[399] Mao, "On Practice," See *Mao Xuan*, Vol. 1, p. 301.

[400] Mao, "Classroom Notes" (October-December, 1913), See *Mao' Road*, Vol. 1, p. 16-17.

[401] Mao, "Marginal Notes to: Friedrich Paulsen, *A System of Ethics*" Ibid. Vol. 1, p. 306.

[402] Ibid. p. 284.

[403] Ibid. p. 284.

[404] It would not be too difficult for Mao to make such a switch because as we indicated before, Mao had a dualistic attitude toward the philosophical issue of subject-object relation from the time of his youth.

[405] Mao, "On Contradiction" (August, 1937), See *Mao Xuan*, Vol. 1, p. 315.

[406] Samuel S. Kim made a clear and specific description of the connection between Mao's theory of contradiction (world outlook) and his vision of the

international world (world view). The cases Kim picked were post-Yanan era. Nevertheless, the linkage would be similarly true if one took the earlier instances mentioned in this thesis. See Samuel S. Kim, *China, the United Nations, and World Order*, pp. 55-58.

[407] In his youth Mao expressed his desire for consistent change. As for humans, he wrote: "Human beings cannot be without change for long." Indicating that a long period of peace world be unbearable to human life, it would be inevitable that peace would give birth to waves of change. As for the world, he wrote: "All phenomena in the world are simply a state of constant change for which there is no birth and death, no formation and demise. Life and birth are both change." As for nations, he praised the German philosopher's idea, "As nations evolved, they were then able to form ideals from their past history....a nation does not reckon the cost of its ideal. It strives for freedom, or power, or glory, without calculating how much happiness is gained or lost." As for a state, Mao said: "The demise of a state is a change in its manifestation. Its land is not destroyed, nor are its people. Changes in a state are the germ of its renewal that is necessary for the evolution of society." The rule of change was also true for individuals. Mao partially agreed with Paulsen's points: "Biology and psychology tell us that every action tends to be cyclical....cyclical actions invariably lead to contraction or involution, and finally torpor." But for Mao cyclical actions are also a type of change. It is always delightful. Even the transformation between life and death is just a change of experience in two great worlds. Therefore, the exciting goal of human life should be to promote change, a complete and consistent change in states, nationalities, societies, and humanities. See Mao, "Marginal Notes to: Friedrich Paulsen, *A System of Ethics*," *Mao's Road*, Vol.1, pp.219, 249, 223, 250, 244-245.

[408] Mao, "Marginal Notes to: Friedrich Paulsen, *A System of Ethics*," Ibid. Vol. 1, p. 238.

[409] Mao, "Dialectical Materialism" (1938), See *Mao Bu*, Vol. 5, p. 205.

[410] In the 1950's and 1960's, Mao used the concept of wave-like more often and deliberately to explain movement, or development, in a philosophical sense. Compared with Engels' spiral-like form, this fact drew the noticeable attention of Chinese scholars in the 1980's in their studies of Mao.

[411] Mao, "Classroom Notes" See *Mao's Road*, Vol. 1, p. 37.

[412] Mao, "On Practice," See *Mao Xuan*, Vol.1, p. 304.

[413] Mao, "On Contradiction" Ibid. Vol. 1, p. 343.

[414] Samuel Kim has used the term "value-oriented thinker" to characterize Mao in his *China, United Nations, and World Order* (p. 52-53). Borrowing this term, our explanation is under a broader context, rather than merely in the context of Mao's revolutionary causes or values, as Kim has done.

[415] Mao, "Marginal Notes to: Friedrich Paulsen, *A System of Ethics*," See *Mao's Road*, Vol. 1, p. 223.

[416] See *Mao's Road* Vol. 1 p. 240.

[417] Mao, "Classroom Notes" Ibid. Vol. 1, p. 39.

[418] Mao said: "I take from history whatever may be used as resources in the fulfillment of my life. Nor do I believe that I have a responsibility to reproduce. If I myself desire to reproduce, this becomes one fragment of my entire life." Mao, "Marginal Notes to: Friedrich Paulsen, *A System of Ethics*," Ibid. Vol. 1, pp. 252-253.

[419] Mao wrote: "I am responsible only for my own subjective and objective reality;...Nor do I believe the saying that historically human beings are responsible for continuing the past and leading the way to the future....because it belongs to the future and not to my present reality." Ibid. p. 252.

[420] Mao, "Classroom Notes" Ibid. Vol. 1, p. 39.

[421] Mao, "On Protracted War," See *Mao Xuan*, Vol. 2, pp. 167-168.

Conclusion

[422] Samuel S. Kim, *China, the United Nations, and World Order*, p. 52.

[423] John Gittings, *The World and China*, 1922-1972, p. 9.

[424] Ibid. p. 269.

[425] Ibid. p. 269.

[426] Mao Zedong's writings and speeches on foreign affairs from 1937 on, were officially announced to be published on the centenary celebration of Mao's birth at the end of 1993. Actually, it had not been available until the proofreading of this thesis in December 1994, no explanation has been made for the one-year delay. Still, the newly coming book, entitled *Mao Zedong Waijiao Wenxuan* (Selected Diplomatic Writings of Mao Zedong) has not released most of Mao's conversations with foreigners in Yanan. See *Mao Zedong Waijiao Wenxua*, complied by the Foreign Ministry of the PRC and the Department for Research on Party Literature (Beijing: Central Party's Literature Press & World Knowledge Press, 1994).

[427] That was exactly what the CCP did. They announced the beginning of their official *wai jiao* was in 1944, by receiving America's Dixie Mission, as cited before.

[428] For instance, the agrarian problem was a crucial but sore point in Communist policy. The importance of the issue could be illustrated by another name for this period in the history of the CCP, namely, "The domestic war of land revolution." Numerous answers were given out by different partisans in Moscow and among Chinese communists. In 1929, when the "Leftist" trend prevailed in Moscow, the Executive Committee of the Comintern often had occasion to reprimand the Chinese Central Committee, who was censuring Mao for his radical treatment of the rich peasantry and gave support to the revolutionary tactics of Mao.

[429] The Zunyi Conference of 1935, a turning point for Mao's rising to the top in the CCP, was known as an occasion for Mao to condemn the erroneousness of

Russian returned students. Mao drafted a conclusive resolution on behalf of the Central Committee of the CCP. He quoted several instructions of the Comintern and used them as authority to criticize people who had responsibilities for the defeat of Red Army in Chiang Kai-shek's Fifth Encirclement Campaign.

[430] A vivid reminiscence of the first meeting between Mao and Stalin on December 16, 1949, evidenced the unforgettable unhappiness Mao experienced fifteen years earlier. Shi Ze, who was the interpreter, recalled that when the two Communist leaders were shaking hands, Stalin made many complimentary remarks to Mao, but Mao's immediate response was full of complaints. He said: "I am a person being attacked and elbowed aside for a long time. There was nowhere for me to speak out on what I wanted to say." Mao's bad feeling was interrupted by Stalin. Seven years later, Mao took another chance to get his grievance off his chest. While he was hosting a Party delegation from Soviet Russia, he told his Soviet guests that "We have had some complaints about the behaviors of the Comintern and Soviet Russian Communist Party at that time (i.e. the Jiangxi period). It was improper to speak out before, but we should start now, even to scold. You could not seal our mouths." See Shi Ze, *Zhai Lishi Juren Shengbian* (At the Side of the Historical Giants) (Beijing: Central Documents Publishing House, 1991) pp. 434-435, 609.

[431] Although Mao was introduced by the publication of the Comintern in 1935 as merely one of the leaders of Chinese Soviet government and the Red Army, Mao had become a de facto chairman of the CCP Politburo at the beginning of 1935. His leadership was publicly acknowledged by Moscow on the article on Mao in the 1938 edition of the *Bol'shaia Sovetshaia Entsiklopediia*. See John E. Rue, *Mao Tse-tung in Opposition, 1927-1935* P.4

[432] Otto Braun, *A Comintern Agent in China*, 1932-1939, Dick Wilson's "Introduction," (Stanford University Press, 1982), p. x.

[433] Frederic Wakeman, Jr. has done a good job in disclosing various intellectual sources of Mao's thought in his *History and Will, Philosophical Perspectives of Mao Tse-tung's Thought* (Berkeley, University of California Press, 1973). However, the book is relatively old-dated, and does not deal with Mao's world view in particular.

[434] Mao once told people in 1965, that in his school time, "all I believe in was Kant's dualism, particularly his idealism. "* However, in his youth Mao's reading was, in fact, not limited to Immanuel Kant and as he admitted the impact of these readings was not so superficial and shallow. The problem is how to evaluate the influence of western learning on Mao.

* Mao, "Chairman Mao's Conversation with Comrades Ch'en Po-ta and K'ang Sheng" (1965), See Frederic Wakeman, Jr., *History and Will, Philosophical Perspectives of Mao Tse-tung's Thought*, p. 182.

[435] Samuel S. Kim provides, in "New Directions and Old Puzzles in Chinese Foreign Policy," a comprehensive description of conflicting assumptions and arguments about both the continuities and the changes, one of the enduring puzzles in the field. He also offered his own approach. See Samuel S. Kim, ed., *China and the World, New Directions in Chinese Foreign Relations*, Second Edition (Westview Press, 1989), pp. 3-30.

REFERENCES

Original source of Mao's writings

A Documentary History of Chinese Communism, edited by Brandt, Conrad, Benjamin Schwartz and John Fairbank (New York: Atheneum, 1971).

Documents of Dissent: Chinese Political Thought Since Mao, translated by J. Chester Cheng (Stanford: Hoover Institution Press, 1980).

Mao Zedong Ji Bujuan, Vol. 1-9 (Chinese) (*Supplements to Collected Writings of Mao Zedong*), edited by Takeuchi Minoru (Tokyo: Sososha, 1986).

Mao Zedong, 1917-1927: Documents, edited by M. Henri Day (Stockholm, 1975).

Mao Zedong Shuxin Xuanji (Chinese) (*Selected Letters of Mao Zedong*), compiled by the Department for Research on Party Literature, Central Committee of the Communist Party of China (Beijing: People's Publishing House, 1983).

Mao Zedong Ji, Vol. 1-10 (Chinese)(*Collected Writings of Mao Zedong*), edited by Takeuchi Minotu (Tokyo: Hokubosha, 1970).

Mao Papers, Anthology and Bibliography, edited by Jerome Ch'en (London: Oxford University Press, 1970).

Mao Zedong Nianpu, Vol. 1-2 (Chinese) (*A Chronicle of Mao Zedong's Life*), edited by the Department for Research on Party Literature, Central Committee of the Communist Party of China (Beijing: People's Publishing House and Central Party's Literature Press, 1993).

Mao Zedong Waijiao Wenxuan (Chinese) (*Selected Diplomatic Writings of Mao Zedong*), complied by the Foreign Ministry of People's Republic of China & the Department for Research on Party Literature, (Beijing: Central Party's Literature Press & World Knowledge Press, 1994).

Mao Zedong Zaoqi Wengao (Chinese) (*Draft Writings by Mao Zedong for the Early Period*), edited by the Department for Research on Party Literature, Central Committee of Communist Party of China, 1989).

Mao Zedong Xuanji, (Chinese) (*Selected Works of Mao Zedong*), complied by the committee for the publication of the Selected Works of Mao Zedong, Central Committee of the Communist Party of China (Beijing: People's Publishing House, 1966), and its English translation--*Selected Works of Mao Tse-tung* (Beijing: Foreign Language Press, 1975).

Mao's Road to Power, Revolutionary Writings, 1912-1949, Vol.1, (The Pre-Marxist Period, 1912-1920) edited by Stuart R. Schram (New York: M. E. Sharpe, Publishers, 1992).

Reverberation, A New Translation of Complete Poems of Mao Tse-tung, translated by Nancy T. Lin (Hong Kong: Joint Publishing Co., 1980).

The Political Thought of Mao Tse-tung, edited by Stuart R.Schram (Praeger Publishers, 1971).

The Poems of Mao Tse-tung, translated by Willis Barnstone, (New York: Harper & Row, Publishers, 1972).

The Writings of Mao Zedong, 1949-1976, Vol.1-2, edited by John K. Leung & Michael Y. M. Kau, (New York: M. E. Sharpe, 1992).

Secondary sources about Mao's life and thought

Band, Claire, *Two Years with the Chinese Communists* (New Haven: Yale University Press, 1948).

Bertram, James, *Unconquered. Journal of A Year's Adventures Among the Fighting Peasants of North China* (New York: The John Day Company, 1939).

------ *North China Front* (London: Macmillan and Co., Limited, 1939).

Bisson, T. A., *Yenan in June 1937: Talks with the Communist Leaders* (Berkeley: University of California, 1973).

Carlson, Evans Fordyce, *Twin Stars of China, A Behind-the-scenes Story of China's Valiant Struggle for Existence, By A U.S. Marine Who Lived & Moved with the People* (New York: Dodd, Mead & Company, 1940).

Gong Yuzhi, Pang Xianzhi and Shi Zhongquan, *Mao Zedong de Dushu Shenghuo* (Chinese), (*Mao Zedong's Reading Life*), (Beijing: Three Joint Publishing House, 1986).

Gunther, Stein, *The Challenge of Red China* (New York: McGraw-Hill Book Company, Inc., 1945).

Huang Yuchuan, *Mao Zedong Shengping Zhiliao Jianbian, 1893-1969* (Chinese) (*Concise Edition of Mao Zedong's Biographical Materials*), (Hong Kong: You Lian Institute, 1970).

Lawrance, Alan, *Mao Zedong: A Bibliography* (New York: Greenwood Press, 1991).

Li, Jui, *The Early Revolutionary Activities of Comrade Mao Tse-tung* (White Plains, N. Y.: M. E. Sharpe, 1977).

Shi Zhe, *Zai Lishi Jiuren Shengbian, Shi Zhe Huiyiluo* (Chinese) (*Beside the Hisotrical Giants, Shi Zhe Memoirs*), (Beijing: Central Party's Literature Press, 1991).

Siao Yu, *Mao Tse-tung and I Were Beggars* (Syracuse University Press, 1959).

Smedley, Agnes, *Battle Hymn of China* (New York: A. A. Knopf, 1943).

Snow, Edgar, *Random Notes on Red China, 1936-1945* (Cambridge, Mass.: Harvard University Press, 1957).

------- *Red Star Over China* (New York: Grove Press, Inc., 1961).

Strong, Anna Louise, *The Chinese Conquer China* (Garden City, N. Y. : Doubleday, 1949).

------- *One-fifth of Mankind* (New York: Modern Age Books, 1938).

Wales, Nym, *Inside Red China* (New York: Doubleday, Doran & Company, Inc., 1939).

Zhang Yijiu, *Mao Zedong He Si* (Chinese) (*Mao Zedong and Poem*), (Beijing: Spring and Autumn Publishing House, 1987).

Studies of Mao and China's international relations

1. Books

Adel, Daljit Sen, *China and Her Neighbors: A Review of Chinese Foreign Policy* (New Delhi: Deep & Deep Publications, 1984).

Armstrong, J. D., *Revolutionary Diplomacy: Chinese Foreign Policy and the United Front Doctrine* (Berkeley: University of California Press, 1977).

Bloodworth, Dennis, *The Chinese Looking Glass* (New York: Farrar, Straus and Giroux, 1967).

------- *The Messiah and the Mandarins: Mao Tse-tung and the Ironies of Power* (New York: Atheneum, 1982).

Braun, Otto, *A Comintern Agent in China 1932-1939* (Stanford: Stanford University Press, 1982).

Burlatskii, Fedor Mikhailovich, *Mao Tse-tung: An Ideological and Psychological Portrait* (Moscow: Progress Publishers, 1980).

Ch'en, Jerome, *Mao and the Chinese Revolution* (London: Oxford University Press, 1972).

Chang, Feng-chen, *The Diplomatic Relations Between China and Germany Since 1898* (Taipei: Ch'eng Wen Publishing Co., 1971).

Chang, Kuo-tao, *The Rise of the Chinese Communist Party; the Autobiography of Chang Kuo-tao* Vol.1 & 2 (Lawrence: University Press of Kansas, 19710-72).

Chang, Luke T., *China's Boundary Treaties and Frontier Disputes* (London: Oceana Publications, 1982).

Cheng, Tien-fang, *A History of Sino-Russian Relations* (Washington: Public Affairs Press, 1957).

Chi, Madeleine, *China Diplomacy, 1914-1918* (Cambridge, Mass.: Harvard University Press, 1970).

Chou, Eric, *Mao Tse-tung, the Man and the Myth* (London: Cassell, 1982). Corrigan, Philip Richard D. Ramsay, Harvie and Sayer, Derel: *For Mao: Essays in Historical Materialism* (London: Macmillan, 1979).

Creel, Herrlee Glessner, *Sinism: A Study of the Evolution of the Chinese World-view* (Westport, Conn.: Hyperion Press, 1975).

Dallin, David J., *The Rise of Russia in Asia* (New Haven:Yale University Press, 1949).

Djang, Feng Djen, *The Diplomatic Relations Between China and Germany Since 1898* (Shanghai, China: The Commercial Press, Ltd.,1936).

Dorothy Borg and Shumpei Okamoto, (ed.) *Pearl Harbor As History, Japanese-American Relations 1931-1941* New York: Columbia University Press, 1973).

Elegant, Robert S., *The Center of the World; Communism and the Mind of China* (London: Methuen, 1963).

Esherick, Joseph W. (ed.) *Lost Chance in China, the World War II Despatches of John S. Service* (New York: Random House, 1974).

Fairbank, John K., *Chinese-American Interactions: A Historical Summary* (New Brunswick, N.J.: Rutgers University Press, 1975).

Fairbank, John K. and Feuerwerker, Albert: *The Cambridge History of China*, Vol. 13 (Cambridge: Cambridge University Press, 1986).

-------(ed.) *The Chinese World Order, Traditional China's Foreign Relations* (Cambridge, Mass.: Harvard University Press, 1968).

-------(ed.) *The Cambridge History of China*, Vol. 12, Reppublican China 1921-1949, Part 1 (Cambridge: Cambridge University Press).

Fitzgerald, C. P., *The Chinese View of Their Place in the World* (London: Oxford University Press, 1966).

Gittings, John, *The World and China, 1922-1972* (New York: Harper & Row, 1974).

Gladue, E. Ted, *China's Perception of Global Politics* (Washington, D. C. : University Press of America, 1982).

Han, Suyin, *The Morning Deluge; Mao Tse-tung and the Chinese Revolution, 1893-1954* (Poston: Little, Brown, 1972).

Hao, Yufan (1st ed.) *The Chinese View of the World* (New York: Pantheon Books, 1989).

Hsiao, Tso-liang, *Power Relations Within the Chinese Communist Movement, 1930-1934, A Study of Documents* (Seattle: University of Washington Press, 1961).

Hsiung, James Chieh, *The Logic of "Maoism"; Crittiques and Explication* (New York: Praeger, 1974).

------- *Ideology and Practice; the Evolution of Chinese Communism* (New York: Praeger Publishers, 1970).

Hsu, Immanuel C. (ed.) *Reading in Modern Chinese History* (London: Oxford University Press, 1971).

------- *China's Entrance into the Family of Nations: The Diplomatic Phase, 1858-1880* (Cambridge, Mass.: Harvard University Press, 1966).

Huang, Philip C., *Liang Chi-chao and Modern Chinese Liberalism* (Seattle: University of Washington Press, 1972).

Huang, Philip C., Bell, Linda Schaefer and Walker, Kathy Lemons, *Chinese Communist and Rural Society, 1927-1934* (Berkeley: University of California, 1978).

Hunt, Michael, *The Making of A Special Relationship: the United States and China to 1914* (New York: Columbia University Press, 1983).

Iriye, Akira, *Across the Pacific, An Inner History of American-East Asia Relations* (New York: Harcourt, Brace & World, Inc., 1967).

Kapur, Herish, *As China Sees the World: Perceptions of Chinese Scholars* (London: Pinter, 1987).

Kataoka, *Resistance and Revolution in China, The Communists and the Second United Front* (Berkeley, University of California, 1974).

Kim, Samuel S., *China In and Out of the Changing World Order* (Princeton, N.J. : Princeton University, 1991).

------- *China, the United Nations, and World Order* (Princeton: Princeton University Press, 1979).

------- *China and the World, New Directions in Chinese Foreign Relations,* (2nd. edition) (Westview Press, 1989).

Lee, Robert, *France and the Exploitation of China 1885-1901* (Hong Kong: Oxford University Press, 1989).

Leng, Shao Chuan, *Changes in China: Party, State, and Society* (Lanham, MD.: University Press of America, 1989).

Levenson, Joseph R., *Confucian China and Its Modern Fate, the Problem of Intellectual Continuity* (Berkeley and Los Angeles: University of California Press, 1958).

Lewis, Charlton M., *Prologue to the Chinese Revolution: the Transformation of Ideas and Institutions in Hunan Province, 1891-1907* (Cambridge, Mass.: Harvard University Press, 1976).

Liabng, Hsi-huey, *The Sino-German Connection:Alexander von Falkenhausen Between China and Germany 1900-1941*(Assen: Van Gorcum, 1978).

Mancall, Mark, *China at the Center, 300 Years of Foreign Policy* (New York: The Free Press, 1984).

McDonald, Angus W. JR., *The Urban Origins of Rural Revolution, Elites and the Masses in Hunan Province, China, 1911-1927* (Berkeley: University of California Press, 1978).

Mclane, Charles B., *Soviet Policy and the Chinese Communists, 1931-1946* (New York: Columbia University Press, 1958).

Meissner, Werner, *Philosophy and Politics in China: the Controversy Over Dialectical Materialism in the 1930s* (Stanford: Stanford University Press, 1990).

Metha, Narinder, *Foreign Policies of Great Powers: U.S.A., U.S.S.R., U.K., China, France & India* (Jullundur: New Academic Pub. Co., 1977).

Payne, Robert, *Mao Tse-tung, Ruler of Red China* (London: Secker and Warburg, 1951).

Pye, Lucian W., *Mao Tse-tung: the Man in the Leader* (New York: Basic Books, 1976).

Reardon-Anderson, James, *Yenan and the Great Powers: the Origins of Chinese Communist Foreign Policy, 1944-1946* (New York: Columbia University Press, 1980).

Rosinger, Lawrence Kaelter, *China's Wartime Politics, 1937-1944* (Princeton: Princeton University Press, 1944).

Rue, John E., *Mao Tse-tung in Opposition, 1927-1935* (Stanford: Stanford University Press, 1966).

Schaller, Michael, *The United States and China in the Twentieth Century* (New York: Oxford University Press, 1979).

Schram, Stuart R., *Mao Zedong, A Preliminary Reassessment* (New York: St. Martin's Press, 1983).

------- *Mao Tse-tung* (England: Penguin Books, 1970).

------- *The Thought of Mao Tse-tung* (Cambridge: Cambridge University Press, 1989).

Schwartz, Harry, *Tsars Mandarins and Commissars, A History of Chinese-Russian Relations* (Anchor Books, 1973).

Schwartz, Benjamin I., *Chinese Communism and the Rise of Mao* (Cambridge, Mass.: Harvard University Press, 1968).

------- *The World of Thought in Ancient China* (Cambridge, Mass.: Belknap Press of Harvard University Press, 1985).

Shaffer, Lynda, *Mao and the Workers: the Hunan Labor Movement, 1920-1923* (Armonk, N. Y.: M. E. Sharpe, 1982).

Shai, Aron, *Britain and China, 1941-47: Imperial Momentum* (London: Macmillan, 1984).

Shewmaker, Kenneth E., *Americans and Chinese Communists, 1927-1945: A Persuading Encounter* (Conell University Press, 1971).

Shih, Chih-yu, *The Spirit of Chinese Foreign Policy, A Psychocultural View* (The Macmillan Press Ltd., 1990).

Snow, Edgar, *The Pattern of Soviet Power* (New York: Random House, 1945).

Starr, John Bryan, *Continuing the Revolution, the Political Thought of Mao* (Princeton University Press, 1979).

Teng, Ssu-yu and Fairbank, John King, *China's Response to the West: A Documentary Survey, 1839-1923* (Cambridge: Harvard University Press, 1954).

Terrill, Ross, *Mao: A Biography* (New York: Harper & Row, 1980).

Treadgold, Donald W. (ed.) *Soviet and Chinese Communism, Similarities and Differences* (Seattle: University of Washington Press, 1967).

Tsou, Tang, *America's Failure in China, 1941-50* (Chicago:University of Chicago Press, 1963).

Tuchman, Barbara W., *Notes From China* (Macmillan Publishing Co., Inc., 1972).

------- *Stilwell and the American Experience in China, 1911-1945* (Toronto: Bantam Books, 1971).

Twitchett, Denis Crispin and Fairbank, John King (ed.) *The Cambridge History of China*, Vol. 10, Later Ching from c.1800 to c.1870 (Cambridge: Cambridge University Press, 1978).

Vertzberger, Yaacov, *The World in Their Minds: Information Processing, Cognition, and Perception in Foreign Policy Decisionmaking* (Stanford: Stanford University Press, 1990).

Wakeman, Frederic E., *History and Will;Philosophical Perspectives of Mao Tse-tung's Thought* (Berkeley, University of California Press, 1973).

Waller, Derek J., *The Kiangsi Soviet Republic: Mao and the National Congresses of 1931 and 1934* (Berkeley:University of California, 1973).

Wei, Henry, *China and Soviet Russia* (Princeton, New Jersey: D. Van Nostrand Company, Inc., 1956).

Whiting, Allen Suess and Sheng, Shih-tsai, *Sinkiang: Pawn or Pivot?* (East Lansing: Michigan State University Press, 1958).

Whiting, Allen S., *Soveit Policies in China 1917-1924* (New York: Columbia University Press, 1954).

Wilbut, C. Martin and How, Julie Lien-ying, *Documents on Communism, Naticnalism, and Soveit Advisers in China, 1918-1927* (NewYork: Columbia University Press, 1956).

Wilson, Dick, *The Long March, 1935; the Epic of Chinese Communism's Survival* (New York: Viking Press, 1971).

------- (ed.) *Mao Tse-tung in the Scales of History: A Preliminary Assessment* (Cambridge: Cambridge University Press, 1977).

Womack, Brantly, *The Foundations of Mao Zedong's Political Thought, 1917-1935* (Honolulu: University Press of Hawaii, 1982).

Wu, Tien-wei, *The Sian Incident: A Pivotal Point in Modern Chinese History* (Ann Arbor: University of Michigan, 1976).

------- *Mao Tse-tung and the Tsunyi Conference: An Annotated Bibliography* (Washington: Associate of Research Libraries, 1974).

Wylie, Raymond Finlay, *The Emergence of Maoism: Mao Tse-tung, Ch'en Po-ta, and the Search For Chinese Theory, 1935-1945* (Stanford: Stanford University Press, 1980).

Zhang, Yongjin, *China in the International System, 1918-20: The Middle Kingdom at the Periphery* (Macmillan, 1991).

2. Articles

Bedeski, Rober E., "Concept of the State: Sun Yat-sen and Mao Tse-tung", *China Quarterly* No.70, June 1977.

Elleman, Bruce A., "The Soviet Union's Secret Diplomacy Concerning the Chinese Eastern Railway, 1924-1925", *The Journal of Asian Studies*, Vol. 53, No. 2, May 1994.

Garver, John W., "Ther Origin of the Second United Front, The Comitern and the Chinese Communist Party", *China Quarterly*, No. 113, March 1988.

Heinzig, Dieter, "The Otto Brann Memories and Mao's Rise to Power", *China Quarterly*, No. 46, June 1971.

Herrmann, Richard, "The Empirical Challenge of the Cognitive Revolution: A Strategy for Drawing Inferences about Perceptions", *International Studies Quarterly*, Vol. 32, No. 2, June 1988.

Li, Jing, "China's America: Chinese Perceptions of the United States, 1900-1989", *Journal of Oritental Studies*, Vol. xxix, No. 1, 1991 (Hong Kong).

Okazaki, S., "Moscow, Yenan, Chungking", *Pacific Affairs* No.14, March 1941.

Schwartz, Benjamin, "Maoist Image of World Order", *Journal of International Affairs* No. 21, January 1967.

------- "On the `Originality' of Mao", *Foreign Affairs*, No.34, October 1955.

3. Chinese sources

Fan Xianchao, *Mao Zedong Shixiang Fazhan de Lishi Guiji* (*The Historical Orbit of the Development of Mao Zedong Thought*), (Hunan: Hunan People's Publishing House, 1993).

Gao Jucheng, etc., *Qingnian Mao Zedong* (*The Young Mao Zedong*), (Beijing: Historical Literatures of the Chinese Communist Party Press, 1990).

Jincheng, *Yanan Jiaojichu Huiyilu* (*Memoirs of Yanan Association Department*), (Beijing: Chinese Youth Publishing House, 1986).

Li Rui, *Mao Zedong de Zhaonian yu Wannian*, (*Mao Zedong's Early Age and Old Age*), (GuiYang: Gui Zhou People's Publishing House, 1992).

------- *Mao Zedong Zhaonian Dushu Shenghuo*, (*Readings in Mao Zedong's Early Age*), (Shengyang: Liaoning People's Publishing House, 1992).

Li Yongshou, *Zhong Xi Wenhua yu Mao Zedong Zhaoqi Shixian* (*Sino-Western Cultures and Mao Zedong's Early Thinking*), (Shichuan: Shichuan University Press, 1989).

------- *Mao Zedong Yu Dageming* (*Mao Zedong and the Great Revolution*), (Shichuan: Shichuan People's Publishing House, 1991).

Shima Changfeng, *Mao Zedong Pingzhuan, 1893-1927* (*The Life and Times of Mao Zedong*), (Hong Kong: Culture Book House, 1975).

Shu Yand (ed.), *Zhongguo Chulege Mao Zedong, Zhongwai Mingren de Pingshou* (*China Had A Mao Zedong, the Commentaries of Famous Persons within and without China*), (Beijing: People's Liberal Army's Publishing House, 1991).

Wang Shubai, *Mao Zedong Shixian de Zhongguo Jiyi The Chinese Gene of Mao Zedong Thought*), (Beijing: Commercial Press, 1990).

Yu Jiundao and Li Jie, (ed.), *Mao Zedong Jiaowanglu* (*Records of Mao Zedong's Associatin Activities*), (Beijing: People's Publishing House, 1991).

Zhang Xixian, etc. (ed.), *Mao Zedong Zai Yanan* (*Mao Zedong in Yanan*), (Beijing: Education for Police Officers Publishing House, 1993).

INDEX